The Encyclopedia of

Coca-Cola® Trays

An Unauthorized Collector's Guide

The Encyclopedia of
Coca-Cola® Trays
An Unauthorized Collector's Guide

Frank Laughlin

4880 Lower Valley Road, Atglen, PA 19310 USA

Dedication

To my grandfather Abraham, who I did not know, but who in 1907, as a recent immigrant to the United States, somehow managed to acquire a small Coca-Cola bottling plant in southern West Virginia; to MAV; and to the good friends who encouraged me to write, tolerated the endless trips to flea markets, and endured the hours I spent creating this book.

Coca-Cola, Coke, the Dynamic Ribbon Device, the Contour Bottle, the design of the Coca-Cola Santa, and the design of the Coca-Cola Polar Bear are trademarks of The Coca-Cola Company. eBay is a trademark of eBay Inc.

The Coca-Cola Company did not authorize this book nor specifically furnish or approve of any of the information contained herein. This book is derived from the author's independent research.

Dollar value ranges is this book are intended only as a guide. Values from reference materials and dealer/collectors were compiled by the author and are subject to condition variations, price differentials in different geographic locations, unusual supply/demand circumstances, and error.

Internet auction prices in this book are intended only as a guide. Values were recorded from auctions viewed on random days and may not represent an accurate price. Condition variations, supply/demand, other concurrent auctions, and recording error can influence a listed price.

Every attempt has been made to provide the information listed for trays accurately and without any bias. Any errors or omissions are due to a lack of knowledge at the time of writing.

Neither the Author nor the Publisher assumes any responsibility for any issues arising from the use of the data in this publication.

Copyright © 2001 by Frank Laughlin
Library of Congress Card Number: 2001088399

Designed by John P. Cheek
Type set in ZapfHumanist Dm BT/Humanist 521 BT

ISBN: 0-7643-1331-2
Printed in China
1 2 3 4

Published by Schiffer Publishing Ltd.
4880 Lower Valley Road
Atglen, PA 19310
Phone: (610) 593-1777; Fax: (610) 593-2002
E-mail: Schifferbk@aol.com
Please visit our web site catalog at **www.schifferbooks.com**
We are always looking for people to write books on new and related subjects. If you have an idea for a book, please contact us at the above address.

This book may be purchased from the publisher.
Include $3.95 for shipping.
Please try your bookstore first.
You may write for a free catalog.

In Europe, Schiffer books are distributed by
Bushwood Books
6 Marksbury Avenue
Kew Gardens
Surrey TW9 4JF England
Phone: 44 (0) 20 8392 8585
Fax: 44 (0) 20 8392 9876
E-mail: Bushwd@aol.com
Free postage in the UK. Europe: air mail at cost.

Contents

Acknowledgments

A comment that many of us frequently hear, *If I knew then what I know now . . .* , seems overused, but that comment is certainly a correct description of my feelings as the ten months of effort on this book came to a close.

In January, 2000, when the idea was first developed, only vague thoughts existed as to how the material would be compiled. My personal collection of Coca-Cola trays numbered over two hundred, which could, of course, be used. However, my collection contained only a very modest number of early trays. But, I thought, certainly pictures of trays being auctioned on the Internet could be downloaded, printed, and, with proper agreement, utilized in the book. Probably The Coca-Cola Company archives could be used for other pictures of early trays. Maybe the Coca-Cola Collectors Club had some material. Perhaps even one of the prominent tray manufacturers would provide information.

It took a little bit of time to work through all of these initial thoughts, but in the end *none* of those options for material (except my own collection, now close to three hundred trays) was available to be used. The reasons were sometimes clear and sometimes *not* so clear, but the book project would have to find other approaches. Obviously, other approaches were found—and I think a better, more beautiful, and more complete book has resulted.

The captions with each tray pictured in the chronological chapters of the book note the person(s) who provided the tray or its picture. Following are a special few that I wish to acknowledge for contributions that, in total, are really what made the book possible.

The *Schmidts, Bill and Jan*, from Elizabethtown, Kentucky responded to someone they did not know and provided pictures of their beautiful, world-class collection of classic trays. Mr. and Mrs. Schmidt and the Schmidt Museum have a well-known collection including much more than trays. Many of the Schmidt's items were included in a 1983 book they authored, entitled *The Schmidt Museum of Coca-Cola Memorabilia*. The condition of trays in *The Schmidt Collection* is as good as most of us will ever see and I feel most fortunate to be able to have pictures of them included!

The collection of *John E. Peterson* is about as remarkable as the Schmidt collection, but in a different way. John has accumulated (and continues to accumulate) what I believe is another world-class collection of Coca-Cola trays. His collection already contains many of the classic Coca-Cola trays. But John is also attracted to Coca-Cola trays from around the world, including some of the beautiful Mexican trays of the 1950s-1970s, *and* to recent trays issued in the 1970s-1990s. His collec-tion is well over four hundred trays . . . and growing. John Peterson also responded to someone he did not know and opened his Illinois home to me for a frenetic couple of days spent photographing his collection. Many trays only referenced in previous collector books now have pictures in this book. And, many of the unique and beautiful trays from the last thirty years are pictured in this book for the *first time* anywhere. Most are from John's collection. *John Peterson* is interested in advancing the activity of collecting *all* Coca-Cola trays and I thank him for his most generous help and support.

It was a little discouraging at first, trying to find trays to photo-graph. Then Dave Sherrod answered my e-mail. *Dave and Ann Poppenheimer Sherrod* have *POP'S Mail Order Collectibles* in Bells, Ten-nessee (popsmailorder.com or Popsmail1@aol.com). Dave promptly mailed me twenty trays to photograph and return, no questions asked. I photographed them all, returned about half, and bought the rest. *POP'S* is a great source for recent Coca-Cola trays and other collectibles at fair prices.

Trademark Marketing and its President, *Barbara Brim*, distribute many of the licensed Coke Brand trays from the 1990s. Ms. Brim and her staff provided me with sales volumes and verified the issue dates for trays they distributed. They were very helpful.

Leslie Cope, the American artist who created a series of 1980s trays from Zanesville, Ohio, and his wife *Velma* opened their gallery in Roseville, Ohio on a day when it was closed. They provided trays to complete the set and talked with me about the works. It was a special visit.

Other individuals provided one or more trays and they are noted in the captions. Thanks to all.

Friends helped. A little legal advice from Jim Rhodes and Patti Evans, Jim Badzik's aid after a couple of nasty computer crashes, and a little design and photography assistance from Michele LaMarca and Ava Barbour were much appreciated.

Finally, the people from Schiffer Publishing could not have been more helpful and supportive. Bruce Waters gave me a crash course and ongoing assistance in photography and my editor, Donna Baker, patiently and quickly answered each and every question and edited out at least a few hundred errors from what I thought was a perfect manuscript. Her support and advice could not have been better.

Introduction

This Introduction first briefly describes the objectives of this book then follows with three short sections covering recent types of trays, terms used in this book to describe trays, and definitions used for tray condition. Next is a section describing the process used to document Internet auctions. The Introduction ends with a sample caption used to describe each tray with a description of each item contained in the caption. Since the captions contain much detail (including dollar values) it will be especially useful for readers to spend a few minutes familiarizing themselves with the way the information is presented.

Chapters One through Six cover all trays in chronological order from 1897 through the 1990s. Chapter Seven groups together and lists trays with similar themes, such as all commemorative trays and all Santa Claus trays. Chapter Eight provides a small review of tip trays. The Appendix contains several summary lists of trays, all Internet auction data, and captions for trays identified in Chapters One through Six but not pictured.

Objectives

This book's main objective has always been to create a reference guide for *all* Coca-Cola trays but to especially capture the variety and attractiveness of trays issued in the last thirty-five years—and to do so without detracting from the special beauty of the original classic trays. Another objective was to include dollar value data from the many trays that were being sold each day in Internet auctions.

Quite a few reference books have provided details on the *classic* trays, from the first one in 1897 through those of the early 1960s. To the extent possible, this guide has attempted to provide the same level of detail on the hundreds of trays issued *since* the 1960s AND to relate these two groups. That means instead of just noting that a classic tray has been reproduced, details and pictures will be found on the 84 trays actually reproduced from these classic trays . . . as well as the more than 150 trays reproduced from other Coca-Cola ad images, including 46 Santa trays.

Fulfilling these objectives developed into quite a large amount of work. The number and variety of trays exceeded expectations and kept on growing. When it was necessary to stop adding new trays due to publishing deadlines the count was *582 identified trays*. That total includes not only 373 U.S. trays, but also 82 Canadian trays, 62 Mexican, 41 Italian, 8 German, and 16 from ten additional countries. Are there more trays out there? The answer is without a doubt, YES. Photographs in this book show 517 trays, more than have ever appeared in *any* Coca-Cola memorabilia reference book. About 160 of these trays have *never* appeared in any of the nineteen reference books containing pictures or words about Coca-Cola trays that were researched in preparation of this book. Trays never before pictured are from the 1950s, 1960s, 1970s, and 1980s, as well as all identified trays through 1999.

Many books and other materials listed in the Bibliography have done a thorough job of providing a detailed history of The Coca-Cola Company, including its early use of a unique franchised bottler system and its rich tradition of advertising excellence. Archives of The Company were used in the preparation of many of these efforts. Since the archives were not available for this book, the other materials listed may better serve the reader interested in specific and detailed historical information on topics beyond this book's stated objectives.

New Types of Trays

Serving trays were originally very functional items that also provided a good way to advertise. Their sturdy construction, while subject to chipping and rust, was durable and held the colors over many years of use. But, as sales of Coca-Cola in bottles increased, vending machines proliferated, and home consumption increased, the need for serving trays decreased, resulting in the end of new company-issued advertising trays in the 1960s. Serving trays continue to be issued, however, and at least three new types have emerged.

One new type of tray was developed or commissioned by the local franchised bottler in conjunction with The Company. It is called a *commemorative* tray, issued to celebrate something. Bottler anniversaries, sports events, and other activities were all reasons to generate trays. But the franchise system consolidated and technology allowed bottles to be more easily issued as commemoratives than trays. Today, this type of tray has become a dying breed.

A second type of tray comes under the generic heading of *promotional*. The 1976 Santa tray for Long John Silver Sea Food Shoppes is one example of a promotional tray. Another example is the reproduction of classic trays that were offered as a promotion through The Company in 1973 and 1974 for a nominal fee and that were very successful. Logo trays and trays packaged with product, such as the Italian trays of the early 1990s, are additional examples.

The third group of recent trays are those *licensed* by The Coca-Cola Company for retail sale. Instead of a bottler paying the company a few cents for each tray and then giving them away to customers, a manufacturer and/or distributor pays The Company for licensing rights and makes the trays available through various retail outlets.

Regardless of the type of tray, many recent issues are very attractive and relatively inexpensive. While some are easy to find, many are already scarce items.

A Few Terms

What is (and isn't) a tray? It was a little surprising to realize that this is not a simple question. A great variety of shapes and materials exist in items that someone will call a tray. This book has generally *not* considered glass platters and light or thin non-durable plastic items as trays. Usually if the item is metal or durable plastic and contains an image it was listed as a tray.

A uniform language for describing trays doesn't really exist, especially when describing anything after the classic tray period. Following, however, are some definitions of terms as used in this guide. If a term is used by a reader in a different way, apologies.

• A tray comes into being at some point and ends up being included in this book. The terms used are that the tray was *issued*, *found*, *located*, *identified*, or *listed*.

•Trays contain a picture and/or at least some words. Sometimes more than one tray will have the same picture or words. Therefore, the terms used in the text are intended to differentiate between a tray and the tray's *image*. If three trays have the same picture the text will identify *three trays* but only *one image*. Sometimes the noun *picture* will be used as a verb, *pictured*.

• The flat, center part of a tray, the part containing the image, is usually called the *face*. The outside of the tray usually has a color change from the face and/or has a different angle or slope. That part of the tray is called the *border* and the end of the border is an *edge* or *rim*.

Tray Condition

Most collectors of Coca-Cola memorabilia sooner rather than later gain familiarity with the uniform terms used for describing the condition of trays or other types of collectibles. Applying these terms to a specific tray is a somewhat subjective matter—and where the *fun* begins. Trying to accurately determine condition by viewing a computer image in an Internet auction doesn't make the process any easier or any more precise.

The general grading categories of *condition* are described below. In addition to these terms many collectors prefer to assign a number from one to ten, worst to best, to describe condition, usually in .5 increments. This approach allows a little more preciseness. For example, assigning a Very Good or Excellent rating is deciding which of *two* words will be used, while the numbering system provides many more choices (6.5, 7.0, 7.5, 7.6, 7.7 etc.).

MINT. Mint *is* mint. No marks, no scratches, unused. *Mint except for one small chip is not mint.* Period. Numerically, Mint is 10. Not 9.7, not 9.9, but 10. Obviously not many items are mint.

NEAR MINT. Near Mint condition will have a *very* few minor marks, chips, or other slight imperfections that are not even easy to see and that do not detract from the overall look of the item. Numerically, Near Mint is about 9.5 to 9.9.

EXCELLENT. Excellent condition means minor marks, chips, or scratches that can be seen but are not what the eyes first see. Good color has been maintained and no rust spots are visible on the face or border. Numerically, Excellent is about 8.5 to 9.5.

VERY GOOD. Very Good is similar to Excellent but with a few more problems, such as a small area of paint bubbling or flaking (not right on the nose of a beautiful model, of course). *Small* rust spots or pitting may also be present. Numerically, Very Good can range from around 7.0 to 8.5.

GOOD. An item in Good condition may have a small dent, scratches, flaking, pitting, minor color fading, or a little rust, *but not all of these* on one tray and not placed so as to detract from part of the primary image of the tray. Any nail hole places a tray no higher than Good. Sometimes a condition will be stated as Good+ or Good-. Numerically, Good can range from around 6.0/6.5 to 7.0.

FAIR. Fair condition will be similar to the problems of a Good tray, only more of them. The tray should have a mostly complete image with reasonable colors. Unless it is something very special, a Fair condition tray should not be considered for purchase. Numerically, Fair ranges from about 4.5/5.0 to 6.0/6.5.

POOR. Lots of pitting, fading, rust spots, flaking, scratches, and dents. Not a tray to show to anyone. In other words, worthless.

Buyers of *recent* trays should apply the above condition guidelines in a slightly different manner, as described below.

• A tray dated past the early 1990s should *not* be considered for purchase unless it can easily be considered in *Excellent* condition or better. The reasons must be obvious but are stated here for the record. Enough of these trays are around, somewhere. It will be seen again. And, prices for a *Near Mint* versus a *Very Good* tray of this age won't vary that much.

• Some trays from the 1970s, 1980s, and early 1990s are scarce. Many were not produced in volume. For these trays, a collector could con-sider purchasing a tray in *Very Good* condition. Many of the other trays from these years are readily available and should not be considered unless *Excellent* or better.

• Some trays from the 1940s through the 1970s are as scarce as trays from the early part of the century, especially some of the beautiful Mexican deep round trays. Trays from these years could be considered for purchase in *Fair* to *Good* condition, but probably as a *filler* (see below). Others, such as the U.S. version of *Menu Girl* are readily available every day in Internet auctions.

• A *filler* is the term used to describe a tray that a collector would like to acquire but that is below the desired condition. The thinking is that the buyer would at least have the tray represented in the collection, even if it is in less desirable condition, and then trade up when a better one comes along, selling off the *filler* tray. This practice can work but requires discipline. Don't overpay for the *filler*. Be conscious of the condition versus the price. Consult reference books for suggested price ranges and the volumes produced.

After all the information on condition is absorbed, buyers should realize that the entire process is mostly an art and not a science. Collectors who are interested in trays of the 1970s through today are looking at prices *below* fifty dollars for most trays. If you are looking at an Internet auction that ends tomorrow or shopping at a flea market somewhere you won't be again and you see a specific tray that is in your area of collecting, grab it! But, as a last comment, remember that *Poor/Worthless* trays are not *fillers*. Some Internet auctions have pictured trays in such bad condition that it makes one flinch to view them. Yet some of these trays, even ones not classics, are sold. Resist that urge!

The Internet

The Internet has been thoroughly discussed and dissected in great detail in every type of media. How will it change things in the future? How will it affect us? Without question, many collectors have already seen a significant change in the way to build a collection. Suppose a collector had the time, the money, and the energy to travel around North America, visit hundreds of sellers, and sit through dozens of auctions, all at once. That collector then *might* get an opportunity to bid on the variety of items that are usually available in just *ONE DAY* of Internet auctions on just a few of the Internet auction sites.

In the preparation of data for this book, several auction sites were searched for Coca-Cola memorabilia listings and then specifically for Coca-Cola serving trays. One certainty is that the number and variety of auction sites and the types of auctions are expanding and changing almost daily. But, at the time the material in this book was created, the auction site at ebay.com had, by far, the greatest number of Coca-Cola memorabilia items in auction each day.

Auctions of Coca-Cola Memorabilia were reviewed from seventy specific days, chosen at random, during ten months in the year 2000. From this review the tray auctions were identified and documented, with results shown in the Internet dollar values that are part of the caption for each tray. Over 97,000 auctions were reviewed, an average of almost 1,400 each day. From that review *5,028* tray auctions containing *11,374* bids were documented!

Documenting an auction means (1) reviewing items such as tray name, date issued, color, and any other relevant details; (2) estimating the tray's condition from viewing the auction's picture and as stated in the description; (3) if the tray was sold, recording final bid price and number of bids; and (4) if the tray was not sold, noting whether the reason was that *no bids* were received or if the bids received did not meet the seller's required price (*reserve not met*).

The 5,028 auctions featured 409 different trays in at least one auction (over seventy percent of the total trays listed in this book). A total of 2,193 sales were recorded and are listed in the captions of 333 different trays. Note that over one-half of total tray auctions are no bid, some trays auctioned in unacceptable condition are not listed, and some auctions were dropped for other miscellaneous reasons. However, trays were auctioned and sales were recorded from every decade. The earlier classic trays (through the 1960s) represent twenty-seven percent of the auctions, thirty-six percent of the sales, and sixty-one percent of the bids (and, since trays of these years have a higher value, they recorded ninety percent of the total of *"reserve not met"* auctions).

Extrapolating results of the documented seventy days of auctions out to a full year shows that in the year 2000 it is most likely that over 25,000 Internet auctions of Coke trays were held, resulting in over 58,000 bids and the sale of over 11,000 trays!

Did the review gather data on every tray auction on the selected days? Probably not. The process is manual, time consuming, and tedious. But, the data recorded does provide a unique and comprehensive look at Internet auctions of Coke trays. Over sixty percent of the sales were at prices within the dollar value range of the expert references for that tray. Complete details on Internet auction data can be found in the Appendix.

Captions

One of the objectives of this book is to provide thorough details about each tray in a consistent format. The caption accompanying every picture contains this detail. A sample caption is shown below, followed by descriptions of the listings. A *dash* indicates any item where the information is not available.

Sample Caption

Name: Good Boys and Girls; **Issued:** 1983
Comments: Reproduction of 1951 ad, by Haddon Sundblom; **Shape:** Standard Rectangle; **Size:** 10.5" x 13.5"; **Story:** Yes; **Country:** US; **Mfr/Dist:** Ohio Art Company, distributed by Trademark Marketing; **Border/Edge:** Green with Holiday Trim; **Quantity:** 10,500; *Courtesy of John E. Peterson.*
$ Value, References: $5-20 (1,2,5,7,x);
$ Value, Internet Auctions: $12; **# Sales:** 5

1. Name. Each caption begins with a name for the tray. Identifying the commonly used name helps in defining and communicating descriptions of specific trays in a consistent manner. For example, *Good Boys and Girls,* in the sample caption above, is the name of the 1951 Santa ad. To use a name that describes other elements of the picture such as *Santa at a Desk* or *Santa with a List* could cause confusion and/or misidentification. At least *forty-six* Santa trays have been reproduced from over twenty different Santa ads; *five* trays reproduce this specific ad. Tray names are compiled (1) from information in the reference materials listed in the Bibliography, (2) from a name or slogan indicated on the tray, or (3) from a theme on the tray, based on its image.

2. Issued. The year or years during which a tray was newly issued obviously establishes that tray's age. Determining the year issued is often simple, more difficult at other times, and sometimes nearly impossible.

Some trays have a date printed on the face of the tray or on the rim (easily subject to wear). Many recent trays have the year of issue listed on the back of the tray. Trays sometimes list a copyright year, which may or may not be the year issued. Other trays have an image similar to dated advertising materials, such as a calendar. In some cases, a slogan or logo can help provide clues to the year issued. But, a number of trays have been issued with absolutely no marking or clues anywhere to identify the year issued.

If the year of issue is not clear, the *circa* notation, meaning *about that time*, will be used (e.g., c.1956 or c.1940s). Also, trays issued as new over more than one year will have the beginning and ending years listed in the caption.

3. Comments. Comments include a variety of items, such as the source of the image, the name of an artist, and other miscellaneous details. The comments are intended to provide additional information of interest on that specific tray.

4. Shape. Trays have four shapes: round, rectangle, square, and oval. But, to further differentiate trays, those shapes not in the most

common or *standard* size are noted with additional descriptive terms such as *large, small,* or *long.* Also, descriptions will frequently list tray depth, as measured from the top edge of the border to the tray's face. The standard depth is .75" to 1.0." Trays with less depth are called *flat,* while trays with more depth are indicated as *deep.* Details of a tray's shape are useful in identifying specific trays, since several images have been reproduced in more than one shape. As an example, the 1910 *The Coca-Cola Girl* tray can be found reproduced in at least four shapes.

5. Size. Each tray shape also has size variations, stated in inches.

6. Story. A *"Yes"* indicates that some words about the image or the commemorative can be found on the tray. The information can range from a few words on the face or the rim up to a few hundred words on the back. Beginning around the late 1980s, trays, notably those licensed and distributed by *Trademark Marketing,* began to have useful information printed on the back.

7. Country. The country of issue helps identify and categorize tray collections. Some licensed trays issued from the 1970s to today are U.S. trays with trademark and story information printed in English *and* French to allow for distribution in Canada. Most trays issued in Canada are noted as either English Canadian or French Canadian. A few early images were issued in English in two similar but separate trays, one U.S. and one Canadian. The differentiation, if any, is usually only a small detail on the rim.

8. Mfr./Dist. This information is another aid in helping collectors accurately identify trays. The manufacturer's name and city are clearly listed on many early trays. In the 1980s and 1990s trays list *Coke Brands* as the Coca-Cola corporate licensing organization and many also list a manufacturer and/or distributor.

9. Border/Edge. This detail lists the color of the tray's border and/or rim. Other border details and words are also listed in many cases. This information provides collectors with a checkpoint. It is important for a collector to be able to look at a tray or at least a picture or computer image. But, pictures may not always show colors accurately and even the actual tray may be sun-bleached or had its colors distorted in some other way.

10. Quantity. The number of trays produced will be listed if available. Most quantities of *classic* trays have never been accurately determined and/or made available. But, for such trays that are fifty to one hundred years old, the condition, by far, is the most important variable in determining value.

The quantity produced is of more importance on recent trays. A high percentage should still be in *Very Good* or better condition since these trays were not generally used at soda fountains, drive-ins, bars, or other places where they would have daily use (some might have the remnants of a sticky hanger on the back). Therefore, suppose two different 1977 trays are both in *Very Good* condition but that 150,000 copies is the volume produced for one and 800 the volume produced for the other. It is reasonable to assume that the tray produced in the lower quantity is, or will be, harder to find over time and thus should have a greater dollar value.

Quantity information in the captions was obtained from (1) printed volumes on the tray, (2) volumes provided by the manufacturer or distributor, or (3) volumes identified in the reference materials.

11. Courtesy of. This acknowledges contributions of others who provided photographs or trays to be photographed. Without their support the book would not have been possible.

12. $ Value, References. The Bibliography lists all references researched for this book. *Dollar value* ranges in the caption represent a composite of values from any of eight specific sources (all published in the last four years) that list the specific tray.

As mentioned previously, a tray's condition is critical in determining value. For the dollar values shown, trays from the *1960s and earlier* should be in *Good* to *Excellent* or better condition. A *Good* condition tray would be at the lower end of the range; *Excellent* would be towards the higher end. Trays in *Near Mint* condition will typically have higher values than those shown while those in *Fair* or *Poor* condition will have values below the range. More recent trays from the *1970s to the early 1990s* should be in *Very Good* or better condition for the dollar values shown. Trays issued from the *mid-1990s to today* should be at least in *Excellent* condition.

Numbers in parenthesis after the dollar value range correspond to the eight numbered references in the Bibliography used in determining the value range (see page 157). This detail allows further pursuit of information about a specific tray. An "*x*" in the parenthesis notes that one or more collector or dealer quotes were included in the dollar value range.

If less than three references are listed, the dollar value range will note that fact by adding the abbreviation "*est.*" The intention of this added abbreviation is to further alert readers that the dollar value is not to be used as a firm guide.

13. $ Value, Internet Auctions. The Internet section earlier in this chapter provides information on how auctions were reviewed. The dollar value reflects an *average* of final bid amounts from completed Internet auctions for that specific tray. The amount does *not* include shipping/handling, insurance, postage, or any other costs associated with money orders, checks, or credit cards. These extras can add several dollars to the price paid. The dollar value follows the same tray condition guidelines outlined in the previous section. Tray condition is somewhat harder to determine accurately from Internet auction pictures and descriptions.

14. # Sales. This detail lists the total number of *completed Internet auctions* that were reviewed in determining the dollar value. Excluded are auctions where (1) the tray was outside the guidelines for condition, (2) the tray did not meet the minimum reserve price established by the seller, and (3) no bids were made.

If less than three sales were recorded, the dollar value will note that fact by adding the words "*for info only*." The intention of the added words is to further alert readers that the dollar value is not to be used as a firm guide.

A reader may not need every detail for every tray . . . at least not today. But, the number of identified trays continues growing, including multiple versions of the same image. And, based on data from Internet auctions, collector interest in recent trays is growing as well.

## Chapter One

The First Classics (The Untouchables) 1897-1919

This period of less than twenty-five years produced twenty-two identified trays. Trays issued during these years contain sixteen different images (fifteen are women) and they have become the first group of familiar classics. The remaining six trays are variations of the sixteen images. Pictured in this chapter are twenty-one of the twenty-two identified trays. During these years, Coca-Cola expanded from a fledgling fountain drink into a beverage sold throughout the United States and countries around the world.

The classic images on trays issued in these early years will be prominent on reproduction trays in future years. Reproduction trays picture an image from an earlier tray, not necessarily in the same shape, size, or color. They are first identified in the late 1960s. From then through 1999, *eighty-four* tray reproductions have been identified and are listed in Chapter Seven of this book. Eleven of the sixteen images from 1897-1919 have at least one tray reproducing the image. The trays from these years eventually appear on *fifty-six* other trays, or two-thirds of all the identified reproductions!

Trays from these years are scarce and command the highest dollar values. Condition of all the classic early trays is most important in determining dollar value. Many examples, in excellent or better condition, are the highlights of Coca-Cola collections and are seldom seen for sale. Some of the trays might even be called *untouchables* since availability at *any* price is very limited.

Comments will be placed in each Chapter regarding Internet auctions for trays from the years reviewed in that Chapter. Trays from 1897-1919 are not frequently seen in Internet auctions. In the auctions reviewed for this book, thirty-four were found. Nineteen of those auctions did not conclude in a sale since the bids did not meet the seller's reserve price or the tray just did not get any bids. Fifteen trays did successfully sell, but all of those sales were trays in Good or worse condition. Sales of trays in Good or worse condition will *not* be listed in future Chapters, but *will* be included in this Chapter's caption details due to the scarcity of these earliest classic trays.

NOTE that many of the trays shown in this chapter are considered to be in as good a condition as *any* that will be seen—the book is fortunate to be able to present these images. However, many collectors interested in acquiring trays from the classic period will not always be able to find (or afford the acquisition of) trays in the top condition of these images. Therefore, a collector may acquire a *filler* tray in pursuit of the eventual perfect collection. (See the complete comments on filler trays in the Introduction, page 8.) The first two Chapters of this book display additional pictures for certain trays to demonstrate condition differences and to show the reasonable quality levels that can be found in *filler* trays. Chapter One has pictures of six such trays.

1897-1899

Two trays are identified from the 1800s. Both are images used in the calendar of that year as well as in other advertising materials.

Many collectors know of *Victorian Girl*, 1897, but few have one. Only a few examples of this tray exist.

The 1899 *Hilda with The Pen* is the first of four years of *Hilda* trays. Hilda Clark, a musical celebrity of that time, was pictured on many types of advertising items.

Name: Victorian Girl; **Issued:** 1897, also on calendar
Comments: Note on the desk reads: *This card entitles you to one glass of Coca-Cola, free, at the fountain of any dispenser of Coca-Cola;* **Shape:** Round; **Size:** 9.375"; **Story:** —;
Country: US; **Mfr/Dist:** —; **Border/Edge:** Red, with cola beans; **Quantity:** —; *Courtesy of Bill and Jan Schmidt.*
$ Value, References: $14,000-$37,500 (1,4,5,7)
$ Value, Internet Auctions: —; **# Sales:** —

Name: Hilda with The Pen; **Issued:** 1899, also on calendar
Comments: First year of Hilda trays; **Shape:** Round; **Size:** 9.625"; **Story:** —;
Country: US; **Mfr/Dist:** Standard Advertising Company; **Border/Edge:** Red, cola beans; **Quantity:** —; *Courtesy of Bill and Jan Schmidt.*
$ Value, References: $9,500-$20,000 (1,4,5)
$ Value, Internet Auctions: —; **# Sales:** —

1900-1909

Fourteen trays are identified from the first decade of the twentieth century, including three additional *Hilda* images. Thirteen of the trays are pictured in this section. The 1900 *Hilda with Glass and Note* is the reproduction champ with nineteen identified reproduction trays, all issued in the late 1970s and all but one to commemorate various bottler anniversaries. Although more bottler anniversary trays used the *Hilda with Glass and Note* than any other image, *Hilda with The Roses*, 1901, *Bottle 5¢*, 1903, the 1905 *Lillian Nordica with Bottle*, and *Relieves Fatigue*, 1907, were also reproduced on a total of eleven additional bottler anniversary trays.

Hilda with Glass and Note, 1900; *Hilda with The Roses,* 1901; and *Hilda with The Glass,* 1903 complete the four years of trays from this celebrity. The 1903 *Hilda* is additionally found in two large oval trays, also called *Big Hilda* (one pictured). Never again will any person or any other image equal *Hilda* either in the number of years on a tray or in the number of new trays issued! Mr. and Mrs. William B. Schmidt generously provided the picture of the tray, *Hilda with Glass and Note,* 1900, from their collection (along with providing many other pictures). This tray is the actual one photographed for the many reproduction commemorative trays of the late 1970s.

The border of trays during this decade was usually decorated with drawings of cola beans and other colorful flourishes. Any words were on the face of the tray. The 1903 *Hilda with The Glass* trays are the first to include words on the border, with the script *Coca-Cola* centered on the tray's bottom border.

Name: Hilda with The Roses; **Issued:** 1901, ©1900, also on calendar
Comments: First tray to show a price for Coca-Cola, branches are listed in Philadelphia, Chicago, Los Angeles, and Dallas; **Shape:** Round; **Size:** 9.75"; **Story:** —; **Country:** US; **Mfr/Dist:** Meek & Beech Company; **Border/Edge:** Yellow with cola beans, blue/red edge; **Quantity:** —; *Courtesy of Bill and Jan Schmidt.*
$ Value, References: $3,350-$7,600 (1,2,4,5,8)
$ Value, Internet Auctions: —; **# Sales:** —

Name: Hilda with Glass and Note; **Issued:** 1900, ©1899, also on calendar
Comments: Note reads: *Coca-Cola makes flow of thought more easy and reasoning power more vigorous.* Book on table indicates branches in Philadelphia, Chicago, Los Angeles, and Dallas; **Shape:** Round; **Size:** 9.625"; **Story:** —; **Country:** US; **Mfr/Dist:** Standard Advertising Company; **Border/Edge:** Yellow with cola beans, blue/red edge; **Quantity:** —; *Courtesy of Bill and Jan Schmidt.*
$ Value, References: $7,700-$12,250 (1,4,5,7,8)
$ Value, Internet Auctions: —; **# Sales:** —

Name: Hilda with The Glass (Pewter Holder); **Issued:** 1903, also on calendar
Comments: Fourth year of Hilda trays, branch list adds Baltimore, New York and Boston; **Shape:** Round; **Size:** 9.75"; **Story:** —; **Country:** US; **Mfr/Dist:** Chas. W. Shonk Company; **Border/Edge:** Gold, flower trim; **Quantity:** —; *Courtesy of Bill and Jan Schmidt.*
$ Value, References: $2,700-$7,300 (1,2,3,4,5,7,8)
$ Value, Internet Auctions: $2,325 (for info only); **# Sales:** 1 (Good)

Name: Hilda with The Glass (Pewter Holder), *or* Big Hilda; **Issued:** 1903, also on calendar
Comments: Largest of the classic trays; **Shape:** Large Oval; **Size:** 15.125" x 18.625"; **Story:** —; **Country:** US; **Mfr/Dist:** Chas. W. Shonk Company; **Border/Edge:** Gold, flower trim; **Quantity:** —; *Courtesy of Bill and Jan Schmidt.*
$ Value, References: $3,500-$8,400 (1,2,3,4,5,7,8,x)
$ Value, Internet Auctions: —; **# Sales:** —

Bottle 5¢, c.1903-1912, is the only company-issued tray to feature a bottle as the central image. It is also the last flat round tray to be issued until the reproduction trays of the late 1970s, sixty-five years later. U.S., Mexican and German round trays are identified beginning in the 1950s, but these trays have a depth of 1.25" or more. The *Bottle 5¢* tray was distributed over several years by local bottlers to their customers.

Many trays, as expected, have an image of someone with a drink of Coca-Cola. Most tray images of this period show a glass, signaling a drink of Coca-Cola from a soda fountain. Only three trays from 1897 to 1919 (the years covered in this Chapter) feature a bottle. One is the 1903 *Bottle 5¢*. Another is *Topless Girl*, c.1905, issued by Western Coca-Cola Company, a bottler. The third bottle tray, issued in 1905, features another musical celebrity and is titled *Lillian Nordica with Bottle*. The companion tray is *Lillian Nordica with Glass*. Over the years, calendars and other advertising items were issued in multiple versions, with a glass in some and a bottle in others. But, these 1905 trays are the first of only two classic tray images to be issued in versions for both the fountain and the bottle market.

Name: Bottle 5¢; **Issued:** c.1903-1912
Comments: Tray words: *The Most Refreshing Drink in the World.* Last classic round shape; **Shape:** Round; **Size:** 9.75"; **Story:** —; **Country:** US; **Mfr/Dist:** Chas. W. Shonk Company; **Border/Edge:** Gold; **Quantity:** —; *Courtesy of Bill and Jan Schmidt.*
$ Value, References: $4,500-$10,000 (1,3,4,5,7,8)
$ Value, Internet Auctions: —; **# Sales:** —

Name: Hilda with The Glass (Pewter Holder), *or* Big Hilda; **Issued:** 1903
Comments: Second picture, lower condition grade; **Shape:** Large Oval; *Courtesy of John E. Peterson.*

Name: Lillian Nordica with Glass; **Issued:** 1905, ©1904, also on calendar
Comments: Fountain version, *Drink Coca-Cola at Soda Fountains;* **Shape:** Oval;
Size: 10.625" x 12.875"; **Story:** —; **Country:** US; **Mfr/Dist:** Meek Company;
Border/Edge: Red edge, four cola beans; **Quantity:** —; *Courtesy of Bill and Jan Schmidt.*
$ Value, References: $2,200-$5,000 (2,3,4,5,7,8)
$ Value, Internet Auctions: —; **# Sales:**—

Name: Lillian Nordica with Bottle; **Issued:** 1905, ©1904, also on calendar
Comments: Bottle version, *Drink Carbonated Coca-Cola in Bottles;* **Shape:**
Oval; **Size:** 10.625" x 12.875"; **Story:** —; **Country:** US; **Mfr/Dist:** Meek
Company; **Border/Edge:** Red edge, four cola beans; **Quantity:** —;
Courtesy of Bill and Jan Schmidt.
$ Value, References: $2,200-$5.000 (1,3,4,5,7,8,x)
$ Value, Internet Auctions: —; **# Sales:** —

Topless Girl, c.1905-1907, is the only known exception in the group of company-issued trays from the first one (1897) until at least the 1940s, since it was issued by the Western Coca-Cola Bottling Company, head-quartered in Chicago. Western Coca-Cola Bottling was a parent bottler, working with franchised bottling operations. The tray's purpose was to encourage the use of Coca-Cola as a mixer in cocktails. This company also issued a number of Vienna Plates, not pictured here.

Juanita, 1906, *Relieves Fatigue,* 1907, and *Exhibition Girl,* 1909, are three additional familiar images that were also on calendars for the same years. The latter two images were issued in both oval and large oval shapes.

Name: Topless Girl; **Issued:** c.1905-1907
Comments: Not company-issued; **Shape:** Round; **Size:** 12.25"; **Story:** —; **Country:** US;
Mfr/Dist: Distributed by Western Coca-Cola Bottling Company; **Border/Edge:** Brown,
gold trim; **Quantity:** —; *Courtesy of Bill and Jan Schmidt.*
$ Value, References: $3,600-$9,200 (1,2,3,4,5,7,8,x)
$ Value, Internet Auctions: $800 (for info only); **# Sales:** 2 (Poor)

Name: Topless Girl; **Issued:** c.1905-1907
Comments: Second picture, lower condition grade; **Shape:** Round;
Courtesy of John E. Peterson.

Name: Juanita; **Issued:** 1906, ©1905, also on calendar
Comments: Named for a song with popular sheet music, from painting by Wolf & Company, Philadelphia. First tray with someone drinking Coca-Cola; **Shape:** Oval; **Size:** 10.875" x 13"; **Story:** —; **Country:** US; **Mfr/Dist:** N.Y. Metal Ceiling Company;
Border/Edge: Gold, cola beans, red/black edge; **Quantity:** est 36,000; *Courtesy of Bill and Jan Schmidt.*
$ Value, References: $1,950-$3,900 (1,3,4,5,7,8,x)
$ Value, Internet Auctions: —; **# Sales:** —

Name: Relieves Fatigue; **Issued:** 1907, also on calendar
Comments: Tray named for words printed on the tray; **Shape:** Oval; **Size:** 10.875" x 13.25"; **Story:** —; **Country:** US; **Mfr/Dist:** Chas. W. Shonk Company; **Border/Edge:** Gold, cola beans, red edge; **Quantity:** —; *Courtesy of Bill and Jan Schmidt.*
$ Value, References: $1,900-$4,300 (1,3,4,5,7,8,x)
$ Value, Internet Auctions: —; **# Sales:** —

Name: Juanita; **Issued:** 1906
Comments: Second picture, lower condition grade; **Shape:** Oval; *Courtesy of John E. Peterson.*

Name: Relieves Fatigue; **Issued:** 1907, also on calendar
Comments: Tray named for words printed on the tray; **Shape:** Large Oval; **Size:** 13.75" x 16.625"; **Story:** —; **Country:** US; **Mfr/Dist:** Chas. W. Shonk Company; **Border/Edge:** Gold, cola beans, red edge; **Quantity:** —; *Courtesy of Bill and Jan Schmidt.*
$ Value, References: $2,700-$6,750 (4,5,8)
$ Value, Internet Auctions: $4,600 (for info only); **# Sales:** 2 (Good)

Name: Exhibition Girl; **Issued:** 1909, ©1908, also on calendar
Comments: Image for many years thought to be at St. Louis World's Fair, but is not; **Shape:** Oval; **Size:** 10.625" x 13"; **Story:** —; **Country:** US; **Mfr/Dist:** H. D. Beech Company; **Border/Edge:** Blue, cola beans, gold stripe; **Quantity:** —; *Courtesy of Bill and Jan Schmidt.*
$ Value, References: $1,150-$2,900 (2,4,5,7,x)
$ Value, Internet Auctions: $720 (for info only); **# Sales:** 1 (Good)

Name: Exhibition Girl; **Issued:** 1909
Comments: Second picture, lower condition grade; **Shape:** Large Oval; *Courtesy of John E. Peterson.*

Name: Exhibition Girl; **Issued:** 1909, ©1908, also on calendar
Comments: Image for many years thought to be at St. Louis World's Fair, but is not; **Shape:** Large Oval; **Size:** 13.625" x 16.625"; **Story:** —; **Country:** —; **Mfr/Dist:** H. D. Beech Company; **Border/Edge:** Blue, cola beans, gold stripe; **Quantity:** —; *Courtesy of Bill and Jan Schmidt.*
$ Value, References: $1,800-$4,200 (1,3,4,5,7,8,x)
$ Value, Internet Auctions: $1,525 (for info only); **# Sales:** 1 (Good)

1910-1919

The second decade of the century contained only six identified trays, with four different images—all of women. All four were featured on calendars and other advertising materials of the same year. No new trays were issued in this decade after 1916-1917, due to World War I material restrictions. Each image has been reproduced on a later tray at least once. All the trays from this decade are pictured in this section.

Hamilton King is the first noted artist to create and sign an image featured on a tray. His drawings of beautiful and elegantly dressed women were featured on calendars for 1910, 1911, 1912, and 1913. Trays issued in 1910 and 1913 contain that year's calendar picture. Names for these images are frequently confused. The 1910 tray, signed by the artist, is correctly named *The Coca-Cola Girl*, and that name appears on the face of the tray. It is also the first tray issued in a rectangle shape that will become the most used tray shape for the next *ninety* years. No information is found that discusses why this tray shape was first created. But, considering the width of the hat on *The Coca-Cola Girl*, one can wonder whether or not it was a design decision: in trays with both standard rectangle and oval versions, examples can be found where parts of the image are in the rectangle tray but not in the oval one.

The 1913 woman, issued in both a rectangle and large oval shape and also signed by the artist, is correctly titled *The Hamilton King Girl*. *The Coca-Cola Girl* has been identified on eight reproduction trays while *The Hamilton King Girl* is found on two.

Name: The Coca-Cola Girl;
Issued: 1910
Comments: Second picture,
lower condition grade; **Shape:**
Std Rectangle; *Courtesy of John E.
Peterson.*

Name: The Coca-Cola Girl; **Issued:** 1910, ©1909, also on calendar
Comments: By Hamilton King, with signature and tray name on tray, first rectangle
shape; **Shape:** Std Rectangle; **Size:** 10.5" x 13.25"; **Story:** —; **Country:** US; **Mfr/
Dist:** The American Artworks; **Border/Edge:** Red, with trim; **Quantity:** —;
Courtesy of Bill and Jan Schmidt.
$ Value, References: $450-$1,750 (1,2,3,4,5,7,8,x)
$ Value, Internet Auctions: $120 (for info only); **# Sales:** 1 (Poor)

Name: The Hamilton King Girl; **Issued:** 1913, ©1912, also on calendar
Comments: By Hamilton King, with signature on tray; **Shape:** Std Rectangle; **Size:**
10.25" x 13.25"; **Story:** —; **Country:** US; **Mfr/Dist:** Passaic Metalware Company;
Border/Edge: Black, gold stripe; **Quantity:** —; *Courtesy of Bill and Jan Schmidt.*
$ Value, References: $500-$1,050 (3,4,5,7,8)
$ Value, Internet Auctions: —; **# Sales:** —

Name: The Hamilton King Girl; **Issued:** 1913, ©1912, also on calendar
Comments: By Hamilton King, with signature on tray; **Shape:** Large Oval; **Size:** 12.5"
x 15.25"; **Story:** —; **Country:** US; **Mfr/Dist:** Passaic Metalware Company; **Border/
Edge:** Black, gold stripe; **Quantity:** —; *Courtesy of Bill and Jan Schmidt.*
$ Value, References: $550-$1,150 (3,4,5,7,8,x)
$ Value, Internet Auctions: —; **# Sales:** —

Name: The Hamilton King Girl;
Issued: 1913
Comments: Second picture,
lower condition grade; **Shape:**
Std Rectangle; *Courtesy of John E.
Peterson.*

Betty or *Betty Girl*, 1914, is a beautiful and familiar image that is also on the 1914 calendar. Unlike trays issued in the years just before and after Betty, no known issues or confusion exists.

Elaine, pictured on a calendar and a tray, with a 1916 copyright, was issued as a tray in 1916-1917. *Elaine* is notable for several reasons. First, just as with the earlier images by Hamilton King, arriving at the correct name is confusing. The artwork was copyrighted *Girl With a Basket of Flowers*, which would usually become the *correct* identification. But that name never really caught on with collectors (maybe because the flowers in the picture are not in a basket). Referring back to 1914, the calendar picture was named Betty and that name, sensibly, was adopted for the 1914 tray with the same image. In the two years following Betty, 1915 and 1916, calendars both feature *Elaine*, but each calendar has a different image. Clearly, the 1916 calendar and tray have the same image. But the name Elaine is on the 1915 calendar and not on the 1916 version (the calendar with the same image as the tray but copyrighted with a different title). Therefore, while the tray image matches the 1916 calendar that has a copyrighted name seldom used, the commonly used name matches the one on the 1915 calendar, which never had a tray. Got it? Adding to the confusion is a third name, *The World War I Girl*, which has sometimes been used. That name might relate to material restrictions imposed for World War I that also made this tray the decade's last.

Elaine is the name, correct or not. The tray is the first long rectangle tray (8.5" x 19.0") issued by The Coca-Cola Company. It is also the last long rectangle tray; in fact it is the *only* long rectangle tray issued until the *Elaine* reproductions of 1973, fifty-seven years later. *Elaine* has eight identified reproductions, the same number as *The Coca-Cola Girl*, 1910.

Name: Betty *or* Betty Girl; **Issued:** 1914, also on calendar
Comments: Name used on calendar; **Shape:** Large Oval; **Size:** 12.375" x 15.5"; **Story:** —; **Country:** US; **Mfr/Dist:** Passaic Metalware Company; **Border/Edge:** Black, gold stripe; **Quantity:** —; *Courtesy of John E. Peterson.*
$ Value, References: $275-$850 (1,2,3,4,5,7,8,x)
$ Value, Internet Auctions: $302; **# Sales:** 3 (Good)

Name: Betty *or* Betty Girl; **Issued:** 1914, also on calendar
Comments: Name used on calendar; **Shape:** Std Rectangle; **Size:** 10.625" x 13.375"; **Story:** —; **Country:** US; **Mfr/Dist:** Passaic Metalware Company; **Border/Edge:** Black, gold stripe; **Quantity:** —; *Courtesy of Bill and Jan Schmidt.*
$ Value, References: $350-$1,000 (1,2,3,4,5,7,8,x)
$ Value, Internet Auctions: —; **# Sales:** —

Name: *Popular name*: Elaine *or* Elaine Girl, © *Name*: Girl With a Basket of Flowers, *also* World War I Girl; **Issued:** 1916, also on calendar
Comments: Only classic tray issued in this shape; **Shape:** Long Rectangle; **Size:** 8.5" x 19"; **Story:** —; **Country:** US; **Mfr/Dist:** Stelad Signs Passaic Metalware Company; **Border/Edge:** Gold, with trim; **Quantity:** —; *Courtesy of John E. Peterson.*
$ Value, References: $300-$600 (1,2,3,4,5,7,8,x)
$ Value, Internet Auctions: $260; **# Sales:** 4 (3 Good, 1 Fair)

Chapter Two

The Classic Beauties, 1920-1949

Forty-three trays have been found in the three decades of trays reviewed in this chapter. This group of trays contains thirty-one different images and, for many collectors, these beauties are the ones most identified with classic Coca-Cola trays. Included in the trays of this era are the *red-bordered* standard rectangle trays, issued from 1926 to the early 1950s, which provide a color recognition that instantly makes the viewer think *Coke*. Also identified are the first known trays issued into the Canadian and Mexican markets—with language changes but in the same image—*and* the first identified trays issued by a market outside the U.S. (Mexico). Twenty-five reproduction trays have been identified from the 1970s to the 1990s using ten of the images from trays of these decades.

Twenty-seven of the thirty-one images and thirty-one of the forty-three trays from 1920 to 1949 are pictured in this chapter.

Internet auctions for trays in Chapter Two are found more frequently than auctions for earlier trays. Four hundred forty-six auctions were reviewed, about thirteen times as many as for trays in Chapter One. Fifty percent of the trays in Chapter One were involved in at least one auction, while sixty-seven percent of the trays in this Chapter were found in at least one auction. In these Chapters, the rate of successful sales of trays in acceptable condition averages about thirty-eight percent of the total number of tray auctions.

NOTE that as with Chapter One, many of the trays shown in this chapter are considered to be in as good a condition as any that will be seen. Again, the book is fortunate to be able to present these images. As noted previously, however, many collectors interested in acquiring trays from the classic period will not always be able to find (or afford the acquisition of) trays in the top condition of these images. Therefore, a collector may acquire a *filler* tray in pursuit of the eventual perfect collection. (See the complete comments on filler trays in the Introduction, page 8.)

Chapters One and Two display additional pictures for certain trays to demonstrate condition differences and to show the *very good* quality levels that can be acquired in *filler* trays. Chapter Two has ten such examples pictured in addition to the six shown in Chapter One.

1920-1929

Six *Girls* are pictured on trays from 1920 to 1925. Four of them have more than one name (see the caption detail). All six were also featured on that year's calendar and other advertising items. All the images of the 1920s and thirteen of the fifteen trays are pictured here.

Golfer Girl or *Garden Girl*, 1920, is noted for several reasons. *Golfer Girl* is the last company-issued tray in an oval shape *and* the last to be issued in multiple shapes or sizes until *Picnic Cart* in 1958, over thirty-five years later. The golf activity that resulted in the tray's name is in the picture on the calendar and can be seen on the standard rectangle tray but *not* on the oval version. *Golfer Girl* is the first in a procession of at least one tray a year, totaling thirty-nine trays, over the next twenty-three years.

Summer Girl and *Autumn Girl* are two trays that do not have a consensus on the year of issue. One is from 1921, the other from 1922. Calendars from both years with both images have been identified in reference materials, adding to the confusion. Since summer is ahead of autumn and at least two noted collectors independently agree, *Summer Girl* is listed here as issued in its copyright year, 1921, with *Autumn Girl* dated in 1922. A 1976 issue of the Coca-Cola Collector Newsletter listed information, provided by The Company, on 1970s reproduction trays. That information also dated *Autumn Girl* as 1922.

Summer Girl has small gold squares around the border. These are a unique detail to this rectangle tray but are similar to parts of the border design on earlier round trays.

Flapper Girl, 1923, is the most reproduced tray of the 1920s, with eight trays identified.

Smiling Girl, 1924, is the only tray of this period identified in two versions with the *same* image, shape, and size, differing only in the color of the border. One is pictured.

Party Girl, 1925, is the last image for several years to also be on that year's calendar. Of the twenty images on trays issued from *Victorian Girl* in 1897 to *Party Girl*, only two were *not* featured on that year's calendar. One is the bottler-issued tray, *Topless Girl*, c.1905, and the other is the c.1903-1912 *Bottle 5¢*. The *Party Girl* calendar also shows a bottle of Coke on a table at her side. Having both a bottle and a glass eliminates the need for two versions of the calendar. The original tray does not show the bottle. *Party Girl* is elegant in her fox fur and jewelry, but she doesn't make eye contact with us.

Name: Golfer Girl or Garden Girl; **Issued:** 1920, also on calendar
Comments: Golf game in background of tray image, first rectangle tray with words in the border; **Shape:** Std Rectangle; **Size:** 10.5" x 13.25"; **Story:** —;
Country: US; **Mfr/Dist:** —; **Border/Edge:** Brown, gold stripe; **Quantity:** —; *Courtesy of Bill and Jan Schmidt.*
$ Value, References: $350-$1,150 (2,3,4,7,8)
$ Value, Internet Auctions: $523 (for info only); **# Sales:** 2

Name: Golfer Girl *or* Garden Girl; **Issued:** 1920, also on calendar
Comments: Last year of classic oval trays; **Shape:** Large Oval; **Size:** 13.75"
x 16.75"; **Story:** —; **Country:** US; **Mfr/Dist:** —; **Border/Edge:** Brown,
gold stripe; **Quantity:** —;
Courtesy of Bill and Jan Schmidt.
$ Value, References: $350-$1,100 (2,3,4,5,7,8)
$ Value, Internet Auctions: —; **# Sales:** —

Name: Autumn Girl *or* Navy Girl; **Issued:** 1922, also on calendar
Comments: Navy name from style of hat. Question on year issued, 1922
vs. 1921; **Shape:** Std Rectangle; **Size:** 10.5" x 13.25"; **Story:** —; **Country:**
US; **Mfr/Dist:** —; **Border/Edge:** Brown, gold stripe; **Quantity:** —;
Courtesy of Bill and Jan Schmidt.
$ Value, References: $350-$1,100 (1,2,3,4,5,7,8,x)
$ Value, Internet Auctions: $456 (for info only); **# Sales:** 2

Name: Summer Girl *or* Baseball Girl; **Issued:** 1921, ©1921, also on calendar
Comments: Baseball in tray name based on background in calendar image.
Question on year issued, 1921 versus 1922; **Shape:** Std Rectangle; **Size:** 10.5" x
13.25"; **Story:** —; **Country:** US; **Mfr/Dist:** H. D. Beech Co.; **Border/Edge:**
Brown, gold stripe, small square gold dots on interior of border; **Quantity:** —;
Courtesy of Bill and Jan Schmidt.
$ Value, References: $350-$1,100 (1,2,3,4,5,7,8,x)
$ Value, Internet Auctions: $595; **# Sales:** 3

Name: Flapper Girl; **Issued:** 1923, also on calendar
Comments: Tray has © but with no year listed, calendar picture has additional details,
such as a feathery fan in her left hand; **Shape:** Std Rectangle; **Size:** 10.5" x 13.25"; **Story:**
—; **Country:** US; **Mfr/Dist:** The American Artworks; **Border/Edge:** Brown, gold stripe;
Quantity: —; *Courtesy of Bill and Jan Schmidt.*
$ Value, References: $225-$675 (1,2,3,4,5,7,8,x)
$ Value, Internet Auctions: $235; **# Sales:** 5

Name: Smiling Girl; **Issued:** 1924, also on calendar
Comments: Issued in two versions, differing only in border colors. Calendar picture has a glass *and* bottle; **Shape:** Std Rectangle; **Size:** 10.5" x 13.25"; **Story:** —; **Country:** US; **Mfr/Dist:** The American Artworks; **Border/Edge:** Brown, gold stripe; **Quantity:** —; *Courtesy of Bill and Jan Schmidt.*
$ Value, References: $350-$1000 (1,2,3,4,5,7,8,x)
$ Value, Internet Auctions: $479; **# Sales:** 3

Name: Party Girl *or* Girl at Party; **Issued:** 1925, also on calendar
Comments: Detailed background party scene, calendar picture has glass *and* bottle; **Shape:** Std Rectangle; **Size:** 10.5" x 13.25"; **Story:** —; **Country:** US; **Mfr/Dist:** The American Artworks; **Border/Edge:** Brown, gold stripe; **Quantity:** —; *Courtesy of Bill and Jan Schmidt.*
$ Value, References: $250-$600 (1,2,3,4,5,7,8,x)
$ Value, Internet Auctions: $273 (for info only); **# Sales:** 2

Name: Smiling Girl; **Issued:** 1924
Comments: Second picture, lower condition grade; **Shape:** Std Rectangle; *Courtesy of John E. Peterson.*

The first distinctive red border tray is *Golfers* or *Golfing Couple*, 1926, created by Fred Mizen. With one exception in 1936, the red border was used on the next thirty-five company-issued trays over the next twenty-seven years. It is also the first tray in twenty-one years to picture a bottle.

Curb Service, 1927, is the first rectangle tray with a *horizontal* image. *Soda Jerk*, also issued in 1927, makes that year only the second in which trays were issued with more than one image (counting the 1905 *Lillian Nordica* with glass *and* bottle as two images). In contrast, during the 1970s, 1980s, and 1990s several years have over *twenty* different images.

In 1928 the *Girl With The Bobbed Hair* is the first identified tray also issued to the Mexican market (not pictured). The logo reads "Tome Coca-Cola" or "Drink . . ."

Girl in Swimsuit, 1929, is the first tray since *Lillian Nordica*, 1905, to be issued in a bottle version to promote bottle sales *and* a version with a glass to promote fountain sales. It is also the *last* identified set of trays to have these two versions. In 1929, bottle sales of Coca-Cola exceeded fountain sales for the first time.

It may be hindsight, but the decline in the importance of Coca-Cola fountain sales versus bottle consumption, together with the emerging home market, were no doubt important factors that mark the beginning of the end of company-issued serving trays. In the next year, 1930, the *last* tray promoting fountain sales would be issued.

Name: Curb Service; **Issued:** 1927, ©1927
Comments: First tray with image in a horizontal position, first person pictured on a tray sipping Coca-Cola (from a glass) through a straw; **Shape:** Std Rectangle; **Size:** 10.5" x 13.25"; **Story:** —; **Country:** US; **Mfr/Dist:** Tindeco; **Border/Edge:** Red, gold edge band; **Quantity:** —; *Courtesy of Bill and Jan Schmidt.*
$ Value, References: $400-$1050 (1,2,3,4,5,7,8,x)
$ Value, Internet Auctions: —; **# Sales:** —

Name: Golfers *or* Golfing Couple; **Issued:** 1926, ©1926
Comments: By Fred Mizen, signature on tray. First of the red border trays, first with words in the top and bottom borders; **Shape:** Std Rectangle; **Size:** 10.5" x 13.25"; **Story:** —; **Country:** US; **Mfr/Dist:** The American Artworks; **Border/Edge:** Red, gold edge band; **Quantity:** —; *Courtesy of Bill and Jan Schmidt.*
$ Value, References: $300-$1,050 (1,2,3,4,5,7,8,x)
$ Value, Internet Auctions: $442; **# Sales:** 3

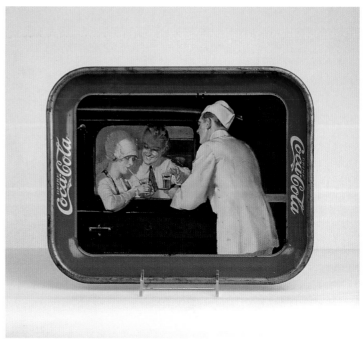

Name: Curb Service; **Issued:** 1927
Comments: Second picture, lower condition grade; **Shape:** Std Rectangle; *Courtesy of John E. Peterson.*

Name: Girl With The Bobbed Hair *or* Bobbed Hair Girl; **Issued:** 1928, ©1927 **Comments:** First person pictured on a tray sipping Coca-Cola (from a bottle) through a straw; **Shape:** Std Rectangle; **Size:** 10.5" x 13.25"; **Story:** —; **Country:** US; **Mfr/Dist:** The American Artworks; **Border/Edge:** Red, gold edge band; **Quantity:** —; *Courtesy of Bill and Jan Schmidt.*
$ Value, References: $275-$950 (1,2,3,4,5,7,8,x)
$ Value, Internet Auctions: $300 (for info only); **# Sales:** 2

Name: Soda Jerk *or* Soda Person; **Issued:** 1927, ©1927
Comments: First rectangle tray image that overlaps into part of the border; **Shape:** Std Rectangle; **Size:** 10.5" x 13.25"; **Story:** —; **Country:** US; **Mfr/Dist:** The American Artworks; **Border/Edge:** Red, gold edge band; **Quantity:** —; *Courtesy of Bill and Jan Schmidt.*
$ Value, References: $300-$950 (1,2,3,4,5,7,8,x)
$ Value, Internet Auctions: $500 (for info only); **# Sales:** 2

Name: Girl in Swimsuit (with Glass) *or* Girl in Yellow Bathing Suit; **Issued:** 1929, ©1929
Comments: First tray since 1905 issued in both bottle and glass versions; **Shape:** Std Rectangle; **Size:** 10.5" x 13.25"; **Story:** —; **Country:** US; **Mfr/Dist:** The American Artworks; **Border/Edge:** Red, gold edge band; **Quantity:** —; *Courtesy of Bill and Jan Schmidt.*
$ Value, References: $300-$800 (1,2,3,4,5,7,8,x)
$ Value, Internet Auctions: —;
 # Sales: —

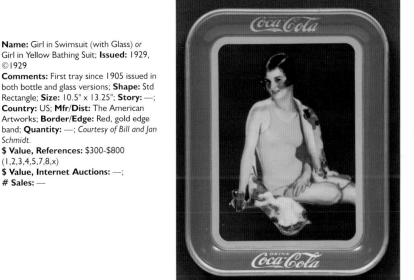

Name: Soda Jerk *or* Soda Person; **Issued:** 1927
Comments: Second picture, lower condition grade; **Shape:** Std Rectangle; *Courtesy of John E. Peterson.*

Name: Girl in Swimsuit (with Bottle) *or* Girl in Yellow Bathing Suit; **Issued:** 1929, ©1929
Comments: First tray since 1905 issued in bottle and glass versions; **Shape:** Std Rectangle; **Size:** 10.5" x 13.25"; **Story:** —; **Country:** US; **Mfr/Dist:** Tindeco; **Border/Edge:** Red, brown edge stripe; **Quantity:** —; *Courtesy of Bill and Jan Schmidt.*
$ Value, References: $300-$825 (2,3,4,5,7,8,x)
$ Value, Internet Auctions: $229; **# Sales:** 3

1930-1939

In this decade seventeen trays with eleven different images have been identified. Nine of the images are of beautiful women. Each tray is the standard rectangle shape and manufactured by The American Artworks, Coshocton, Ohio. All eleven images and thirteen of the seventeen trays are pictured. This group contains some of The Coca-Cola Company's most famous advertising images. As a group they certainly are desirable to many collectors since they have classic beauty and prices that make them affordable to a greater number of interested buyers than many of the earlier trays.

Noted artists produced over fifty percent of the decade's images. Haddon Sundblom and Hayden Hayden each created two images; Norman Rockwell and Bradshaw Crandell each created one. Four of the eleven images from the 1930s have been reproduced. The 1938 *Girl at Shade* leads the decade with three identified reproductions.

In 1930 two trays were issued. One is *Bather Girl*, a bottle version and one, the *Telephone Girl*, is for fountain sales. These trays represent the *only* time that two images were used for bottle/fountain versions. *Telephone Girl* is the *last* company-issued tray to promote fountain sales.

Barefoot Boy is the only *original* company-issued tray from a painting by Norman Rockwell. Although the quantity manufactured of specific trays is not generally known, Petretti's *Classic Trays* estimates that close to two million *Barefoot Boy* trays could have been made. It was a *very* popular tray and calendar. Rockwell produced several other paintings used for calendars in the 1930s.

Girl in the Yellow Bathing Suit or *Girl on Beach*, 1932, is a tray with minimal information but no controversy or confusion. Hayden Hayden created the beautiful image.

Name: Bather Girl *or* Bathing Beauty; **Issued:** 1930, ©1930
Comments: Bottle tray for the year, last of fountain/bottle versions;
Shape: Std Rectangle; **Size:** 10.5" x 13.25"; **Story:** —; **Country:** US; **Mfr/Dist:** The American Artworks; **Border/Edge:** Red, with gold edge; **Quantity:** —; *Courtesy of Bill and Jan Schmidt.*
$ Value, References: $200-$625 (1,2,3,4,5,7,8,x)
$ Value, Internet Auctions: $382; **# Sales:** 4

Name: Telephone Girl *or* Girl with Phone; **Issued:** 1930, ©1930
Comments: *Meet me at the soda fountain*, fountain tray for the year, last year of fountain/bottle versions; **Shape:** Std Rectangle; **Size:** 10.5" x 13.25"; **Story:** —; **Country:** US; **Mfr/Dist:** The American Artworks; **Border/Edge:** Red, with gold edge; **Quantity:** —; *Courtesy of Bill and Jan Schmidt.*
$ Value, References: $250-$550 (1,2,3,4,5,7,8,x)
$ Value, Internet Auctions: $230; **# Sales:** 3

Name: Bather Girl *or* Bathing Beauty; **Issued:** 1930
Comments: Second picture, lower condition grade; **Shape:** Std Rectangle; *Courtesy of John E. Peterson.*

Name: Barefoot Boy, Boy with Dog, *or* The Rockwell Tray; **Issued:** 1931
Comments: By Norman Rockwell, only *classic* Rockwell tray; **Shape:** Std Rectangle;
Size: 10.5" x 13.25"; **Story:** —; **Country:** US; **Mfr/Dist:** The American Artworks;
Border/Edge: Red, with gold edge; **Quantity:** est 2,000,000; *Courtesy of Bill and Jan
Schmidt.*
$ Value, References: $375-$1,000 (1,2,3,4,5,7,8,x)
$ Value, Internet Auctions: $450; **# Sales:** 4

Name: Girl in the Yellow Bathing Suit *or* Girl on Beach; **Issued:** 1932, ©1932
Comments: By Hayden Hayden, with signature; **Shape:** Std Rectangle; **Size:** 10.5" x
13.25"; **Story:** —; **Country:** US; **Mfr/Dist:** The American Artworks; **Border/Edge:** Red,
with gold edge; **Quantity:** —; *Courtesy of Bill and Jan Schmidt.*
$ Value, References: $300-$900 (1,2,3,4,5,7,8,x)
$ Value, Internet Auctions: —; **# Sales:** —

Name: Barefoot Boy, Boy with Dog, *or* The Rockwell Tray; **Issued:** 1931
Comments: Second picture, lower condition grade; **Shape:** Std Rectangle;
Courtesy of John E. Peterson.

Name: Girl in the Yellow Bathing Suit *or* Girl on Beach; **Issued:** 1932
Comments: Second picture, lower condition grade; **Shape:** Std Rectangle;
Courtesy of John E. Peterson.

Celebrities are featured on three trays, beginning with the movie star *Frances Dee* in 1933. The previous celebrity pictured on a tray was *Lillian Nordica*, twenty-eight years earlier, in 1905. *Tarzan*, with *Johnny Weissmuller and Maureen O'Sullivan*, 1934, is the second celebrity tray and also the second with a horizontal image. *Madge Evans*, a movie star in a 1935 party scene, is the third celebrity tray and also the *last* celebrity to ever appear on any identified tray.

Name: Tarzan; **Issued:** 1934, ©1934
Comments: Second horizontal tray, first with words top and bottom borders on long ends. Tray face words: *Maureen O'Sullivan and Johnny Weissmueller, Metro-Goldwyn-Mayer Featured Players*; **Shape:** Std Rectangle; **Size:** 10.5" x 13.25"; **Story:** —; **Country:** US; **Mfr/Dist:** The American Artworks; **Border/Edge:** Red, with gold edge; **Quantity:** —; *Courtesy of Bill and Jan Schmidt.*
$ Value, References: $350-$1,000 (1,2,3,4,5,7,8,x)
$ Value, Internet Auctions: $365; **# Sales:** 6

Name: Frances Dee; **Issued:** 1933, ©1933
Comments: First celebrity on a tray since 1905. Tray words: *a Paramount Player*; **Shape:** Std Rectangle; **Size:** 10.5" x 13.25"; **Story:** —; **Country:** US; **Mfr/Dist:** The American Artworks; **Border/Edge:** Red, with gold edge; **Quantity:** —; *Courtesy of Bill and Jan Schmidt.*
$ Value, References: $250-$775 (1,2,3,4,5,7,8,x)
$ Value, Internet Auctions: $245 (for info only); **# Sales:** 2

Name: Tarzan; **Issued:** 1934
Comments: Second picture, lower condition grade;
Shape: Std Rectangle;
Courtesy of John E. Peterson.

Name: Frances Dee; **Issued:** 1933, ©1933;
Comments: Second picture, lower condition grade; **Shape:** Std Rectangle; *Courtesy of John E. Peterson.*

Name: Madge Evans; **Issued:** 1935, ©1935
Comments: Last known celebrity on a classic tray. Tray face words: *Madge Evans, Metro-Goldwyn-Mayer*; **Shape:** Std Rectangle; **Size:** 10.5" x 13.25"; **Story:** —; **Country:** US; **Mfr/Dist:** The American Artworks; **Border/Edge:** Red, with gold edge; **Quantity:** —; *Courtesy of Bill and Jan Schmidt.*
$ Value, References: $175-$475 (1,2,3,4,5,7,8,x)
$ Value, Internet Auctions: $240; **# Sales:** 5

Hostess Girl is a beautiful 1936 tray from the artist Hayden Hayden. It is the exception tray in the red border series; this tray reverses the color order. In c.1936-1937 *Hostess Girl* was also the first identified tray to be issued into the Canadian Market, with both English and French versions (not pictured). The French Canadian tray reads *Buvez Coca-Cola* in the logo.

Running Girl, 1937, is a beach scene with particularly beautiful colors. Various reference books discuss whether or not the tray's image was originally by an illustrator named Rolf Armstrong and the accuracy of a woman's claim to be the model.

Girl at Shade, 1938, is by Bradshaw Crandell. The tray was also issued in English Canadian (not pictured) and French Canadian versions.

Springboard Girl, 1939, is by Haddon Sundblom and is the ninth and last swimsuit image in the red border series. A silver edge rim instead of gold is introduced. *Springboard Girl* is the first identified tray to also be issued in a French Canadian version (not pictured) *and* a Mexican version.

Name: Running Girl; **Issued:** 1937, ©1937
Comments: Image attributed to illustrator Rolf Armstrong; **Shape:** Std Rectangle; **Size:** 10.5" x 13.25"; **Story:** —; **Country:** US; **Mfr/Dist:** The American Artworks; **Border/Edge:** Gold, with red edge; **Quantity:** —; *Courtesy of Bill and Jan Schmidt.*
$ Value, References: $150-$375 (1,2,3,4,5,7,8,x)
$ Value, Internet Auctions: $170; **# Sales:** 9

Name: Hostess Girl *or* Hostess Tray; **Issued:** 1936, ©1936
Comments: By Hayden Hayden, tray reverses the colors of red border trays; **Shape:** Std Rectangle; **Size:** 10.5" x 13.25"; **Story:** —; **Country:** US; **Mfr/Dist:** The American Artworks; **Border/Edge:** Gold, with red edge; **Quantity:** —; *Courtesy of Bill and Jan Schmidt.*
$ Value, References: $175-$500 (1,2,4,5,7,8,x)
$ Value, Internet Auctions: $388; **# Sales:** 5

Name: Girl at Shade, Girl in the Afternoon, *or* Girl in Yellow Hat; **Issued:** 1938, ©1938, *similar to* calendar image **Comments:** By Bradshaw Crandell, with signature on tray. Calendar model has different dress and hat, and hands on legs leaning right; **Shape:** Std Rectangle; **Size:** 10.5" x 13.25"; **Story:** —; **Country:** US; **Mfr/Dist:** The American Artworks; **Border/Edge:** Gold, with red edge; **Quantity:** —; *Courtesy of Bill and Jan Schmidt.*
$ Value, References: $125-$325 (1,2,3,4,5,6,7,8,x)
$ Value, Internet Auctions: $128; **# Sales:** 24

Name: Hostess Girl *or* Hostess Tray; **Issued:** 1936
Comments: Second picture, lower condition grade; **Shape:** Std Rectangle; *Courtesy of John E. Peterson.*

Name: Girl at Shade, Girl in the Afternoon, *or* Girl in Yellow Hat; **Issued:** 1938, ©1938, *similar to* calendar image
Comments: By Bradshaw Crandell, with signature on tray. Calendar model has different dress and hat, and hands on legs leaning right, *Buvez or Drink*; **Shape:** Std Rectangle; **Size:** 10.5" x 13.25"; **Story:** —; **Country:** US for Canadian (French) market; **Mfr/Dist:** The American Artworks; **Border/Edge:** Gold, with red edge; **Quantity:** —; *Courtesy of John E. Peterson.*
$ Value, References: $125-$325 (4,5,x)
$ Value, Internet Auctions: —; **# Sales:** —

1940-1949

Three of the standard rectangle red border trays, all featuring beautiful women, were issued in 1940, 1941, and 1942. World War II restrictions prevented additional U.S. trays from being issued until either 1948 or 1950, depending on one's view of the year that *Girl with Wind in Hair* was issued, as described in the next chapter. No reproductions have been identified for trays of this decade. Eleven trays with eight images have been listed from the 1940s. Pictures of four images on five trays are shown.

Sailor Girl, 1940, is the third horizontal tray to be issued and the first horizontal image also issued to the Canadian market, in English (not pictured) and French versions.

The first tray to include words and/or a logo on *all four* borders is the beautiful 1941 *Skater Girl*, by Haddon Sundblom. The small logo on the left and right borders is an outline of a woman drinking a bottle of Coca-Cola and is called *Silhouette Girl*. That logo is still in use today by the Coca-Cola Collectors Club.

Two logo trays were identified in one reference book but are not pictured here. And a third logo tray is listed, also without a picture.

Name: Springboard Girl; **Issued:** 1939, ©1939
Comments: By Haddon Sundblom, with signature on tray. Ninth and last of red border *swimsuit* trays, expanded top logo drops below border; **Shape:** Std Rectangle; **Size:** 10.5" x 13.25";
Story: —; **Country:** US; **Mfr/Dist:** The American Artworks;
Border/Edge: Red, thin silver lines, with silver edge; **Quantity:** —; *Courtesy of Bill and Jan Schmidt.*
$ Value, References: $175-$325 (1,2,3,4,5,7,8,x)
$ Value, Internet Auctions: $230; **# Sales:** 14

Name: Sailor Girl; **Issued:** 1940, ©1940
Comments: Third horizontal image issued on a tray; **Shape:** Std Rectangle; **Size:** 10.5" x 13.25"; **Story:** —; **Country:** US; **Mfr/Dist:** The American Artworks;
Border/Edge: Red, thin silver lines, with silver edge; **Quantity:** —; *Courtesy of Bill and Jan Schmidt.*
$ Value, References: $100-$350 (1,3,4,5,7,8,x)
$ Value, Internet Auctions: $219; **# Sales:** 23

Name: Springboard Girl; **Issued:** 1939, ©1939
Comments: *Deliciosa y Refresca*; **Shape:** Std Rectangle; **Size:** 10.5" x 13.25"; **Story:** —; **Country:** US for Mexican market; **Mfr/Dist:** The American Artworks; **Border/Edge:** Red, thin silver lines, with silver edge; **Quantity:** —; *Courtesy of John E. Peterson.*
$ Value, References: $125-$325 (4,5,x)
$ Value, Internet Auctions: —; **# Sales:** —

Name: Sailor Girl; **Issued:** 1940, ©1940
Comments: Third horizontal image; **Shape:** Std Rectangle; **Size:** 10.5" x 13.25"; **Story:** —; **Country:** US for Canadian (French) market; **Mfr/Dist:** The American Artworks; **Border/Edge:** Red, thin silver lines, with silver edge; **Quantity:** —; *Courtesy of John E. Peterson.*
$ Value, References: $75-$300 (4,5,x)
$ Value, Internet Auctions: —; **# Sales:** —

Name: Skater Girl *or* Ice Skater; **Issued:** 1941, ©1941
Comments: By Haddon Sundblom, first tray to include words or logos on all four sides. Silhouette Girl logo used on left and right sides; **Shape:** Std Rectangle; **Size:** 10.5" x 13.25"; **Story:** —; **Country:** US; **Mfr/Dist:** The American Artworks; **Border/Edge:** Red, with gold edge; **Quantity:** —; *Courtesy of Bill and Jan Schmidt.*
$ Value, References: $150-$375 (1,2,3,4,5,6,7,8,x)
$ Value, Internet Auctions: $224; **# Sales:** 12

Name: Woman in White Dress with Beads; **Issued:** c.1940s
Comments: Early Mexican tray; **Shape:** Std Rectangle; **Size:** 10.5" x 13.25"; **Story:** —; **Country:** Mexico; **Mfr/Dist:** —; **Border/Edge:** Red, with white edge; **Quantity:** —; *Courtesy of John E. Peterson.*
$ Value, References: $250-$675 (4,x)
$ Value, Internet Auctions: $250 (for info only); **# Sales:** 1

Two Girls at Car is the last tray identified as manufactured by The American Artworks. That business manufactured many of the 1920s trays, *all* of the 1930s trays, and the three red bordered trays of the 1940s. Al Mitchell, a noted Coca-Cola memorabilia collector, related to the author that the model for the woman standing by the car visited the 1979 Coca-Cola Collectors Club Convention held in Elizabethtown, Kentucky.

Three trays issued in Mexico have been identified from this decade. These are the *first* trays with images not also on U.S. trays of the same time period. Based on the general quality, the logo, and other small print on the tray, it appears that these were company-issued in Mexico. One of these trays is pictured.

Name: Two Girls at Car; **Issued:** 1942
Comments: Second picture, lower condition grade; **Shape:** Std Rectangle; *Courtesy of John E. Peterson.*

Name: Two Girls at Car; **Issued:** 1942, ©1942
Comments: Last US classic tray until after World War II, last tray from The American Artworks; **Shape:** Std Rectangle; **Size:** 10.5" x 13.25"; **Story:** —; **Country:** US; **Mfr/Dist:** The American Artworks; **Border/Edge:** Red, thin silver lines, with silver edge; **Quantity:** —; *Courtesy of Bill and Jan Schmidt.*
$ Value, References: $125-$375 (1,2,3,4,5,7,8,x)
$ Value, Internet Auctions: $212; **# Sales:** 18

## Chapter Three

The End of the Classics, 1950-1969

This two-decade period includes seventy-two identified trays. The trays contain forty-seven images with twenty-five additional trays having the same images but with variations in shape, size, or language. This period is the most difficult in terms of locating the known trays. Several infrequently seen Canadian and Mexican trays are the primary reason that more of the identified trays are not pictured. This chapter does show thirty-eight of the forty-seven images and fifty-four of the seventy-two trays.

While some data about pre-1950 trays is not available, the group from Chapters One and Two at least had some orderliness to it. The trays have had expert research on the year of issue and other details. Most of the sixty-five previously identified trays, dating from 1897 through the 1940s, are company-issued U.S. trays. Over sixty-six percent are the standard rectangle shape. More than forty percent of the images were also used on the calendar of the same year. The decade of the 1930s was a model of orderliness: every tray the same shape, from the same manufacturer, and with the year of issue not a question.

In contrast, the decades of the 1950s and 1960s are anything but orderly in items such as date of issue. Many of the U.S. trays don't have any date, though some clues can be found by looking at the tray for clothing, hairstyles, type of logo, and advertising phrases. It is not always clear whether or not The Coca-Cola Company even authorized them.

Mexican trays are the most numerous of these twenty years—both Mexican and Canadian trays outnumber the identified U.S. trays. This period has the first *reproductions*, both of earlier trays and earlier ads. Also found are the first trays from outside North America and the first trays that commemorate the anniversary of a Coca-Cola bottler, issued in Mexico more than a decade before any similar U.S. trays.

A measurement used in the first two Chapters to help characterize Internet auction activity is how many of the identified trays were seen in at least one auction. Even with the scarce trays of this Chapter, sixty-five percent of the identified trays were auctioned at least once, about the same as the the sixty-seven percent for Chapter Two. Over seven hundred tray auctions were logged. But, just *two trays* from the 1950s (*Menu Girl* and *Snacks*) account for *forty-five percent* of the total auctions!

A note of interest for sellers in the Internet auctions involves *pricing*. The 1956 TV tray, *Snacks*, is an example. In thirty-one auctions the tray, in good to excellent condition, sold for an average price of $9.35. But, in thirty-five other auctions the tray received *no bids* at the requested minimum price. Zero, none. The average minimum price requested by the sellers was $11.55, a mere twenty-three percent higher than the average sale price in the successful auctions.

Please review the comments about *Dollar Values* shown in the captions. They are covered in the Introduction, pages 9-10.

1950-1959

Thirty-two trays have been identified from the 1950s. Only nine trays are U.S. issues, while twenty are Canadian or Mexican trays *or* U.S. trays issued into those markets. Twenty-five trays with fifteen of the seventeen images have photographs.

Many 1950s U.S. trays are frequently available even today in *Very Good* or better condition. The abundance of these trays, fifty years later, suggests that some of them were issued over multiple years and in very, very large quantities.

A c.1950 U.S. tray (not pictured) was shown and described in one reference book, *The Illustrated Guide to the Collectibles of Coca-Cola*, by Cecil Munsey.

From a rare tray to a more available one, the *Girl with Wind in Hair* or *Girl with Red Hair*, by Haddon Sundblom, is the first metal U.S. tray issued after the lifting of World War II restrictions. Reference books and other collectors do not agree on 1948 versus 1950 as the year this tray was first issued. The consensus year used here is 1950. The image did appear on the 1948 U.S. calendar (March/April page) and the 1948 Canadian calendar (January/February page). The question is, why would this tray be the first of twenty trays spanning fifty years that was *not* issued in the same year as the calendar? Perhaps materials restrictions after World War II delayed production; perhaps the actual manufacturing of the tray was an issue since The American Artworks, primary manufacturer of trays for three decades, went out of business in 1950. A persuasive argument for 1950 seems to be that *two* subsequent U.S. trays that have general agreement on the year issued also were images from calendars or ads appearing two years earlier. *Menu Girl*, 1953, was an image on the 1951 U.S. calendar and *Pansy Garden*, 1961, appeared first in 1959 magazine ads.

Girl with Wind in Hair has been identified in at least five variations, more than any other tray to date. The two U.S. versions (one pictured) differ in the background screen, with the more common version being lighter at the bottom. At least one version was issued for the Canadian market (French). A Mexican version reads *Deliciosa and Refrescante*. One last version is a very unique tray. With the same image and English wording, this version also has *oriental* characters, probably Chinese, on the left and right borders. The colors and clarity of this tray suggest it is not a reproduction. Could this tray have been issued by some Coca-Cola operation serving the armed forces in the Far East during this time? This newly identified version is clearly similar to the other original versions, versus the reproduction tray identified in the 1980s.

Name: Girl with Wind in Hair *or* Girl with Red Hair; **Issued:** 1950-1952, on 1948 calendar, US (Mar/Apr page) and Canada (Jan/Feb page) **Comments:** By Haddon Sundblom, some disagreement on issue date vs. 1948, first tray with ad words on all four sides; **Shape:** Std Rectangle; **Size:** 10.5" x 13.25"; **Story:** —; **Country:** US; **Mfr/Dist:** —; **Border/Edge:** Red, with silver edge; **Quantity:** —; *Courtesy of John E. Peterson.* **$ Value, References:** $50-$125 (1,3,4,5,6,7,8,x) **$ Value, Internet Auctions:** $54; **# Sales:** 41

Name: Girl with Wind in Hair *or* Girl with Red Hair; **Issued:** 1950-1952, on 1948 calendar, US (Mar/Apr page) and Canada (Jan/Feb page)
Comments: By Haddon Sundblom, tray words: *Delicieux* and *Refraichissant*; **Shape:** Std Rectangle; **Size:** 10.5" x 13.25"; **Story:** —; **Country:** US for Canadian (French) market; **Mfr/Dist:** —; **Border/Edge:** Red, with silver edge; **Quantity:** —; *Courtesy of John E. Peterson.*
$ Value, References: $75-$150 (4,5,8,x)
$ Value, Internet Auctions: $65 (for info only); **# Sales:** 2

A familiar face, *Menu Girl* or *Girl with Menu* is first pictured on the 1951 U.S. calendar, but the consensus is that this tray was issued in 1953 and was a new issue for several years (probably until the end of the decade), and undoubtedly in millions of copies. The U.S. version of this tray is, by far, the most frequently offered tray in Internet auctions.

The *Menu Girl* is sometimes confused with various *real* people, such as actresses Jane Wyman or Claudette Colbert. Al Mitchell, a noted Coca-Cola collector, related a conversation he had with the artist in which it was stated that this image is a composite of the *best* facial features from three models. Claudette Colbert did appear in advertising material for The Coca-Cola Company in the early 1930s, but no celebrity images have been identified since *Madge Evans* in 1935. Ms. Colbert did appear during the 1940s in ads for Royal Crown Cola.

The Mexican version of *Menu Girl* (not pictured) continues use of the familiar red border. But, on the U.S. and two Canadian versions (one pictured), after twenty-seven years and thirty-five trays, the red border is replaced by one filled with fourteen small images of outdoor activities. This detailed border was used *only* on this tray. Also, in some reference books, *Menu Girl* is said to have versions with alternate wording in one of the border banners (not pictured).

Name: Girl with Wind in Hair *or* Girl with Red Hair; **Issued:** 1950-1952, on 1948 calendar, US (Mar/Apr page) and Canada (Jan/Feb page)
Comments: By Haddon Sundblom, tray words: *Deliciosa* and *Rafrescanta*; **Shape:** Std Rectangle; **Size:** 10.5" x 13.25"; **Story:** —; **Country:** US for Mexican market; **Mfr/Dist:** —; **Border/Edge:** Red, with silver edge; **Quantity:** —; *Courtesy of John E. Peterson.*
$ Value, References: $55-$150 (4,5,x)
$ Value, Internet Auctions: —; **# Sales:** —

Name: Menu Girl *or* Girl with Menu; **Issued:** 1953-c.1960, on 1951 calendar, US (Mar/Apr page)
Comments: End of red border trays, slight change in rectangle size. Banners in border read: *Have a Coke* and *Thirst knows no season*; **Shape:** Std Rectangle; **Size:** 10.625" x 13.25"; **Story:** —; **Country:** US; **Mfr/Dist:** —; **Border/Edge:** Fourteen small pictures of year around activities; **Quantity:** —; *Courtesy of Bill and Jan Schmidt.*
$ Value, References: $45-$125 (1,2,3,4,5,7,8,x)
$ Value, Internet Auctions: $29; **# Sales:** 134

Name: Girl with Wind in Hair *or* Girl with Red Hair; **Issued:** 1950-1952, on 1948 calendar, US (Mar/Apr page) and Canada (Jan/Feb page)
Comments: By Haddon Sundblom, logo left and right in *oriental* language, probably Chinese; **Shape:** Std Rectangle; **Size:** 10.5" x 13.25"; **Story:** —; **Country:** US for international market, probably Far East; **Mfr/Dist:** —; **Border/Edge:** Red, with silver edge; **Quantity:** —; *Courtesy of John E. Peterson.*
$ Value, References: est $120-$180 (x)
$ Value, Internet Auctions: —; **# Sales:** —

Name: Menu Girl *or* Girl with Menu; **Issued:** 1953-c.1960, on 1951 calendar, US (Mar/Apr page) **Comments:** End of red border trays, slight change in rectangle size. Banners in border read: *Prenez un Coke* and *La soif aja pos de salson*; **Shape:** Std Rectangle; **Size:** 10.625" x 13.25"; **Story:** —; **Country:** US for Canadian (French) market; **Mfr/Dist:** —; **Border/ Edge:** Fourteen small pictures of year around activities; **Quantity:** —; *Courtesy of John E. Peterson.*
$ Value, References: $40-$100 (1,4,5,7,8,x)
$ Value, Internet Auctions: $64 (for info only); **# Sales:** 2

Name: Picnic Cart *or* Picnic Basket; **Issued:** c.1958 **Comments:** Horizontal Image; **Shape:** TV; **Size:** 13.5" x 18.75"; **Story:** —; **Country:** US; **Mfr/Dist:** Donaldson Art Company; **Border/Edge:** Brown faux wood, brown edge; **Quantity:** —; *Courtesy of Bill and Jan Schmidt.*
$ Value, References: $20-$50 (2,3,4,6,x)
$ Value, Internet Auctions: $21; **# Sales:** 10

TV Trays and Drive-in Car Trays

TV trays have a large rectangle shape, usually 13.625" x 18.75" in size, and can be distinguished by a wavy edge design. Six U.S. TV trays and ten Mexican images have been identified from the 1950s through the 1970s.

Snacks is the name used for the first identified TV tray, c.1956. Cooking utensils and snack plates appear to be pasted onto the surface. *Snacks* does not make an especially attractive appearance compared to other classic trays, but it is the most frequently seen TV tray in Internet auctions.

One other 1950s TV tray, issued c.1958, is *Picnic Cart*. A standard rectangle U.S. version was also issued with a rectangle logo, while the English Canadian (not pictured) and French Canadian versions are the first trays identified that use the logo commonly referred to as the *fish-tail*, but properly called the *arciform* logo. The logo was used from 1958 through the early 1960s.

Name: Picnic Cart *or* Picnic Basket; **Issued:** c.1958 **Comments:** Rectangle Logo, *Drink Coca-Cola*; **Shape:** Std Rectangle; **Size:** 10.75" x 13.25"; **Story:** —; **Country:** US; **Mfr/Dist:** Donaldson Art Company; **Border/Edge:** Brown short lines with a wicker look; **Quantity:** —; *Courtesy of Bill and Jan Schmidt.*
$ Value, References: $20-$60 (1,3,4,5,6,7,8,x)
$ Value, Internet Auctions: $22; **# Sales:** 26

Name: Snacks *or* Assortment; **Issued:** c.1956 **Comments:** First TV tray; **Shape:** TV (Large Rectangle with wavy edges); **Size:** 13.625" x 18.75"; **Story:** —; **Country:** US; **Mfr/Dist:** —; **Border/Edge:** Black, gold vine trim; **Quantity:** —;
Courtesy of Bill and Jan Schmidt.
$ Value, References: $10-$20 (1,2,3,4,7,x)
$ Value, Internet Auctions: $9.35; **# Sales:** 31

Name: Picnic Cart *or* Picnic Basket; **Issued:** c.1958 **Comments:** Fishtail or Arciform Logo, *Servez Coca-Cola*; **Shape:** Std Rectangle; **Size:** 10.75" x 13.25"; **Story:** —; **Country:** US for Canadian (French) market; **Mfr/Dist:** Donaldson Art Company; **Border/Edge:** Brown short lines with a wicker look; **Quantity:** —; *Courtesy of John E. Peterson.*
$ Value, References: $20-$75 (4,8,x)
$ Value, Internet Auctions: $15; **# Sales:** 8

Two German deep round trays reading *Trink*, the German word for "Drink" (one pictured), are the first trays identified from outside North America and the first two trays found from Germany.

TV trays were meant for those staying at home. But baby boomers and increasing automobile usage created the drive-in restaurant for eating away from home. Two 1950s *Drive-in trays* have been identified. One is a c.1959 U.S. tray with the fishtail logo. The second is Canadian and has wooden hooks or handles used to attach it to a car window. The tray is stainless steel and very attractive.

Name: Drive-In Tray; **Issued:** c.1959
Comments: Yellow oval with Coke bottle, wooden handles and hooks on tray back for attaching to car window; **Shape:** Large Rectangle; **Size:** 12.25" x 16.75"; **Story:**—; **Country:** Canada; **Mfr/Dist:** —; **Border/ Edge:** Stainless Steel; **Quantity:** —; *Courtesy of John E. Peterson*
$ Value, References: est $200-$300 (x)
$ Value, Internet Auctions: —; **# Sales:** —

Mexican and Canadian Trays

Five Mexican and nine Canadian trays have been identified from the 1950s in addition to the previously listed six U.S. trays that were issued into the Mexican and Canadian markets. Four of the Mexican and all the Canadian trays are pictured in this section.

A beautiful 1951 Mexican tray (not pictured) has the image of a woman with long black braids, dressed for a party and drinking a bottle of Coke. The same picture has been reproduced in a 1997 U.S. tray distributed by Trademark International for Coke Brands, called *Reanimese!* or *Refresh!*

The remaining four Mexican trays are from three different years. Three portray beautiful women in assorted activities—with Coke of course! The fourth is a logo or product tray with graphics and a bottle.

Name: Mach mal Pause . . .Trink Coca-Cola; **Issued:** 1950s
Comments: One of two logo trays that are the first known trays from outside North America, first trays identified from Germany; **Shape:** Deep Round; **Size:** 13.5" dia. x 1.75" depth; **Story:**—; **Country:** Germany; **Mfr/Dist:** —; **Border/Edge:** White with red back; **Quantity:** —; *Courtesy of John E. Peterson.*
$ Value, References: est $150-$225 (x)
$ Value, Internet Auctions: —; **# Sales:** —

Name: Drive in for Coke; **Issued:** 1959
Comments: Large Fishtail Logo, *Coca-Cola Goes Good with Food*; **Shape:** Large Rectangle; **Size:** 12.5" x 17.5"; **Story:** —; **Country:** US; **Mfr/Dist:** —, **Border/ Edge:** Light green; **Quantity:** —; *Courtesy of John E. Peterson.*
$ Value, References: $100-$350 (3,4,7,x)
$ Value, Internet Auctions: —; **# Sales:** —

Name: Coca-Cola with Bottle; **Issued:** 1953
Comments: An early logo tray; **Shape:** Deep Round; **Size:** 13.5" dia. x 1.75" depth; **Story:** —; **Country:** Mexico; **Mfr/ Dist:** —; **Border/Edge:** Red with gold edge; **Quantity:** —; *Courtesy of John E. Peterson.*
$ Value, References: est $175-$250 (4,x)
$ Value, Internet Auctions: —; **# Sales:** —

Name: Woman in White Blouse with Bottle; **Issued:** 1954, also on calendar
Comments: Bottom of tray has the letters *Z.H.*; **Shape:** Deep Round; **Size:** 13.25" dia. x 1.5" depth; **Story:** —; **Country:** Mexico; **Mfr/Dist:** —; **Border/Edge:** Red; **Quantity:** —; *Courtesy of John E. Peterson.*
$ Value, References: est $175-$250 (4,x)
$ Value, Internet Auctions: —; **# Sales:** —

Four 1957 Canadian images each have English and French versions. *Sandwich Tray* and *Girl with the Umbrella* are traditional images. *Rooster Tray* and *Birdhouse Tray* are unique collections of items that are the first collage trays.

Name: Sandwich Tray *or* Sandwiches; **Issued:** 1957
Comments: All food, horizontal image, border words: *Sign of Good Taste*; **Shape:** Std Rectangle; **Size:** 10.5" x 13.25"; **Country:** Canada (English); **Mfr/Dist:** —; **Border/Edge:** Green, gold edge; **Quantity:** —; *Courtesy of John E. Peterson.*
$ Value, References: $30-$140 (3,4,5,8,x)
$ Value, Internet Auctions: $66 (for info only); **# Sales:** 1

Name: Dark Hat and Gloves with Bottle; **Issued:** 1959
Comments: *Coca-Cola Grande de la Mucho Mas*; **Shape:** Deep Round; **Size:** 13.25" dia. x 1.5" depth; **Story:** —; **Country:** Mexico; **Mfr/Dist:** —; **Border/Edge:** Yellow with red edge; **Quantity:** —; *Courtesy of John E. Peterson.*
$ Value, References: est $175-$250 (4,x)
$ Value, Internet Auctions: —; **# Sales:** —

Name: Sandwich Tray *or* Sandwiches; **Issued:** 1957
Comments: All food, horizontal image, *Servez*, border words: *Signe de bon goût*; **Shape:** Std Rectangle; **Size:** 10.5" x 13.25"; **Story:** —; **Country:** Canada (French); **Mfr/Dist:** —; **Border/Edge:** Green, gold edge; **Quantity:** —; *Courtesy of John E. Peterson.*
$ Value, References: $35-$150 (2,4,5,8,x)
$ Value, Internet Auctions: $79 (for info only); **# Sales:** 1

Name: Coca-Cola Grande; **Issued:** 1959
Comments: Woman in skirt carrying tray with two bottles; **Shape:** Deep Round; **Size:** 13.25" dia. x 1.5" depth; **Story:** —; **Country:** Mexico; **Mfr/Dist:** —; **Border/Edge:** White, red edge; **Quantity:** —; *Courtesy of John E. Peterson.*
$ Value, References: est $150-$200 (x)
$ Value, Internet Auctions: —; **# Sales:** —

Name: Girl with the Umbrella *or* The Umbrella Tray; **Issued:** 1957, on calendar, US 1956, (Mar/Apr page)
Comments: Border words: *Delicious, Refreshing*; **Shape:** Std Rectangle; **Size:** 10.5" x 13.25"; **Story:** —; **Country:** Canada (English); **Mfr/Dist:** —; **Border/Edge:** Light green, gold edge; **Quantity:** —; *Courtesy of John E. Peterson.*
$ Value, References: $100-$425 (1,2,3,4,5,8,x)
$ Value, Internet Auctions: $123 **# Sales:** 3

Name: Rooster Tray; **Issued:** 1957
Comments: An early collage, kitchen items. Border words: *Delicieux, Refraichissant*; **Shape:** Std Rectangle; **Size:** 10.5" x 13.25"; **Story:** —; **Country:** Canada (French); **Mfr/Dist:** —; **Border/Edge:** Teal, gold edge; **Quantity:** —; *Courtesy of John E. Peterson.*
$ Value, References: $50-$175 (4,5,7,8,x)
$ Value, Internet Auctions: $50; **# Sales:** 11

Name: Girl with the Umbrella *or* The Umbrella Tray; **Issued:** 1957, on calendar, US 1956, (Mar/Apr page)
Comments: Border words: *Delicieux, Refraichaissant*; **Shape:** Std Rectangle; **Size:** 10.5" x 13.25"; **Story:** —; **Country:** Canada (French); **Mfr/Dist:** —; **Border/Edge:** Light green, gold edge; **Quantity:** —; *Courtesy of John E. Peterson.*
$ Value, References: $100-$425 (4,5,7,8,x)
$ Value, Internet Auctions: $135; **# Sales:** 5

Name: Birdhouse Tray; **Issued:** 1957
Comments: Outdoors, flowers, and Coke, border words: *Delicious, Refreshing*; **Shape:** Std Rectangle; **Size:** 10.5" x 13.25"; **Story:** —; **Country:** Canada (English); **Mfr/Dist:** —; **Border/Edge:** Light blue, gold edge; **Quantity:** —; *Courtesy of John E. Peterson.*
$ Value, References: $50-$175 (1,2,3,4,7,8,x)
$ Value, Internet Auctions: $55; **# Sales:** 11

Name: Rooster Tray; **Issued:** 1957
Comments: An early collage, kitchen items. Border words: *Delicious, Refreshing*; **Shape:** Std Rectangle; **Size:** 10.5" x 13.25"; **Story:** —; **Country:** Canada (English); **Mfr/Dist:** —; **Border/Edge:** Teal, gold edge; **Quantity:** —; *Courtesy of John E. Peterson.*
$ Value, References: $50-$175 (1,2,3,4,5,8,x)
$ Value, Internet Auctions: $60; **# Sales:** 8

Name: Birdhouse Tray; **Issued:** 1957
Comments: Outdoors, flowers, and Coke, border words: *Delicieux, Refraichaissant*; **Shape:** Std Rectangle; **Size:** 10.5" x 13.25"; **Story:** —; **Country:** Canada (French); **Mfr/Dist:** —; **Border/Edge:** Light blue, gold edge; **Quantity:** —; *Courtesy of John E. Peterson.*
$ Value, References: $50-$175 (4,7,8,x)
$ Value, Internet Auctions: —; **# Sales:** —

1960-1969

Forty trays have been identified from the 1960s. Five are U.S. issues, eight are Canadian, twenty-six are from Mexico, and one contains an Arabic language. A c.1960 Mexican TV tray and four Canadian trays represent the first identified trays that reproduce images from earlier trays and ads.

This chapter pictures twenty-nine trays and twenty-three of the thirty images. Two of the trays not pictured are Canadian; the rest are Mexican. After 1962 the rest of the decade contains *only* Canadian or Mexican trays.

Three Mexican trays are listed as 1960s since it has not been possible to make a more accurate identification on the year of issue. The one pictured is a *tip* or *change* tray with a horizontal image, acquired in Uruguay. This book has *not* concentrated on the overall population of tip trays. However, many are listed with details and pictures in Chapter Eight. The larger Mexican tip trays contain beautiful and sometimes unique images. Several have been included in this book as identified trays.

Two Mexican TV trays date from 1960. *Salad Bowl with Bottles* is the first Mexican tray to picture food. The other TV tray, c.1960, is the first identified tray to reproduce *any* earlier image, either from a tray or an ad. The image is the 1941 ad *Sprite Boy with Bottle*. This tray is the first of over *160* trays that will reproduce ads over the next four decades! See Chapter Seven for a review of tray reproductions from both other trays and ads.

A c.1961 tray, *Harvest* or *Thanksgiving*, and *Candlelight, c.1962*, are the last identified U.S. TV trays.

Name: Sprite Boy with Bottle; **Issued:** c.1960
Comments: Reproduction of 1941 ad, by Haddon Sundblom, *first* identified reproduction of an earlier ad; **Shape:** TV; **Size:** 13.25" x 18.5"; **Story:** —; **Country:** Mexico; **Mfr/Dist:** —; **Border/Edge:** Red stripe top and bottom, white border; **Quantity:** —;
Courtesy of John E. Peterson.
$ Value, References: est $50-$100 (x)
$ Value, Internet Auctions: —; **# Sales:** —

Name: Salad Bowl with Bottles; **Issued:** 1960
Comments: All food; **Shape:** TV; **Size:** 13.25" x 18.5"; **Story:** —; **Country:** Mexico; **Mfr/Dist:** Agosta; **Border/Edge:** Beige; **Quantity:** —; *Courtesy of John E. Peterson.*
$ Value, References: est $100-$130 (4,x)
$ Value, Internet Auctions: —; **# Sales:** —

Name: Woman with Bottle; **Issued:** 1960s
Comments: *También . . . en . . . Tamaño Mediano*; **Shape:** Tip Tray; **Size:** 6.5" x 7.5"; **Story:** —; **Country:** South America (Mexico or Uruguay); **Mfr/Dist:** —; **Border/Edge:** Beige; **Quantity:** —; *Courtesy of John E. Peterson.*
$ Value, References: est $60-$75 (x)
$ Value, Internet Auctions: —; **# Sales:** —

Name: Harvest, Farm Theme, *or* Thanksgiving; **Issued:** 1961
Comments: A farm party scene, with music; **Shape:** TV; **Size:** 13.25" x 18.5"; **Story:** —; **Country:** US; **Mfr/Dist:** —; **Border/Edge:** Red, flower trim, gold stripe; **Quantity:** —; *Courtesy of Bill and Jan Schmidt.*
$ Value, References: $15-$25 (1,2,3,4,7,x)
$ Value, Internet Auctions: $11; **# Sales:** 25

Name: Candlelight; **Issued:** 1962
Comments: Ham and Coke by candlelight; **Shape:** TV; **Size:** 13.25" x 18.5";
Story: —; **Country:** US; **Mfr/Dist:** Donaldson Art Company;
Border/Edge: Brown; **Quantity:** 25,000.
$ Value, References: $20-$50 (1,4,6,7,8,x)
$ Value, Internet Auctions: $20; **# Sales:** 14

Pansy Garden, c.1961, is considered the last of the classic trays. The two TV trays from 1961-1962 and *Pansy Garden* are the final U.S. company-issued original or classic-period trays that have been identified in the research for this book.

Six variations of *Pansy Garden* have been found, the most of any tray, surpassing the five versions of *Girl with Wind in Hair*. All six are horizontal images in the standard rectangle shape. Shown below is the original ad from an April, 1959 *National Geographic* magazine.

Three U.S. versions of *Pansy Garden* have variations in logo and border wording. Two trays have the lead words from the magazine advertisement on the top and bottom borders. One of these has the rectangle logo and the other the arciform, or fishtail logo. As noted, the arciform logo was first used in 1958 (*Picnic Cart*), and continued in use through the early 1960s. It is a useful clue to narrowing down the date of a tray. The third U.S. *Pansy Garden* version has the rectangle logo but with *Coke Refreshes You Best* and *Here's a Coke for You* in the border words.

Two Canadian versions, one English and one French, have the arciform logo and *no* border words. The sixth version is a rare tray containing Arabic text. The tray reads *refreshes you best* (in English) on the top border with Arabic text at the bottom, supposedly translating to *here's a Coke for you*. The logo is a variation of both the rectangle and arciform logo.

Name: Pansy Garden; **Issued:** 1961, from 1959 ad
Comments: Rectangle Logo, words: *Coke Refreshes you Best, Here's a Coke for you* in top and bottom border; **Shape:** Std Rectangle; **Size:** 10.75" x 13.25"; **Story:** —; **Country:** US; **Mfr/Dist:** Donaldson Art Company; **Border/Edge:** White; **Quantity:** —;
Courtesy of John E. Peterson.
$ Value, References: $15-$65 (1,2,3,4,5,6,7,8,x)
$ Value, Internet Auctions: $22; **# Sales:** 25

Name: Pansy Garden; **Issued:** 1961, from 1959 ad
Comments: Rectangle Logo, words: *Be Really Refreshed!* in top and bottom border; **Shape:** Std Rectangle; **Size:** 10.75" x 13.25"; **Story:** —; **Country:** US; **Mfr/Dist:** Donaldson Art Company; **Border/Edge:** White; **Quantity:** —;
Courtesy of Bill and Jan Schmidt.
$ Value, References: $20-$65 (3,5,8,x)
$ Value, Internet Auctions: $29; **# Sales:** 24

Name: *Pansy Garden*, back cover *National Geographic Magazine*; **Issued:** April, 1959 **Comments:** Original ad image used for Pansy Garden trays.

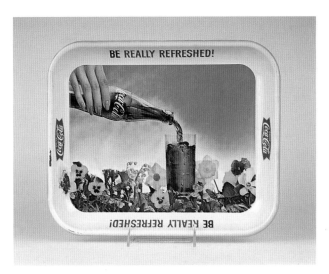

Name: Pansy Garden; **Issued:** 1961, from 1959 ad
Comments: Fishtail or Arciform Logo, words: *Be Really Refreshed!* in top and bottom border; **Shape:** Std Rectangle; **Size:** 10.75" x 13.25"; **Story:** —; **Country:** US; **Mfr/Dist:** Donaldson Art Company; **Border/Edge:** White; **Quantity:** —.
$ Value, References: $25-$65 (1,3,5,6,8,x)
$ Value, Internet Auctions: $18; **# Sales:** 15

Name: Pansy Garden; **Issued:** 1961, from 1959 ad
Comments: Fishtail or Arciform Logo, no words; **Shape:** Std Rectangle;
Size: 10.75" x 13.25"; **Story:** —; **Country:** US for Canadian (English)
market; **Mfr/Dist:** Donaldson Art Company; **Border/Edge:** White;
Quantity: —; *Courtesy of John E. Peterson.*
$ Value, References: est $30-$75 (x)
$ Value, Internet Auctions: $19; **# Sales:** 6

A group of twenty-one Mexican trays are the only trays identified from several years of the 1960s. The dates and number of trays are: 1961(2), 1963(5), 1964(1), 1965(2), 1966(2), 1967(3), 1968(3), and 1969(3). Fourteen of these trays are pictured here. Most are the deep round shape frequently found in Mexican trays, but TV trays and tip trays are also listed. Eight trays (four pictured) feature Coca-Cola bottles in ice and/or with food, consistent with advertising themes of those years. An additional ten trays (eight pictured) feature beautiful women in a variety of fashions, and all with a bottle of Coke!

The remaining three trays (two pictured) in this group are the *first* trays identified that commemorate a Coca-Cola bottler either for an anniversary or the opening of a new plant facility. The first of these, in 1964, is more than a decade ahead of the large group of U.S. bottler commemoratives. That bottler's location is La Laguna, Mexico and the tray begins what will become a total of *seventy-five* trays, through 1995, that celebrate a bottler for some activity. The second tray, in 1967, celebrates fifty years of the *embotelladora*, or bottler, from La Victoria. *Embotelladora Pacifico*, a 1968 TV tray (not pictured) is the first tray found that commemorates a new bottling plant.

Name: Pansy Garden; **Issued:** 1961, from 1959 ad
Comments: Fishtail or Arciform Logo, no words; **Shape:** Std Rectangle;
Size: 10.75" x 13.25"; **Story:** —; **Country:** US for Canadian (French)
market; **Mfr/Dist:** Donaldson Art Company; **Border/Edge:** White;
Quantity: —; *Courtesy of John E. Peterson.*
$ Value, References: est $30-$75 (x)
$ Value, Internet Auctions: $20; **# Sales:** 3

Name: Coca-Cola Grande; **Issued:** 1961
Comments: Coke bottle floating on ice. Back of tray: *Tome*; **Shape:** Deep Round; **Size:** 13.25" dia. x 1.5" depth; **Story:** —; **Country:** Mexico; **Mfr/Dist:** —; **Border/Edge:** White, red edge; **Quantity:** —; *Courtesy of John E. Peterson.*
$ Value, References: est $95-$130 (4,x)
$ Value, Internet Auctions: $65 (for info only); **# Sales:** 1

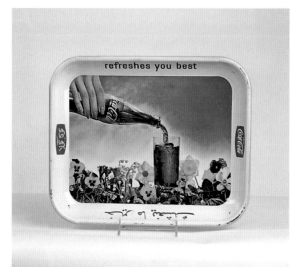

Name: Pansy Garden; **Issued:** 1961, from 1959 ad
Comments: Fishtail or Arciform Logo, right; words: *refreshes you best*, top border; *Arabic* phrases in bottom border and in modified arciform logo on left; **Shape:** Std Rectangle; **Size:** 10.75" x 13.25"; **Story:** —; **Country:** US for Arabic, Middle Eastern market; **Mfr/Dist:** Donaldson Art Company; **Border/Edge:** White; **Quantity:** —; *Courtesy of John E. Peterson.*
$ Value, References: est $65-$125 (x)
$ Value, Internet Auctions: —; **# Sales:** —

Name: Woman in Festive Dress; **Issued:** 1961
Comments: Colorful clothes, outdoor scene; **Shape:** Deep Round;
Size: 13.5" dia. x 1.75" depth; **Story:** —; **Country:** Mexico; **Mfr/**
Dist: —; **Border/Edge:** Red; **Quantity:** —;
Courtesy of John E. Peterson.
$ Value, References: est $120-$160 (4,x)
$ Value, Internet Auctions: —; **# Sales:** —

Name: Woman with Beret; **Issued:** 1963
Comments: Food on a tray with Coke; **Shape:** Deep Round;
Size: 13.5" dia. x 1.75" depth; **Story:** —; **Country:** Mexico; **Mfr/**
Dist: —; **Border/Edge:** White, red edge; **Quantity:** —;
Courtesy of John E. Peterson.
$ Value, References: est $100-$150 (4,x)
$ Value, Internet Auctions: —; **# Sales:** —

Name: Bottler 25th Anniversary,
La Laguna; **Issued:** 1964
Comments: *First* bottler
commemorative, 25th
Anniversary of La Laguna bottler,
1939-1964, *Embotelladora de*
Coahuila A.S.A.; **Shape:** Deep
Round; **Size:** 13.25" dia. x 1.5"
depth; **Story:** Yes; **Country:**
Mexico; **Mfr/Dist:** —; **Border/**
Edge: White, gold edge;
Quantity: —; *Courtesy of John E.*
Peterson.
$ Value, References: est $100-
$130 (4,x)
$ Value, Internet Auctions:
—; **# Sales:** —

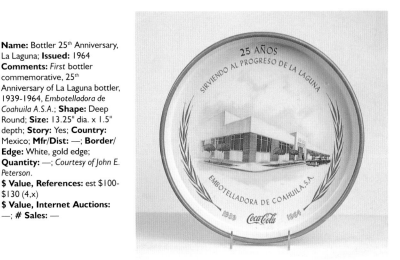

Name: Couple with Bottles; **Issued:** 1963
Comments: Man pouring Coke for a woman; **Shape:** Deep
Round; **Size:** 13.5" dia. x 1.75" depth; **Story:** —; **Country:**
Mexico; **Mfr/Dist:** —; **Border/Edge:** White; **Quantity:** —;
Courtesy of John E. Peterson.
$ Value, References: est $125-$200 (4,x)
$ Value, Internet Auctions: —; **# Sales:** —

Name: Woman with Bottle and
Daisy; **Issued:** 1963
Comments: *Le da mucho mas;*
Shape: Tip tray; **Size:** 6.625" x
7.875"; **Story:** —; **Country:**
Mexico; **Mfr/Dist:** —; **Border/**
Edge: Light Brown; **Quantity:**
—; *Courtesy of John E. Peterson.*
$ Value, References: $55-
$100 (4,8,x)
$ Value, Internet Auctions:
$5 (for info only); **# Sales:** 1

Name: Bottler 25th Anniversary, La Laguna;
Issued: 1964
Comments: Back of La Laguna tray, wheat
stalk and Coke; **Shape:** Deep Round.

Name: Woman with Large Earrings; **Issued:** 1967
Comments: Woman with bottle of Coke. Tray back: *Coca-Cola refresca engrande*; **Shape:** Deep Round; **Size:** 12.5" dia. x 1.25" depth; **Story:** —; **Country:** Mexico; **Mfr/Dist:** —; **Border/Edge:** White, red edge; **Quantity:** —; *Courtesy of John E. Peterson.*
$ Value, References: est $90-$130 (4,x)
$ Value, Internet Auctions: —; **# Sales:** —

Name: Woman in Red Sweater; **Issued:** 1965
Comments: Button Sign, bottle and glass; **Shape:** Tip Tray; **Size:** 6.625" x 7.875"; **Story:** —; **Country:** Mexico; **Mfr/Dist:** —; **Border/Edge:** Beige; **Quantity:** —; *Courtesy of Robyn Ray.*
$ Value, References: est $45-$60 (4,x)
$ Value, Internet Auctions: $96 (for info only); **# Sales:** 1

Name: Fanta Girl; **Issued:** 1966
Comments: Featuring Coca-Cola's orange drink, *Fanta Estabien Buena*; **Shape:** Deep Round; **Size:** 13.25" dia. x 1.75" depth; **Story:** —; **Country:** Mexico; **Mfr/Dist:** —; **Border/Edge:** Teal face, white border; **Quantity:** —; *Courtesy of John E. Peterson.*
$ Value, References: est $45-$70 (x)
$ Value, Internet Auctions: —; **# Sales:** —

Name: Bottles in Ice; **Issued:** 1967
Comments: Bottles in crushed ice. Words on tray, front and back: *Coca-Cola refresca engrande*; **Shape:** Deep Round; **Size:** 13.5" dia. x 1.75" depth; **Story:** —; **Country:** Mexico; **Mfr/Dist:** —; **Border/Edge:** —; **Quantity:** —; *Courtesy of John E. Peterson.*
$ Value, References: est $75-$125 (4,x)
$ Value, Internet Auctions: $65 (for info only); **# Sales:** 1

Name: Bottler 50th Anniversary, La Victoria; **Issued:** 1967
Comments: Old architecture from 1531 and from anniversary years 1917 and 1967. Commemorative tray of 50th Anniversary, La Victoria bottler; **Shape:** Deep Round; **Size:** 13.25" dia. x 1.5" depth; **Story:** Yes; **Country:** Mexico; **Mfr/Dist:** —; **Border/Edge:** White, cobblestone style trim, red edge; **Quantity:** —; *Courtesy of John E. Peterson.*
$ Value, References: est $55-$80 (x)
$ Value, Internet Auctions: —; **# Sales:** —

Name: Woman in V-Neck Dress; **Issued:** c.1966
Comments: Woman with swept back hair and bottle of Coke; **Shape:** Deep Round; **Size:** 13.25" dia. x 1.5" depth; **Story:** —; **Country:** Mexico; **Mfr/Dist:** —; **Border/Edge:** White, red edge; **Quantity:** —; *Courtesy of John E. Peterson.*
$ Value, References: est $75-$125 (4,x)
$ Value, Internet Auctions: $65 (for info only); **# Sales:** 1

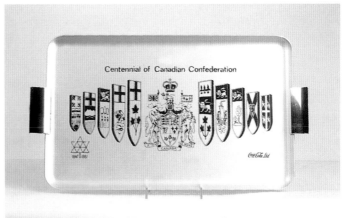

Name: Fruit Arrangement; **Issued:** 1969
Comments: Bowl of fruit, *Tome*; **Shape:** TV; **Size:** 13.5" x 18.75"; **Story:** —; **Country:** Mexico; **Mfr/Dist:** —; **Border/Edge:** Brown; **Quantity:** —; *Courtesy of John E. Peterson.*
$ Value, References: $60-$100 (4,8,x)
$ Value, Internet Auctions: $21 (for info only); **# Sales:** 1

Name: Canadian Federation Centennial; **Issued:** 1967
Comments: Crown, symbols, ten shields, *first* identified tray to commemorate an event; **Shape:** Std Rectangle plus handles; **Size:** 10.25" x 17.25" plus 1.0" each end for handles; **Story:** Yes; **Country:** Canada; **Mfr/Dist:** —; **Border/Edge:** Stainless Steel; **Quantity:** —; *Courtesy of John E. Peterson.*
$ Value, References: est $40-$80 (x)
$ Value, Internet Auctions: —; **# Sales:** —

Name: Ornate Utensils; **Issued:** 1968
Comments: Colorful coffee service, bowl of fruit, dish of bread; **Shape:** TV; **Size:** 13.5" x 18.75"; **Story:** —; **Country:** Mexico; **Mfr/Dist:** —; **Border/Edge:** White; **Quantity:** —; *Courtesy of John E. Peterson.*
$ Value, References: est $55-$75 (4,x)
$ Value, Internet Auctions: —; **# Sales:** —

Six Canadian trays complete the group for this decade. One is the *Canadian Federation Centennial*, an engraved stainless steel tray that is the first identified to commemorate an *event*. A second tray (not pictured) is a small rectangle shape that promoted a short-lived product of frozen Coke *slush*, introduced c.1969.

The first identified reproductions of an earlier tray are from Canada, dated in 1968. The image is *Lillian Nordica with Bottle*, which appeared originally in 1905. The 1968 reproductions have an English (not pictured) and French version. This same 1905 image was reproduced seven years later on the first identified U.S. commemorative tray of a bottler anniversary. Rim markings on the reproductions indicate the copyright year (1904) and list *Lillian Russell* as the subject. Several reference books describe the story of Lillian Nordica and her mistaken identification by experts and collectors over many years as Lillian Russell.

Name: Lillian Nordica with Bottle; **Issued:** 1968
Comments: Reproduction of 1905 tray, *first* identified reproduction of an earlier tray; **Shape:** Flat Std Rectangle; **Size:** 10.75" x 14.75"; **Story:** Rim; **Country:** Canada (French); **Mfr/Dist:** Ballonoff; **Border/Edge:** Green, yellow edge; **Quantity:** 15,000.
$ Value, References: $50-$75 (1,7,8,x)
$ Value, Internet Auctions: $21 (for info only); **# Sales:** 2

Name: Lillian Nordica with Sign; **Issued:** 1969
Comments: Reproduction of 1904 calendar, ©1903; **Shape:** Flat Std Rectangle;
Size: 10.75" x 14.75"; **Story:** Rim; **Country:** Canada (English); **Mfr/Dist:** Ballonoff;
Border/Edge: Yellow; **Quantity:** 50,000.
$ Value, References: $40-$85 (1,3,4,6,7,8,x)
$ Value, Internet Auctions: $16 (for info only); **# Sales:** 2

Name: Lillian Nordica with Sign; **Issued:** 1969
Comments: Reproduction of 1904 calendar, ©1903; **Shape:** Flat Std
Rectangle; **Size:** 10.75" x 14.75"; **Story:** Rim; **Country:** Canada (French);
Mfr/Dist: Ballonoff; **Border/Edge:** Yellow; **Quantity:** 15,000;
Courtesy of John E. Peterson.
$ Value, References: $30-$80 (1,7,8,x)
$ Value, Internet Auctions: $85 (for info only); **# Sales:** 2

A *different* Lillian Nordica image was reproduced on two 1969 trays, again with English and French versions. No original tray exists with this image. The reproduction is from a 1904 calendar, *Lillian Nordica with Sign,* and this image will become the most frequently reproduced tray from an ad, with seven identified reproduction trays.

The introduction in October 1969 of the *original dynamic ribbon* and other new advertising themes marks the end of the Coca-Cola classic collectibles period. The reproduction of many beautiful classic images of Coca-Cola advertising over the following years on trays and other items makes the images more widely available to collec-

tors, many of them new to collecting Coca-Cola memorabilia. The reproductions convey at least some of the power of the original message.

The twenty years from 1950-1969 brought the first trays to reproduce earlier ads, the first trays to reproduce an earlier tray, the first bottler anniversary commemorative trays, the first tray to commemorate a new bottling plant, and the first non-Coke event commemorative tray. While the classic period did end during these years, the same years introduced the types of trays that will be the mainstay of new trays over the next thirty years.

Chapter Four

Commemoratives Galore (Reproductions, Too), 1970-1979

Trays from the three decades after the classic tray period make up a significant portion of this book. From 1897 through 1969, a total of 137 trays have been identified. Yet, in the 1970s—the first full decade of recent trays—115 trays are listed! And, the number of issued trays will increase during the 1980s and increase still more in the 1990s.

For collectors, the 1970s brings new categories and new collecting opportunities, generally at lower prices than earlier trays. The trays of this decade and of the next twenty years are attractive, unique, and definitely collectible. A wide variety of types of trays can be found.

Compared to previous decades the number of tray *shapes* also increases in this decade. The 1897-1919 period had a total of eight shapes; all the trays in the 1920-1949 period except one were in the standard rectangle shape; and in 1950-1969 six different shapes were identified. In the 1970s, trays are listed in at least *twelve* shapes and/or sizes.

The 1970s trays contain seventy-one images. Pictured in this chapter are 101 of the trays and sixty-three of the images.

The 115 trays include sixty-five U.S., twenty-three Canadian, eighteen Mexican, two Italian, two German, three U.K., and two Australian. This decade is the champ for producing reproductions from earlier trays—its total of fifty-six trays represents about sixty-six percent of *all* tray reproductions from 1968-1999. Also, fifty-five of the 1970s trays commemorate something, whether a bottler anniversary, sports event, Olympic Games, Coca-Cola customer, or some other miscellaneous event.

Internet auction numbers are higher for more recent trays. Nine hundred forty-one auctions were logged from trays of the 1970s. Sixty-seven percent of the trays listed in this decade were auctioned at least once and fifty percent of the trays offered for sale were *sold*, at acceptable quality levels. Auction characteristics noted for earlier trays such as offering lower quality trays and placing a reserve, which together equaled about sixty percent of auctions in Chapter One, are only three percent of the auctions for the 1970s.

The 1970s (Unspecified Year)

Seven trays are listed here as dated in the 1970s but without a specific year. All are pictured.

Two Mexican trays include a round tray that pictures a young couple and a tip tray commemorating a new bottling plant at *Embotelladora Mante*. A plastic tray with German words on the Coke bottle features *Rum and Coca-Cola* and is one of two 1970s trays to promote Coke as a highball mixer, the first to do so since *Topless Girl*, c.1905.

Four reproductions include the only known reproductions of *Victorian Girl*, 1897; Weissmuller and O'Sullivan in the 1934 *Tarzan* tray; and *Running Girl*, 1938. A 1916 *Elaine* reproduction is much darker versus the original. None of these trays have any information stating that they are reproductions.

Name: Young Couple with Flowers; **Issued:** 1970s
Comments: A Mexican garden scene; **Shape:** Deep Round;
Size: 13.75" dia. x 1.75" depth; **Story:** —; **Country:** Mexico;
Mfr/Dist: —; **Border/Edge:** White; **Quantity:** —.
$ Value, References: est $40-$75 (x)
$ Value, Internet Auctions: —; **# Sales:** —

Name: New Bottling Plant; **Issued:** 1970s
Comments: *Embotelladora Mante*, artist drawing of new facility;
Shape: Small Rectangle; **Size:** 6.25" x 7.75"; **Story:** Yes; **Country:**
Mexico; **Mfr/Dist:** —; **Border/Edge:** Beige; **Quantity:** —;
Courtesy of John E. Peterson.
$ Value, References: est $90-$140 (4,x)
$ Value, Internet Auctions: —; **# Sales:** —

Name: Rum and Coca-Cola; **Issued:** 1970s
Comments: Coca-Cola bottle pictured with a decanter of rum, words on the bottle are in German, plastic; **Shape:** Flat Round; **Size:** 12.125" dia. x .5" depth; **Story:** —; **Country:** Germany; **Mfr/Dist:** —; **Border/Edge:** White; **Quantity:** —; *Courtesy of John E. Peterson.*
$ Value, References: est $40-$75 (x)
$ Value, Internet Auctions: —; **# Sales:** —

Name: Running Girl; **Issued:** 1970s
Comments: Reproduction of 1937 tray, colors are good but image detail not as sharp as original, no manufacturer listed; **Shape:** Std Rectangle; **Size:** 10.5" x 13.25"; **Story:** —; **Country:** US; **Mfr/Dist:** —; **Border/Edge:** Red, gold edge; **Quantity:** —.
$ Value, References: est $20-$40 (x)
$ Value, Internet Auctions: —; **# Sales:** —

Name: Victorian Girl; **Issued:** 1970s
Comments: Reproduction of the first tray, 1897; **Shape:** Deep Round; **Size:** 12.25" dia. x 1.25" depth; **Story:** —; **Country:** US; **Mfr/Dist:** —; **Border/Edge:** Red; **Quantity:** —.
$ Value, References: est $100-$125 (4,x)
$ Value, Internet Auctions: —; **# Sales:** —

Name: Elaine, Elaine Girl, Girl with a Basket of Flowers, *or* World War I Girl; **Issued:** 1970s
Comments: Reproduction of 1916 tray, with darker details and colors that are not crisp; **Shape:** Long Rectangle; **Size:** 8.5" x 19"; **Story:** —; **Country:** US; **Mfr/Dist:** —; **Border/Edge:** Gold, with trim; **Quantity:** —; *Courtesy of John E. Peterson.*
$ Value, References: est $5-$12 (x)
$ Value, Internet Auctions: —; **# Sales:** —

Name: Tarzan; **Issued:** 1970s
Comments: Reproduction of 1934 tray featuring Johnny Weissmueller and Maureen O'Sullivan. As with a number of reproductions in the 1970s and 1980s, little differentiates this tray from the original at first glance. But, among other clues, the colors are not as clear and sharp and the manufacturer information on the original is not on most reproductions; **Shape:** Std Rectangle; **Size:** 10.5" x 13.25"; **Story:** Yes (partial); **Country:** US; **Mfr/Dist:** —; **Border/Edge:** Red, gold stripe; **Quantity:** —.
$ Value, References: $10-$30 (3,4,x)
$ Value, Internet Auctions: $20; **# Sales:** 24

1970-1972

The first three years of the 1970s contain fifteen identified trays with ten images. Ten trays with six images are pictured in this section.

Three *logo* trays (two pictured) are listed from 1970 since that year was when the slogans on the trays were first used. A 1972 test market reproduction of a 1962 TV tray, *Candlelight,* is not pictured.

Five Mexican trays include three deep round shapes (one pictured) and the *Public Plaza,* Mexico City, pictured on both a TV tray and a tip tray.

Name: Rainbow colored fizz; **Issued:** 1971
Comments: Tray words, front and back: *disfrute la Chispa de la vida;*
Shape: Deep Round; **Size:** 13.25" dia. x 1.5" depth; **Story:** —;
Country: Mexico; **Mfr/Dist:** —; **Border/Edge:** White; **Quantity:** —.
$ Value, References: est $15-$25 (4,x)
$ Value, Internet Auctions: $11 (for info only); **# Sales:** 2

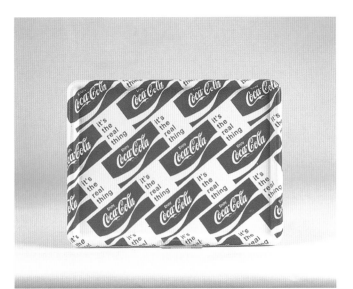

Name: Enjoy, It's the Real Thing; **Issued:** 1970
Comments: A logo tray, plastic, dated as 1970 since the slogan was introduced in the same year; **Shape:** Small Rectangle; **Size:** 9.0" x 11.0"; **Story:** —; **Country:** US; **Mfr/Dist:** —; **Border/Edge:** Design runs into the border; **Quantity:** —; *Courtesy of John E. Peterson.*
$ Value, References: est $15-$25 (x)
$ Value, Internet Auctions: —; **# Sales:** —

Name: Public Plaza with Buildings; **Issued:** 1972, ©1970
Comments: Government buildings, Mexico City, as seen 80-100 years ago. Bottom border: Z.H. Matching tip tray dated 1970;
Shape: TV; **Size:** 13.5" x 18.75"; **Story:** —; **Country:** Mexico; **Mfr/Dist:** —; **Border/Edge:** Brown; **Quantity:** —; *Courtesy of John E. Peterson.*
$ Value, References: est $12-$30 (x)
$ Value, Internet Auctions: —; **# Sales:** —

Name: It's the Real Thing; **Issued:** 1970
Comments: Plastic, molded with handles; **Shape:** Std Rectangle; **Size:** 11.0" x 14.5"; **Story:** —; **Country:** US; **Mfr/Dist:** Tri-Mod Company; **Border/Edge:** Red; **Quantity:** est 5,000; *Courtesy of John E. Peterson.*
$ Value, References: $10-$35 (3,6,x)
$ Value, Internet Auctions: —; **# Sales:** —

Name: Public Plaza with Buildings; **Issued:** 1970
Comments: Government buildings, Mexico City, as seen 80-100 years ago. Bottom border: *Z.H.* Matching TV tray dated 1972;
Shape: Small Rectangle; **Size:** 6.5" x 7.5"; **Story:** —; **Country:** Mexico; **Mfr/Dist:** —; **Border/Edge:** Brown; **Quantity:** —.
$ Value, References: est $15-$30 (4,x)
$ Value, Internet Auctions: —; **# Sales:** —

The 1971 English and French Canadian reproductions of *The Coca-Cola Girl*, 1910, continue what was begun with the *Lillian Nordica with Bottle* trays in 1968. As with the earlier trays, these were in the same flat rectangle shape with the English *Drink . . .* (not pictured) and the French *Buvez . . .* A third, similar reproduction of *The Coca-Cola Girl* in 1972 is the *first* U.S. reproduction of a tray. Over one million copies were issued! A fourth reproduction has a border similar to the original tray but in a different color. Also, this last tray does not have the Hamilton King signature.

English and French Canadian 1972 reproductions of the 1911 ad *Duster Girl* are the first two of four identified trays that reproduce this image.

Name: The Coca-Cola Girl; **Issued:** c.1972
Comments: Reproduction of 1910 tray by Hamilton King, not signed, bottom border: *MX*. Same trim as original 1910 tray but in different color; **Shape:** Std Rectangle; **Size:** 10.5" x 13.25";
Story: —; **Country:** US; **Mfr/Dist:** —; **Border/Edge:** Brown, gold trim, gold edge; **Quantity:** —.
$ Value, References: est $15-$20 (4,x)
$ Value, Internet Auctions: $12 (for info only); **# Sales:** 2

Name: The Coca-Cola Girl; **Issued:** 1971
Comments: Reproduction of 1910 tray by Hamilton King, repro signed, *Buvez* in logo; **Shape:** Flat Standard; **Size:** 11.0" x 15.0"; **Story:** Rim; **Country:** Canada (French); **Mfr/Dist:** Ballonoff; **Border/Edge:** Red; **Quantity:** 15,000; *Courtesy of John E. Peterson.*
$ Value, References: est $15-$35 (4,x)
$ Value, Internet Auctions: $15 (for info only); **# Sales:** 2

Name: Duster Girl *or* Motor Girl;
Issued: 1972
Comments: Reproduction of 1911 ad;
Shape: Flat Rectangle; **Size:** 10.75" x 14.75"; **Story:** —; **Country:** Canada (English); **Mfr/Dist:** Ballonoff; **Border/Edge:** Red; **Quantity:** 35,000.
$ Value, References: $5-$15 (3,4,7,x)
$ Value, Internet Auctions: $9 (for info only); **# Sales:** 2

Name: The Coca-Cola Girl; **Issued:** 1972
Comments: Reproduction of 1910 tray by Hamilton King, repro signed, first US tray reproduction; **Shape:** Flat Standard; **Size:** 11.0" x 15.0"; **Story:** Rim; **Country:** US; **Mfr/Dist:** Ballonoff; **Border/Edge:** Red; **Quantity:** 1,050,000.
$ Value, References: $15-$25 (3,4,x)
$ Value, Internet Auctions: $8; **# Sales:** 29

Name: Duster Girl *or* Motor Girl;
Issued: 1972
Comments: Reproduction of 1911 ad, *Buvez* in logo; **Shape:** Flat Rectangle; **Size:** 10.75" x 14.75"; **Story:** —; **Country:** Canada (French); **Mfr/Dist:** Ballonoff; **Border/Edge:** Red; **Quantity:** 15,000; *Courtesy of John E. Peterson.*
$ Value, References: est $5-$15 (4,x)
$ Value, Internet Auctions: $9; **# Sales:** 4

1973-1974

Interest in collecting Coca-Cola memorabilia increased widely in the 1970s, and the Coca-Cola Collectors Club held their first convention in Atlanta in 1975. While many factors must have led to this increased interest, it is not unreasonable to suppose that the release of a famous group of reproduction trays in 1973 and 1974 stimulated the collecting of Coca-Cola memorabilia. Individuals acquiring these trays might have developed an increased interest in trays and other items from the 1970s and earlier, leading to an increased interest in collecting *original* trays. That, in turn, could have led to interest in the *same images* as they appeared in other advertising materials such as calendars, which, in turn, could have led to more interest in other items, and so on.

In these two years sixteen trays with fourteen images are identified; fifteen are pictured.

What a group! Reproductions of trays were first identified in Canada in 1968, and the first U.S. tray reproduction was in 1972. But, in 1973, tray reproductions became a major event. Three of the classic images from the second decade of this century (1910-1919) were issued as authorized reproductions: *The Hamilton King Girl*, *Betty*, and *Elaine*. The quantity on each of these trays was around four hundred thousand copies. The *Golfers*, a 1926 tray by Fred Mizen, was also reproduced in 1973 for Canada, in both English and French versions.

Three additional trays, this time from the 1920s, were reproduced and issued in 1974: *Autumn Girl*, *Flapper Girl*, and *Party Girl*. The volume on each more than doubles the 1973 trays, with about nine hundred thousand copies produced. These six U.S. trays were company-issued as a marketing promotion, widely advertised, and directly distributed to consumers.

The 1973 reproductions were advertised as *We're Bringing Back the Good Old Trays*, and the 1974 theme was *Recapture the 20's on Trays from Coca-Cola*. The promotion price for each tray was one dollar. The three 1973 releases were reproduced in the same *shapes* as the originals. But, in 1974, *Autumn Girl* and *Flapper Girl* were released in shapes that differed from the 1920s versions. The third 1974 tray, *Party Girl*, was in the same shape as the original tray but now included a bottle in the bottom right corner. This bottle *was not* on the original tray but *was* on the image in the 1925 calendar.

Name: Betty *or* Betty Girl; **Issued:** 1973
Comments: Reproduction of 1914 tray; **Shape:** Large Oval; **Size:** 12.375" x 15.5"; **Story:** Rim; **Country:** US; **Mfr/Dist:** Donaldson Art Company; **Border/Edge:** Black; **Quantity:** 440,000.
$ Value, References: $10-$20 (3,4,x)
$ Value, Internet Auctions: $9; **# Sales:** 55

Name: Elaine, Elaine Girl, Girl with a Basket of Flowers, *or* World War I Girl; **Issued:** 1973
Comments: Reproduction of 1916 tray; **Shape:** Long Rectangle; **Size:** 8.5" x 19.0"; **Story:** Rim; **Country:** US; **Mfr/Dist:** Donaldson Art Company; **Border/Edge:** Gold with trim; **Quantity:** 385,000.
$ Value, References: $10-$15 (3,4,6,x)
$ Value, Internet Auctions: $9; **# Sales:** 48

Name: The Hamilton King Girl; **Issued:** 1973
Comments: Reproduction of 1913 tray, by Hamilton King, repro signed; **Shape:** Std Rectangle; **Size:** 10.5" x 13.25"; **Story:** Rim; **Country:** US; **Mfr/Dist:** Donaldson Company; **Border/Edge:** Green; **Quantity:** 400,000.
$ Value, References: $10-$25 (3,4,x)
$ Value, Internet Auctions: $13; **# Sales:** 32

Name: Golfers *or* Golfing Couple; **Issued:** 1973
Comments: Reproduction of 1926 tray, by Fred Mizen, repro signed; **Shape:** Flat Rectangle; **Size:** 10.75" x 14.75"; **Story:** Yes; **Country:** Canada (English); **Mfr/Dist:** Ballonoff; **Border/Edge:** Red; **Quantity:** 25,000.
$ Value, References: $15-$35 (3,4,x)
$ Value, Internet Auctions: $17; **# Sales:** 4

Name: Golfers *or* Golfing Couple; **Issued:** 1973 **Comments:** Reproduction of 1926 tray, by Fred Mizen, repro signed; **Shape:** Flat Rectangle; **Size:** 10.75" x 14.75"; **Story:** Yes; **Country:** Canada (French); **Mfr/Dist:** Ballonoff; **Border/ Edge:** Red; **Quantity:** 15,000; *Courtesy of John E. Peterson.* **$ Value, References:** est $20- $45 (4,x) **$ Value, Internet Auctions:** $23 (for info only); **# Sales:** 2

Name: Autumn Girl *or* Navy Girl; **Issued:** 1974, printed 1973 **Comments:** Reproduction of 1922 tray; **Shape:** Long Rectangle; **Size:** 8.5" x 19.0"; **Story:** Rim; **Country:** US; **Mfr/ Dist:** Ballonoff and Ohio Art Company; **Border/Edge:** Green; **Quantity:** 910,000. **$ Value, References:** $10-$15 (3,4,x) **$ Value, Internet Auctions:** $8; **# Sales:** 33

Name: Party Girl *or* Girl at Party; **Issued:** 1974, printed 1973 **Comments:** Reproduction of 1925 tray; **Shape:** Std Rectangle; **Size:** 10.5" x 13.25"; **Story:** Rim; **Country:** US; **Mfr/Dist:** Ballonoff and Ohio Art Company; **Border/Edge:** Brown; **Quantity:** 950,000. **$ Value, References:** $10-$15 (3,4,6,x) **$ Value, Internet Auctions:** $9; **# Sales:** 26

This two-year period also has four Mexican trays, including a second tray featuring *Fanta* (Coke's orange drink), as well as a monastery and two trays with groups of young people.

A *1927 Calendar Girl* reproduction was issued in a Canadian Limited Edition. Additionally, a 1974 German tray of *The Flapper Girl,* 1923 (not pictured), is the earliest identified tray reproduction from outside North America.

One of two additional U.S. trays is a unique TV tray dedicated to *Black History Month,* issued in 1972 in a set of two. The other is the first of *forty-six trays* to reproduce the wonderful Santa Claus ads of Haddon Sundblom. Sundblom's ads were prominently featured each year in hundreds of holiday advertising items. No original tray was ever issued. (See Chapter Seven for a review of all Santa trays and the ads they reproduce.) This Santa tray is also the first identified U.S. tray that reproduces an earlier ad.

Name: Flapper Girl; **Issued:** 1974, printed 1973 **Comments:** Reproduction of 1923 tray; **Shape:** Large Oval; **Size:** 12.375" x 15.125"; **Story:** Rim; **Country:** US; **Mfr/Dist:** Ballonoff and Ohio Art Company; **Border/Edge:** Brown; **Quantity:** 998,000. **$ Value, References:** $10- $15 (1,3,4,6,x) **$ Value, Internet Auctions:** $9; **# Sales:** 26

Name: Boy with Dog and Fanta; **Issued:** 1973 **Comments:** Second tray to feature Coca-Cola's orange drink, Fanta, *Fanta Estabien Buena;* **Shape:** Deep Round; **Size:** 13.0" dia. x 2.0" depth; **Story:** —; **Country:** Mexico; **Mfr/Dist:** —; **Border/ Edge:** White; **Quantity:** —; *Courtesy of John E. Peterson.* **$ Value, References:** est $30-$50 (x) **$ Value, Internet Auctions:** —; **# Sales:** —

Name: 1927 Calendar Girl; **Issued:** 1974
Comments: Reproduction of 1927 calendar; **Shape:** Flat Rectangle; **Size:** 10.75" x 14.75"; **Story:** Yes; **Country:** Canada, Ltd Edition; **Mfr/Dist:** Ballonoff; **Border/Edge:** Maroon; **Quantity:** 35,000.
$ Value, References: $15-$35 (3,4,x)
$ Value, Internet Auctions: $10; **# Sales:** 3

Name: Insigne Y Nacional Basillica de Santa Maria de Guadalupe; **Issued:** 1974
Comments: Buildings and mountains, matching TV tray dated 1975; **Shape:** Small Rectangle; **Size:** 6.5" x 7.5"; **Story:** Yes; **Country:** Mexico; **Mfr/Dist:** —; **Border/Edge:** Brown; **Quantity:** —.
$ Value, References: est $15-$30 (4,x)
$ Value, Internet Auctions: $8 (for info only); **# Sales:** 1

Name: People on a Curb; **Issued:** 1973
Comments: Large bottle, tray words: *Disfrute Coca-Cola*; **Shape:** Deep Round; **Size:** 13.25" dia. x 1.5" depth; **Story:** —; **Country:** Mexico; **Mfr/Dist:** —; **Border/Edge:** White, red edge; **Quantity:** —; *Courtesy of John E. Peterson.*
$ Value, References: est $20-$40 (4,x)
$ Value, Internet Auctions: $29 (for info only); **# Sales:** 1

Name: Black History Month; **Issued:** 1972
Comments: Commemorates event, issued originally as sets of two trays with floor standing attachable legs to create a TV tray. Image shows Afro-American leaders and others; **Shape:** TV; **Size:** 13.5" x 18.75"; **Story:** In separate booklet; **Country:** US; **Mfr/Dist:** Ohio Art Company and MarshAllen; **Border/Edge:** White; **Quantity:** 17,600 sets of two.
$ Value, References: est $35-$60 (set of two) (x)
$ Value, Internet Auctions: $49 (for info only); **# Sales:** 2 (set of two)

Name: Coca-Cola y ya!; **Issued:** 1974-1978, ©1973
Comments: People arm in arm, with Coke. Examples of the same tray found dated 04/1974, 05/1977, and 1978; **Shape:** Deep Round; **Size:** 13.25" dia. x 1.5" depth; **Story:** —; **Country:** Mexico; **Mfr/Dist:** —; **Border/Edge:** White; **Quantity:** —; *Courtesy of John E. Peterson.*
$ Value, References: est $20-$45 (4,x)
$ Value, Internet Auctions: —, **# Sales:** —

Name: Dear Santa *or* Santa at Chimney; **Issued:** 1973
Comments: Reproduction of 1963 ad, by Haddon Sundblom, first Santa tray, first US ad reproduction. Rim words: *Merry Christmas from your Coca-Cola Bottler;* **Shape:** Std Rectangle; **Size:** 10.5" x 13.25"; **Story:** Rim; **Country:** US; **Mfr/Dist:** Ohio Art Company; **Border/Edge:** Green, Holiday trim; **Quantity:** 15,000.
$ Value, References: $15-$25 (3,4,6,7,x)
$ Value, Internet Auctions: $9; **# Sales:** 5

1975

Only seven trays are identified in 1975 but they do contain a few firsts. Five are pictured in this section. First, a little background information: the direction of The Coca-Cola Company took an important turn in the late 1890s when two men from Tennessee named Benjamin Thomas and Joseph Whitehead visited Coca-Cola Headquarters in Atlanta. The men obtained a contract, supposedly for one dollar, giving them exclusive bottling rights in most of the United States. The first bottling of Coca-Cola took place in 1894 at the Biedenharn Candy Company, Vicksburg, Mississippi, but it had not spread widely in the following years.

Thomas and Whitehead quickly decided to create franchised bottling operations with exclusive territories. They also soon agreed to disagree over business issues such as the type of bottle and terms of the franchise contract. The resolution to their disagreement was to split the country between them. Thomas kept the populous East and Whitehead went to the spacious West. Each became what was known as a *Parent Bottler*, overseeing and selling syrup and other supplies to their franchised locations. The Western Coca-Cola Company in Chicago, created by Whitehead, was the Parent Bottler that issued the *Topless Girl* tray and the decorative *Vienna Plates* in the first decade of the century. By 1899 the first franchised bottler location opened in Chattanooga, Tennessee. Expansion into other geographic areas began soon thereafter.

As noted, the very first U.S. bottler was in Vicksburg, Mississippi. Chapter Three identifies the first trays commemorating bottler anniversaries as from Mexico, beginning in 1964. But two locations, Nashville, Tennessee and Atlanta, Georgia, become the first identified *U.S.* bottlers to issue commemorative trays, occurring when each location reached its 75th Anniversary as a Coca-Cola bottler. *Hilda with The Roses*, 1901, was the image used by Nashville and *Lillian Nordica with Bottle*, 1905, celebrated the Atlanta event.

In November, 1975 two men coached their last college football game, *Alabama vs. Auburn*. Also, the *Fortitude Valley Rugby Football Club* is identified on an Australian tray (not pictured). These two trays are the first identified to commemorate a specific sports theme.

A Mexican TV tray, another logo tray, and the second identified Santa reproduction (not pictured) complete trays from this year.

Name: Lillian Nordica with Bottle; **Issued:** 1975
Comments: Reproduction of 1905 tray. Together with Nashville, the first US bottler commemoratives, *Atlanta, Georgia*, 75th Anniversary; **Shape:** Std Rectangle; **Size:** 10.5" x 13.25"; **Story:** Yes; **Country:** US; **Mfr/Dist:** Ohio Art Company; **Border/Edge:** Green, gold edge; **Quantity:** 100,000, individually numbered.
$ Value, References: $10-15 (3,4,6,x)
$ Value, Internet Auctions: $10; **# Sales:** 12

Name: Lillian Nordica with Bottle; **Issued:** 1975
Comments: Back of the *Atlanta, Georgia* commemorative tray.

Name: Hilda with The Roses; **Issued:** 1975
Comments: Reproduction of 1901 tray. Together with Atlanta, the first US bottler commemoratives, *Nashville, Tennessee*, 75th Anniversary; **Shape:** Std Rectangle; **Size:** 10.5" x 13.25"; **Story:** Yes; **Country:** US; **Mfr/Dist:** Ohio Art Company; **Border/Edge:** Black; **Quantity:** 35,000, individually numbered.
$ Value, References: $15-$30 (3,4,6,8,x)
$ Value, Internet Auctions: $10; **# Sales:** 5

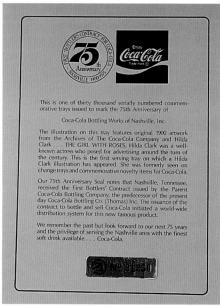

Name: Hilda with The Roses; **Issued:** 1975
Comments: Back of the *Nashville, Tennessee* commemorative tray.

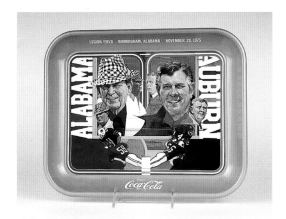

Name: Alabama/Auburn Football Game; **Issued:** 1975
Comments: First sports commemorative tray. Coaches last game, November 29, 1975; **Shape:** Std Rectangle; **Size:** 10.5" x 13.25"; **Story:** Yes; **Country:** US; **Mfr/Dist:** Ohio Art Company; **Border/Edge:** Gold; **Quantity:** 224,000, individually numbered.
$ Value, References: $10-15 (3,4,7,x)
$ Value, Internet Auctions: $10; **# Sales:** 8

Name: Insigne Y Nacional Basillica de Santa Maria de Guadalupe; **Issued:** 1975
Comments: Buildings and mountains, matching tip tray dated 1974; **Shape:** TV; **Size:** 13.5" x 18.75"; **Story:** Yes; **Country:** Mexico; **Mfr/Dist:** —; **Border/Edge:** Brown; **Quantity:** —.
$ Value, References: est $15-$30 (4,x)
$ Value, Internet Auctions: —; **# Sales:** —

Name: Coca-Cola; **Issued:** c.1975
Comments: Logo tray, white graphics on red; **Shape:** Round; **Size:** 11.75" dia. x 1.0" depth; **Story:** —; **Country:** Mexico; **Mfr/Dist:** —; **Border/Edge:** Red; **Quantity:** —; *Courtesy of John E. Peterson.*
$ Value, References: est $25-$40 (x)
$ Value, Internet Auctions: $19.50 (for info only); **# Sales:** 1

1976-1977

Twenty-two trays are identified from 1976 and a record twenty-three from 1977. Thirty-two of these trays commemorate *something*. Forty-two of the forty-five trays from these two years are pictured in this section.

Sports themes represent six of the commemorative trays. Two French Canadian trays issued for the *1976 Montreal Olympic Games* are the first identified Olympic trays. One is a familiar tray with forty-two small squares containing icons representing various Olympics sports and other logos; the other was advertised as a *Limited Edition VIP* tray with only 1,976 copies (clever, since minimum orders from the manufacturer are usually 2,000 trays).

Three U.S. sports trays from 1976 were issued as numbered *Limited Editions,* although the *limits* were pretty high with quantities from seventy thousand to one hundred twenty-five thousand copies of each. The *Arkansas Cotton Bowl* tray commemorates the coach, as do the other two. *Paterno and the Pennsylvania Nittany Lions* introduced the first U.S. large rectangle shape. And, a tray commemorating the *Indiana University* basketball team is round and orange to match the ball. It is the only basketball commemorative tray. Recent activity (late summer of 2000) involving the team's long-time coach, pictured on the tray, might make this tray a more valuable collectible. A second tray, from Australia, is also identified with a rugby sports theme.

Name: Games of the XXI Olympiad, Montreal; **Issued:** 1976
Comments: Commemorates Olympic Games, forty-two squares in checkerboard pattern with twenty-one icons of Olympic disciplines, thirteen of *Drink* in different languages, four of Olympic Logo, four of Coke Logo; **Shape:** Flat Rectangle; **Size:** 10.75" x 14.75"; **Story:** Yes; **Country:** Canada (French); **Mfr/Dist:** —; **Border/Edge:** Dark Yellow; **Quantity:** —.
$ Value, References: $10-$15 (3,4,x)
$ Value, Internet Auctions: $12; **# Sales:** 8

Name: 1976 Olympics, Montreal; **Issued:** 1976
Comments: Commemorates Olympic Games, Ltd VIP Edition, *Getting People Together*; **Shape:** Std Rectangle; **Size:** 10.5" x 13.25"; **Story:** Yes; **Country:** Canada (French); **Mfr/Dist:** —; **Border/Edge:** Black; **Quantity:** 1,976; *Courtesy of John E. Peterson.*
$ Value, References: $75-$175 (2,3,8,x)
$ Value, Internet Auctions: $34 (for info only); **# Sales:** 1

Name: Indiana University, 1976 NCAA Basketball Champions; **Issued:** 1976
Comments: Commemorates sports event, tray in color and shape of a basketball;
Shape: Round; **Size:** 12.5"; **Story:** Yes; **Country:** US; **Mfr/Dist:** Ohio Art Company;
Border/Edge: Orange; **Quantity:** 125,000, individually numbered;
Courtesy of Dr. N. K. Laughlin.
$ Value, References: $5-$25 (3,4,6,7,x)
$ Value, Internet Auctions: $12; **# Sales:** 13

Name: 1976 Arkansas Cotton Bowl; **Issued:** 1976
Comments: Commemorates sports event and Coach Frank Boyles; **Shape:** Std Rectangle; **Size:** 10.5" x 13.25"; **Story:** Yes; **Country:** US; **Mfr/Dist:** Donaldson Art Company; **Border/Edge:** Gold; **Quantity:** 53,600, Ltd. Edition.
$ Value, References: $10-$15 (3,4,x)
$ Value, Internet Auctions: $11; **# Sales:** 5

Name: Indiana University, 1976 NCAA Basketball Champions; **Issued:** 1976
Comments: Back of Indiana University Basketball tray.

Name: Coach Joe Paterno and the Penn State Nittany Lions; **Issued:** 1976
Comments: Commemorates sports event, coach and team, collage, by George I. Parrish, Jr.; **Shape:** Large Rectangle; **Size:** 13.5" x 18.5", with rim .75" wide on top and bottom and 1.25" wide on left and right, .5" depth; **Story:** Yes; **Country:** US; **Mfr/Dist:** —; **Border/Edge:** Gray; **Quantity:** est 75,000, individually numbered.
$ Value, References: est $10-$20 (3,x)
$ Value, Internet Auctions: $16; **# Sales:** 7

Name: Past Brothers Rugby; **Issued:** 1977
Comments: Commemorates sports event, Rugby League football celebration, A Grade, eight pictures of players and rugby scenes; **Shape:** Large Rectangle; **Size:** 11.75" x 16.0"; **Story:** Yes; **Country:** Australia; **Mfr/Dist:** —; **Border/Edge:** White; **Quantity:** —; *Courtesy of John E. Peterson.*
$ Value, References: est $40-$60 (x)
$ Value, Internet Auctions: —; **# Sales:** —

Name: Fred Harvey, 100 Years; **Issued:** 1976
Comments: First tray to commemorate customer. Also, Coca-Cola is ninety years old; **Shape:** Std Rectangle; **Size:** 10.5" x 13.25"; **Story:** Yes; **Country:** US; **Mfr/Dist:** Ohio Art Company; **Border/Edge:** Red; **Quantity:** 10,000, individually numbered.
$ Value, References: $10-$30 (3,4,8,x)
$ Value, Internet Auctions: $17; **# Sales:** 8

Fast food and supermarket chains are some of The Coca-Cola Company's largest customers. Most fast-food chains serve only one brand of soda and grocery chains have a limited resource called shelf space. Over the next twenty-five years several commemorative trays would be issued for and with customers, but two 1976 trays were the *first*. One is the third Santa Claus tray of the 1970s, bearing the same 1963 ad. It was issued as a promotion for Long John Silver Seafood Shoppes, a fast-food chain, to give to its customers. The other tray, *Fred Harvey, 100 Years*, is the first to commemorate a customer relationship. The quantities manufactured reflect each tray's purpose. Forty of the *Santa/ Long John Silver* trays were made for each one of the *Fred Harvey* trays, which was a Limited Edition of ten thousand.

Most bottler anniversary trays are reproductions of classic tray images. The back of the tray contains words about the image, a history of The Coca-Cola Company, and information about the individual bottler. These trays were produced in specific quantities as noted in the narrative and numbered on a sticker that was individually affixed to the back of the tray. The 1900 *Hilda Clark with Glass and Note* was reproduced c.1976 with a plain back. It was *also* issued on eight 1976 bottler 75th Anniversary trays. The back of each tray is pictured in this section and the caption contains additional details.

Name: Dear Santa *or* Santa at Chimney; **Issued:** 1976
Comments: Reproduction of 1963 ad, by Haddon Sundblom, for *Long John Silver Seafood Shoppes*; **Shape:** Small Flat Rectangle; **Size:** 10.5" x 14.0"; **Story:** Rim; **Country:** US; **Mfr/ Dist:** Donaldson Art Company; **Border/Edge:** Green, Holiday trim; **Quantity:** 400,000.
$ Value, References: est $15-$20 (3,x)
$ Value, Internet Auctions: $9; **# Sales:** 7

Name: Hilda with Glass and Note; **Issued:** c.1976
Comments: Reproduction of 1900 tray, blank back, not a commemorative tray; **Shape:** Flat Round; **Size:** 12.25"; **Story:** —; **Country:** US; **Mfr/Dist:** Ohio Art Company; **Border/Edge:** Blue, red edge; **Quantity:** —.
$ Value, References: est $8-$20 (4,x)
$ Value, Internet Auctions: —; **# Sales:** —

Name: Hilda with Glass and Note;
Issued: 1976
Comments: Back of trays shown.
Reproduction of 1900 tray,
commemorates bottler 75th
Anniversary, *see locations below*;
Shape: Flat Round; **Size:** 12.25";
Story: Yes; **Country:** US; **Mfr/Dist:**
Ohio Art Company; **Border/Edge:**
Blue, red edge; **Quantity:** see below,
all individually numbered; *Chicago and
Norfolk, Courtesy of John E. Peterson.*

Campbellsville, Kentucky: 6,000
Chicago, Illinois: 4,000
Cincinnati, Ohio: 80,000
Columbus, Georgia: 6,000
Elizabethtown, Kentucky: 15,000
Louisville, Kentucky: 71,000
Norfolk, Virginia: 41,000
Shelbyville, Kentucky: 8,000

$ Value, References:
Campbellsville: est $12-$20 (x)
Chicago: est $12-$20 (x)
Cincinnati: $7-$12 (3,6,x)
Columbus: est $12-$20 (x)
Elizabethtown: est $10-$18 (x)
Louisville: $7-$12 (3,6,x)
Norfolk: est $8-$15 (3,x)
Shelbyville: est $12-$20 (6,x)

**$ Value, Internet Auctions; #
Sales:**
Campbellsville: $12 (for info only), 1
Sale
Chicago: —; —
Cincinnati: $6; 6 Sales
Columbus: $10 (for info only); 1 Sale
Elizabethtown: $12 (for info only); 2
Sales
Louisville: $7; 3 Sales
Norfolk: $10 (for info only); 2 Sales
Shelbyville: $7.50; 8 Sales

Ten additional *Hilda with Glass and Note* bottler 75th Anniversary trays have been identified from 1977. One is a generic 75th Anniversary issued by the Coca-Cola archives. The backs of nine of these commemoratives are pictured and the caption (see next page) contains additional details.

Some bottlers provided the commemorative tray in a box that contained the tray, four glasses, a full bottle, and a brass belt buckle. All the items had a logo specific to the bottler and the front of the box had a quote from the original contract. An example of this package from Columbia, South Carolina is shown in this section.

Name: Hilda with Glass and Note; **Issued:** 1977
Comments: Columbia, South Carolina, example of boxed set of commemorative tray, a bottle, four glasses (three pictured), and a belt buckle. Top cover calligraphy reads: *The said party of the first part, having the exclusive right within the territory hereinafter described, to put up and sell, in bottles, a carbonated drink, consisting of a mixture of water and the Syrup or preparation known as Coca-Cola . . .*
$ Value, References: est $40-$75 (x)
$ Value, Internet Auctions: $45 (for info only); **# Sales:** 1

Elaine, 1916, has been found in five reproduction trays, all Canadian and all dated 1976. One, a flat oval shape, commemorates the 60th Anniversary of a Canadian bottler. The remaining trays are two flat ovals and two large flat ovals, each with English and French versions.

Name: Hilda with Glass and Note; **Issued:** 1977
Comments: Back of tray shown. Reproduction of 1900 tray, commemorates bottler 75th Anniversary, *see locations below*; **Shape:** Flat Round; **Size:** 12.25"; **Story:** Yes; **Country:** US; **Mfr/Dist:** Ohio Art Company; **Border/Edge:** Blue, red edge; **Quantity:** see below, all individually numbered; *Augusta, Buffalo, Charlotte, Harrisburg, Philadelphia, Savannah, Courtesy of John E. Peterson.*

Augusta, Georgia: 3,000
Buffalo, New York: 6,000
Charlotte, North Carolina: 42,000
Coca-Cola Archives (for all bottler anniversaries): 2,000
Columbia, South Carolina: 5,000
Dallas, Texas: 150,000
Harrisburg, Pennsylvania: 35,000
Meridian, Mississippi: —; (not pictured)
Philadelphia, Pennsylvania: 1,250
Savannah, Georgia: 2,000

$ Value, References:
Augusta: est $12-$20 (3,x)
Buffalo: est $12-$20 (x)
Charlotte: est $8-$15 (x)
Coca-Cola Archives: est $12-$20 (x)
Columbia: est $12-$20 (3,x)
Dallas: est $5-$10 (3,x)
Harrisburg: est $8-$15 (3,x)
Meridian: est $12-$25 (x)
Philadelphia: est $12-$25 (3,x)
Savannah: est $12-$20 (3,x)

$ Value, Internet Auctions; # Sales:
Augusta: —; —
Buffalo: $10; 3 Sales
Charlotte: $12; 4 Sales
Coca-Cola Archives: —; —
Columbia: $10 (for info only); 1 Sale
Dallas: $4; 8 Sales
Harrisburg: $10; 7 Sales
Meridian: —; —
Philadelphia: —; —
Savannah: $8 (for info only); 1 Sale

Name: Elaine *or* Elaine Girl, Girl With a Basket of Flowers, World War I Girl; **Issued:** 1976
Comments: Reproduction of 1916 tray; **Shape:** Flat Oval; **Size:** 10.5" x 12.75"; **Story:** Rim; **Country:** Canada (English); **Mfr/Dist:** —; **Border/Edge:** Brown, gold trim; **Quantity:** —.
$ Value, References: est $10-$25 (3,x)
$ Value, Internet Auctions: $6 (for info only); **# Sales:** 2

Name: Elaine *or* Elaine Girl, Girl With a Basket of Flowers, World War I Girl; **Issued:** 1976
Comments: Reproduction of 1916 tray; **Shape:** Flat Oval; **Size:** 10.5" x 12.75"; **Story:** Rim; **Country:** Canada (French); **Mfr/Dist:** —; **Border/Edge:** Brown, gold trim; **Quantity:** —; *Courtesy of John E. Peterson.*
$ Value, References: est $15-$25 (x)
$ Value, Internet Auctions: —; **# Sales:** —

Name: Elaine *or* Elaine Girl, Girl With a Basket of Flowers, World War I Girl; **Issued:** 1976
Comments: Back of tray. Reproduction of 1916 tray, commemorative of bottler 60th Anniversary, Hamby Beverage Co.; **Shape:** Flat Oval; **Size:** 10.5" x 12.75"; **Story:** Yes; **Country:** Canada (English); **Mfr/Dist:** —; **Border/Edge:** Brown, gold trim; **Quantity:** —; *Courtesy of John E. Peterson.*
$ Value, References: $10-$30 (3,7,x)
$ Value, Internet Auctions: —; **# Sales:** —

The 1905 *Lillian Nordica with Bottle* is reproduced on four 1977 trays. Three commemorate U.S. bottler anniversaries and the fourth version (not pictured) is the first in a series of eight Italian trays issued to begin a commemoration of the 50th Anniversary of Coca-Cola bottling in Italy. The final tray in this Italian series is found eleven years later, in 1988.

Name: Elaine *or* Elaine Girl, Girl With a Basket of Flowers, World War I Girl; **Issued:** 1976
Comments: Reproduction of 1916 tray; **Shape:** Large Flat Oval; **Size:** 13.75" x 17.0"; **Story:** Rim; **Country:** Canada (English); **Mfr/Dist:** —; **Border/Edge:** Brown, gold trim; **Quantity:** —; *Courtesy of John E. Peterson.*
$ Value, References: est $5-$15 (x)
$ Value, Internet Auctions: —; **# Sales:** —

Name: Lillian Nordica with Bottle; **Issued:** 1977
Comments: Reproduction of 1905 tray, commemorative of 75th Anniversary, *Louisiana* (New Orleans and other acquired Louisiana bottlers); **Shape:** Std Rectangle; **Size:** 10.5" x 13.25"; **Story:** Yes; **Country:** US; **Mfr/Dist:** —; **Border/Edge:** Green, gold edge; **Quantity:** 43,400.
$ Value, References: est $10-$20 (x)
$ Value, Internet Auctions: $7 (for info only); **# Sales:** 1

Name: Elaine *or* Elaine Girl, Girl With a Basket of Flowers, World War I Girl; **Issued:** 1976
Comments: Reproduction of 1916 tray; **Shape:** Large Flat Oval; **Size:** 14.25" x 17.25"; **Story:** Rim; **Country:** Canada (French); **Mfr/Dist:** —; **Border/Edge:** Brown, gold trim; **Quantity:** —.
$ Value, References: est $5-$15 (x)
$ Value, Internet Auctions: —; **# Sales:** —

Name: Lillian Nordica with Bottle; **Issued:** 1977
Comments: Back of Louisiana 75th Anniversary Commemorative Tray.

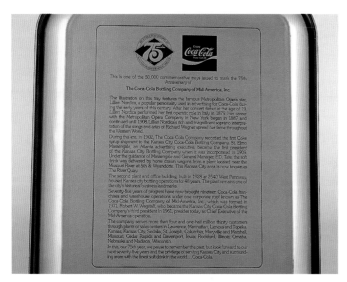

Name: Lillian Nordica with Bottle; **Issued:** 1977
Comments: Back of tray. Reproduction of 1905 tray, commemorative of 75th Anniversary, *Mid-America* (Kansas City and other acquired Kansas bottlers); **Shape:** Std Rectangle; **Size:** 10.5" x 13.25"; **Story:** Yes; **Country:** US; **Mfr/Dist:** —; **Border/Edge:** Green, gold edge; **Quantity:** 50,000.
$ Value, References: est $15-$30 (x)
$ Value, Internet Auctions: —; **# Sales:** —

Name: Lillian Nordica with Bottle; **Issued:** 1977
Comments: Back of tray. Reproduction of 1905 tray, commemorative of 75th Anniversary, *Womecto Bottling Co.* (Roanoke, Virginia) bottler; **Shape:** Std Rectangle; **Size:** 10.5" x 13.25"; **Story:** Yes; **Country:** US; **Mfr/Dist:** —; **Border/Edge:** Green, gold edge; **Quantity:** —; *Courtesy of John E. Peterson.*
$ Value, References: est $15-$40 (x)
$ Value, Internet Auctions: $20 (for info only); **# Sales:** 1

An unusual group of three 1977 trays each has wording on the front reading *The Romance of Coca-Cola*. A sticker on the back reads *Barratt & Sons Mineral Waters*. One tray, *For the Love of Betty*, is a reproduction of *After the Tattoo Artist*, a 1944 Norman Rockwell painting. A second sticker on the back of this tray notes the title (see name on the tattoo in progress) and states that the tray is a Limited Edition. The other two trays, *Romance* and *The Wedding*, have been seen with different versions of labels affixed to the back. The most consistently identified label and the one that also corresponds to the words on the front of the tray is quoted in the caption detail.

Name: For the Love of Betty; **Issued:** 1977
Comments: Reproduction of 1944 ad, *After the Tattoo Artist*, by Norman Rockwell, repro with signature, # three in *Romance of Coca-Cola Series*. Back stickers: (1) Barratt & Sons Mineral Water, (2) sticker with number and name of tray (check the tattoo); **Shape:** Oblong, with rectangle face plate; **Size:** 14.0" x 16.25"; **Story:** Yes; **Country:** United Kingdom; **Mfr/Dist:** Distributed by Pacific Zone of The Coca-Cola Company; **Border/Edge:** Green; **Quantity:** —.
$ Value, References: est $25-$40 (3,x)
$ Value, Internet Auctions: $10 (for info only); **# Sales:** 1

Name: Romance; **Issued:** 1977
Comments: # one in *Romance of Coca-Cola Series*. Back sticker: Barratt & Sons Mineral Water; **Shape:** Oblong, with rectangle face plate; **Size:** 14.0" x 16.25"; **Story:** Yes; **Country:** United Kingdom; **Mfr/Dist:** —; **Border/Edge:** Maroon, gold stripe; **Quantity:** 5,000; *Courtesy of John E. Peterson.*
$ Value, References: $25-$100 (3,4,5,x)
$ Value, Internet Auctions: $45; **# Sales:** 3

Name: Girl at Shade, Girl in the Afternoon, *or* Girl in the Yellow Hat; **Issued:** 1977
Comments: Reproduction of 1938 tray, by Bradshaw Crandell; **Shape:** Large Flat Oval; **Size:** 14.25" x 17.25"; **Story:** Rim; **Country:** Canada (English); **Mfr/Dist:** —; **Border/Edge:** Dark gold, black trim; **Quantity:** —; *Courtesy of John E. Peterson.*
$ Value, References: est $25-$30 (x)
$ Value, Internet Auctions: —; **# Sales:** —

Name: Wedding; **Issued:** 1977
Comments: # two in *Romance of Coca-Cola Series*. Back stickers: (1) Barratt & Sons Mineral Water, (2) *This tray is a Limited Edition produced for the Fellowship of Man and is inspired by the classic "Roots" reproduced from the company's 30th Anniversary series "The Romance of Coca-Cola." Made in the United Kingdom and reproduced for European Area, 1977. 5000 pairs. One of two;* **Shape:** Oblong, with rectangle face plate; **Size:** 14.0" x 16.25"; **Story:** Yes; **Country:** United Kingdom; **Mfr/Dist:** —; **Border/Edge:** Maroon, gold stripe; **Quantity:** 5,000; *Courtesy of John E. Peterson.*
$ Value, References: $25-$100 (3,4,5,x)
$ Value, Internet Auctions: $62; **# Sales:** 3

Additional 1976-1977 trays include a Mexican collage of models (not pictured), three Canadian reproductions of the 1938 *Girl at Shade,* and the first U.S. issued deep round tray, in plastic.

The first commemorative bottler 75th Anniversary tray with a *collage* image is from Los Angeles, California. The pictures are of city scenes, as opposed to a reproduction of an earlier tray or ad. The bottler identified this tray as a *commemorative plate.*

Name: Girl at Shade, Girl in the Afternoon, *or* Girl in the Yellow Hat; **Issued:** 1977
Comments: Reproduction of 1938 tray, by Bradshaw Crandell; **Shape:** Large Flat Oval; **Size:** 14.25" x 17.25"; **Story:** Rim; **Country:** Canada (French); **Mfr/Dist:** —; **Border/Edge:** Dark gold, black trim; **Quantity:** —.
$ Value, References: est $25-$30 (x)
$ Value, Internet Auctions: —; **# Sales:** —

Name: Girl at Shade, Girl in the Afternoon, *or* Girl in the Yellow Hat; **Issued:** 1977
Comments: Reproduction of 1938 tray, by Bradshaw Crandell; **Shape:** Flat Oval; **Size:** 10.5" x 12.75"; **Story:** Rim; **Country:** Canada (English); **Mfr/Dist:** —; **Border/Edge:** Dark gold, black trim; **Quantity:** —; *Courtesy of John E. Peterson.*
$ Value, References: $10-$40 (3,4,6,x)
$ Value, Internet Auctions: $13 (for info only); **# Sales:** 2

Name: Coke Adds Life; **Issued:** 1977
Comments: Collage, eight pictures of people, plastic. First US deep round tray; **Shape:** Deep Round; **Size:** 13.0" dia. x 1.875" depth; **Story:** —; **Country:** US; **Mfr/Dist:** Therma-Serv; **Border/Edge:** White; **Quantity:** —.
$ Value, References: est $10-$20 (3,x)
$ Value, Internet Auctions: $12; **# Sales:** 3

Name: Los Angeles, California, 75th Anniversary; **Issued:** 1977
Comments: Commemorative of 75th Anniversary, Los Angeles, California bottler, first collage on a US bottler commemorative; **Shape:** Flat Round; **Size:** 12.0";
Story: Yes; **Country:** US; **Mfr/Dist:** —; **Border/Edge:** Red; **Quantity:** —; *Courtesy of John E. Peterson.*
$ Value, References: $10-$25 (3,4,x)
$ Value, Internet Auctions: —; **# Sales:** —

Name: Los Angeles, California, 75th Anniversary; **Issued:** 1977
Comments: Presentation box for Los Angeles commemorative tray, showing tray in box.
$ Value, References: $50-$75 (tray and box) (3,7,x)
$ Value, Internet Auctions: $55 (for info only); **# Sales:** 1

1978-1979

The last two years of the 1970s contain twenty-five trays with sixteen images. The rich variety of tray types seen throughout this decade certainly is typified by the trays of these last two years. Pictured in this section are fifteen of the images and twenty-two of the trays.

An unusual tray, dated 1978, may not even be considered by some as a Coca-Cola memorabilia item. The Ohio Art Company of Byron, Ohio manufactured many of the trays from the 1970s and continues to do so today. The *W.C.K. Tribute from the Ohio Art Family* is a collage tray honoring a founder of the company.

Food and drink commemorative trays include a caricature drawing of a family titled *Happy Joe's & Coca-Cola*. Information provided by a collector noted that Happy Joe's Pizza and Ice Cream Parlor is (or was) a chain in Iowa. *Calvert and Coca-Cola* is one of the two trays since *Topless Girl*, 1905, to promote Coca-Cola as a mixer with alcoholic beverages. And a plastic tray with cork liner is shaped as a *Bottle Cap*. No date information appears on this latter tray but it was packaged as a promotion with coasters of the same shape in a box dated 1978.

Name: W.C.K. Tribute from Ohio Art Family; **Issued:** 1978
Comments: Collage of people and logos in the business life of Mr. Killgallen and the company, a primary manufacturer of trays for The Coca-Cola Company. Coca-Cola Account Manager Martin L. Kilgallen II and Coke logo pictured just below center to the right; **Shape:** Std Rectangle; **Size:** 10.5" x 13.25"; **Story:** Yes; **Country:** US; **Mfr/Dist:** Ohio Art Company; **Border/Edge:** Red, white stars trim, gold edge; **Quantity:** —; *Courtesy of John E. Peterson.*
$ Value, References: est $30-$50 (x)
$ Value, Internet Auctions: —; **# Sales:** —

Name: W.C.K. Tribute from Ohio Art Family; **Issued:** 1978
Comments: Back of tray showing key to the collage on front of tray.

Name: Happy Joe's and Coca-Cola; **Issued:** 1978
Comments: Commemorative of customer, caricature of family and *Happy Joe's Pizza & Ice Cream Parlor*, by Patrick J. Costello, signature on tray; **Shape:** Small Flat Oval; **Size:** 10.75" x 12.75"; **Story:** —; **Country:** US; **Mfr/Dist:** —; **Border/Edge:** Yellow; **Quantity:** —;
Courtesy of John E. Peterson.
$ Value, References: est $10-$20 (x)
$ Value, Internet Auctions: —; **# Sales:** —

Name: Bottle Cap; **Issued:** c.1978
Comments: Tray in shape of bottle cap, plastic, cork liner, originally packaged with coasters of same design, tray date from package; **Shape:** Deep Round; **Size:** 12.0" dia. x 1.75" depth; **Story:** —; **Country:** US; **Mfr/Dist:** —; **Border/Edge:** Gray; **Quantity:** —.
$ Value, References: est $12-$25 (without coasters) (4,x)
$ Value, Internet Auctions: —; **# Sales:** —

Name: Calvert & Coca-Cola; **Issued:** c.1978
Comments: Man pushing woman in swing, country scene with Woody Wagon, © of both products on rim; **Shape:** Deep Oval; **Size:** 12.5" x 15.5"; **Story:** —; **Country:** US; **Mfr/Dist:** —; **Border/Edge:** Black, gold edge; **Quantity:** —.
$ Value, References: est $5-$50 (3,x)
$ Value, Internet Auctions: $17; **# Sales:** 3

Name: Bottle Cap; **Issued:** c.1978
Comments: Pictured with Coasters; **Shape:** Deep Round; **Size:** 12.0" dia. x 1.75" depth; **Story:** —; **Country:** US; **Mfr/Dist:** —; **Border/Edge:** Gray; **Quantity:** —.
$ Value, References: est $15-$35 (with coasters) (x)
$ Value, Internet Auctions: $15 (for info only); **# Sales:** 1

Two Canadian commemoratives were issued in 1978. One celebrated the Bicentennial of Captain James Cook's landing in British Columbia and has the British Columbia Proclamation of the anniversary on its back. The other tray is a sports commemorative of the 1978 *Edmonton Commonwealth Games*, shown here in two versions.

Name: Captain James Cook; **Issued:** 1978
Comments: Commemorates event, Bicentennial of Capt. James Cook landing at Nakoota Sound, British Columbia; **Shape:** Flat Oval; **Size:** 10.5" x 13.0"; **Story:** Yes; **Country:** Canada (French); **Mfr/Dist:** —; **Border/Edge:** Gold, brown stripe; **Quantity:** —.
$ Value, References: $15-$35 (3,7,x)
$ Value, Internet Auctions: $8 (for info only); **# Sales:** 1

Name: Captain James Cook; **Issued:** 1978
Comments: Back of tray showing British Columbia Proclamation of the Bicentennial.

Name: Commonwealth Games, Edmonton; **Issued:** 1978
Comments: Commemorative of sports event, collage with locations of nine previous Games. Second tray identified with different color; **Shape:** Std Rectangle; **Size:** 10.5" x 13.25"; **Story:** Yes; **Country:** Canada (French); **Mfr/Dist:** —; **Border/Edge:** Pink, with flags of participating countries; **Quantity:** —.
$ Value, References: $20-$100 (3,4,6,7,x)
$ Value, Internet Auctions: $6 (for info only); **# Sales:** 1

Name: Commonwealth Games, Edmonton; **Issued:** 1978
Comments: Commemorative of sports event, collage with locations of nine previous Games. Same as previous tray except for tan color; **Shape:** Std Rectangle; **Size:** 10.5" x 13.25"; **Story:** Yes; **Country:** Canada (French); **Mfr/Dist:** —; **Border/Edge:** Tan, with flags of participating countries; **Quantity:** —;
Courtesy of John E. Peterson.
$ Value, References: est $40-$60 (x)
$ Value, Internet Auctions: —; **# Sales:** —

Seven additional trays from 1978-1979 are identified from three countries. Five are Mexican trays and include two ad reproductions. One is *1927 Calendar Girl*, a large rectangle tray, the first of that shape with a vertical image. The other, young adults washing an automobile, is shown with an additional picture of the tray's back, bearing words and a logo typical of round Mexican trays. The other three Mexican trays, two pictured, have the same image but different words and shapes.

A 1979 Italian reproduction of *Elaine, 1916*, is the second in the series of eight trays commemorating Coca-Cola bottling in Italy. And a Canadian Limited Edition reproduction of *Flapper Girl, 1923*, might have been part of a promotion, but nothing is noted on the tray.

Name: Tome Coca-Cola Bien Fria; **Issued:** 1979
Comments: Woman in red T-shirt and straw hat drinking Coke through a straw, same image as 1960s Mexican round tray and 1979 Mexican tip tray; **Shape:** Deep Round; **Size:** 13.5" dia. x 1.5" depth; **Story:** —; **Country:** Mexico; **Mfr/Dist:** —; **Border/Edge:** White; **Quantity:** —; *Courtesy of John E. Peterson.*
$ Value, References: est $30-$50 (x)
$ Value, Internet Auctions: —; **# Sales:** —

Name: 1927 Calendar Girl; **Issued:** 1979
Comments: Reproduction of 1927 Calendar, first large rectangle with vertical image; **Shape:** Large Rectangle; **Size:** 14.5" x 18.5"; **Story:** Rim; **Country:** Mexico; **Mfr/Dist:** —; **Border/Edge:** Black; **Quantity:** —; *Courtesy of John E. Peterson.*
$ Value, References: est $10-$45 (x)
$ Value, Internet Auctions: —; **# Sales:** —

Name: de mas Chispa; **Issued:** 1978
Comments: Woman in red T-shirt and straw hat drinking Coke through a straw, same image as 1960s Mexican round tray and 1979 Mexican deep round tray; **Shape:** Small Rectangle; **Size:** 6.5" x 7.5"; **Story:** —; **Country:** Mexico; **Mfr/Dist:** —; **Border/Edge:** Beige; **Quantity:** —; *Courtesy of John E. Peterson.*
$ Value, References: est $30-$80 (5,x)
$ Value, Internet Auctions: —; **# Sales:** —

Name: da mais Chrispa; **Issued:** 1978
Comments: Three young adults washing an automobile; **Shape:** Deep Round; **Size:** 13.5" dia. x 1.75" depth; **Story:** —; **Country:** Mexico; **Mfr/Dist:** —; **Border/Edge:** Red; **Quantity:** —.
$ Value, References: est $25-$50 (8,x)
$ Value, Internet Auctions: —; **# Sales:** —

Name: da mais Chrispa; **Issued:** 1978
Comments: Back of tray showing words and logo, typical of Mexican Deep Round trays.

Name: Elaine *or* Elaine Girl, Girl With a Basket of Flowers, World War I Girl; **Issued:** 1979
Comments: Reproduction of 1916 tray, second in series of eight trays from 1977 through 1988 commemorating fifty years of bottling in Italy. Back of tray has commentary (in Italian) on the series of trays and the anniversary; **Shape:** Std Rectangle; **Size:** 10.5" x 13.25"; **Story:** Yes (in Italian); **Country:** Italy; **Mfr/Dist:** —; **Border/Edge:** Arancio (orange), white trim; **Quantity:** est 100,000; *Courtesy of John E. Peterson.*
$ Value, References: est $40-$60 (x)
$ Value, Internet Auctions: $23 (for info only); **# Sales:** 1

Name: Flapper Girl; **Issued:** 1979
Comments: Reproduction of 1923 tray; **Shape:** Std Rectangle; **Size:** 10.5" x 13.25"; **Story:** —; **Country:** Canada; **Mfr/Dist:** —; **Border/Edge:** Brown; **Quantity:** —.
$ Value, References: est $15-$25 (x)
$ Value, Internet Auctions: —; **# Sales:** —

Nine bottler 75th Anniversary trays are identified from 1978 and 1979. Three from 1978 are the first commemoratives to reproduce the 1904 calendar, *Lillian Nordica with Sign.* Another three, one pictured, are the first reproductions of the 1903 *Bottle 5¢.*

The 1979 bottler trays provide an interesting comparison. The first, a 75th Anniversary commemorative from New York City, is a modest plastic tray with a collage of scenes from the largest U.S. city. Chattanooga, the first *franchised* bottler location, did not have an identified 75th Anniversary tray but now issues one for its 80th Anniversary, using the 1904 *Lillian Nordica with Sign.* And the first Coca-Cola bottling operation, *The Biendenharn Candy Company* in Vicksburg, Mississippi, issued a tray to celebrate its 85th Anniversary in 1979. This operation was not part of the franchised bottler system in its early years.

Finally, two 1979 trays from Canadian bottlers commemorate new plant openings.

Name: Lillian Nordica with Sign; **Issued:** 1978
Comments: Reproduction of 1904 ad, commemorative of 75th Anniversary, *Athens, Georgia* bottler; **Shape:** Std Rectangle; **Size:** 10.5" x 13.25"; **Story:** Yes; **Country:** US; **Mfr/Dist:** —; **Border/Edge:** Yellow; **Quantity:** 2000, individually numbered; *Courtesy of John E. Peterson.*
$ Value, References: est $12-$20 (3,x)
$ Value, Internet Auctions: $10 (for info only); **# Sales:** 1

Name: Lillian Nordica with Sign; **Issued:** 1978
Comments: Back of commemorative tray for Athens, Georgia.

Name: Lillian Nordica with Sign; **Issued:** 1978
Comments: Back of tray. Repro of 1904 ad, commemorative of 75th Anniversary, *Rockwood, Tennessee* bottler; **Shape:** Std Rectangle; **Size:** 10.5" x 13.25"; **Story:** Yes; **Country:** US; **Mfr/Dist:** —; **Border/Edge:** Yellow; **Quantity:** 5000, individually numbered; *Courtesy of John E. Peterson.*
$ Value, References: est $12-$20 (3,x)
$ Value, Internet Auctions: —; **# Sales:** —

Name: 75th Anniversary, New York; **Issued:** 1979
Comments: Commemorative of 75th Anniversary, *New York City* bottler, collage, plastic; **Shape:** Small Rectangle; **Size:** 9.5" x 12.0"; **Story:** Yes; **Country:** Yes; **Mfr/Dist:** Brookpark; **Border/Edge:** Beige; **Quantity:** —.
$ Value, References: est $10-$20 (x)
$ Value, Internet Auctions: $12; **# Sales:** 4

Name: Lillian Nordica with Sign; **Issued:** 1978
Comments: Back of tray. Repro of 1904 ad, commemorative of 75th Anniversary, *Selma, Alabama* bottler; **Shape:** Std Rectangle; **Size:** 10.5" x 13.25"; **Story:** Yes; **Country:** US; **Mfr/Dist:** —; **Border/Edge:** Yellow; **Quantity:** 800, individually numbered.
$ Value, References: est $10-$50 (3,x)
$ Value, Internet Auctions: —; **# Sales:** —

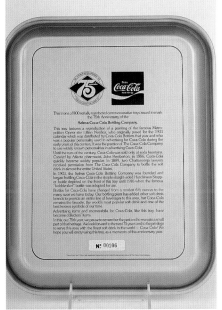

Name: Bottle 5¢; **Issued:** 1978
Comments: Reproduction of 1903 tray, commemorative of 75th Anniversary, *see locations below*; **Shape:** Flat Round; **Size:** 12.5"; **Story:** Yes; **Country:** US; **Mfr/Dist:** —; **Border/Edge:** Yellow, black trim; **Quantity:** *see below.*

Paducah, Kentucky: 8,000
Carolina (South Carolina): — (not pictured)
Jackson, Mississippi: — (not pictured)

$ Value, References:
Paducah: est $12-$20 (3,x)
Carolina (South Carolina): est $12-$25 (3,x)
Jackson: est $12-$25 (3,x)

$ Value, Internet Auctions; # Sales:
Paducah, Kentucky: $17 (for info only); 2 Sales
Carolina (South Carolina): —; —
Jackson, Mississippi: —; —

Name: Bottle 5¢; **Issued:** 1978
Comments: Back of commemorative tray for Paducah, Kentucky. Two other locations not pictured.

Name: Lillian Nordica with Sign; **Issued:** 1979
Comments: Back of tray. Reproduction of 1904 calendar, commemorative of 80th Anniversary, *Chattanooga, Tennessee* bottler; **Shape:** Std Rectangle; **Size:** 10.5" x 13.25"; **Story:** Yes; **Country:** US; **Mfr/Dist:** —; **Border/Edge:** Yellow; **Quantity:** 10,000.
$ Value, References: est $10-$18 (3,x)
$ Value, Internet Auctions: —; **# Sales:** —

Name: Goodwill Bottling; **Issued:** 1979
Comments: Commemorative of new bottling plant, artist rendition; **Shape:** Small Rectangle; **Size:** 9.0" x 14.5"; **Story:** Yes; **Country:** Canada (English); **Mfr/Dist:** —; **Border/Edge:** Blue; **Quantity:** —; *Courtesy of John E. Peterson.*
$ Value, References: est $10-$15 (7,x)
$ Value, Internet Auctions: —; **# Sales:** —

Name: Biedenharn Candy Company; **Issued:** 1979
Comments: Commemorative of 85th Anniversary, Biedenharn Candy Company, *Vicksburg, Mississippi*, the first bottler, collage; **Shape:** Flat Round; **Size:** 12.5"; **Story:** Yes; **Country:** US; **Mfr/Dist:** —; **Border/Edge:** Green; **Quantity:** —.
$ Value, References: $7-$20 (3,4,x)
$ Value, Internet Auctions: $8; **# Sales:** 7

Name: Calgary Plant; **Issued:** 1979
Comments: Commemorative of new bottling plant, artist rendition; **Shape:** Small Rectangle; **Size:** 9.0" x 14.5"; **Story:** Yes; **Country:** Canada (English); **Mfr/Dist:** —; **Border/Edge:** Green, gold line; **Quantity:** —.
$ Value, References: est $10-$15 (x)
$ Value, Internet Auctions: —; **# Sales:** —

## Chapter Five

The New Beauties, 1980-1989

In the 1980s tray variety continues the pace started in the late 1970s. The total number of trays increases by thirty-five percent to *155*. Trays of this decade have an attractiveness that surpasses both the previous decade of the 1970s and the following decade of the 1990s.

As seen in Chapter Four, most commemorative trays from the 1970s were reproductions of earlier trays and most celebrated a bottler anniversary or sporting event. In the 1980s, local franchised bottlers continued sponsoring and/or creating trays for advertising use. The trays commemorated local events and activities and at the same time creatively promoted Coca-Cola. By the early 1990s, many of the local franchised bottlers were gone. Bottlers merged or sold their business to other bottlers. One business reason for this consolidation was the need to deal with the capital demands required to bottle and distribute the increasing number of products with different sizes and types of packaging.

Retail sales of trays increased in prominence during the second half of the 1980s. Changes were occurring in the franchised bottler, customers, types of communications, and competition. As a result, trays, calendars, glasses, letter openers, and similar items were just not going to be the advertising methods that Coke needed to reach its desired audience. But, why not continue to provide these kinds of items (and more)? Instead of selling to bottlers the company began to *license* businesses to create, market, and distribute branded items, all to company specifications (a form of outsourcing). These new businesses worked to find or create sales channels (replacing the function of the bottler). The sales channels then worked at selling the advertising items, now considered *Coke Memorabilia* or collectibles, to people who would pay money for them (instead of a promise to drink Coke).

The Ohio Art Company was manufacturing and distributing trays in the 1970s and early 1980s. The first company identified solely as a distributor, beginning in the 1980s, was a Georgia company called Markatron. The official license program began in 1985-1986. Within a few years thousands of items were being created and sold in thousands of outlets.

Of the 155 trays issued in the 1980s, 103 are U.S. trays, 31 are Canadian, 4 are Mexican, 11 are Italian, 3 are German, and 1 each come from Scandinavia, Belgium, and Chile. The trays contain 135 images. Note that the number of Mexican trays is down significantly from rates found in the 1950s, 1960s, and 1970s. Pictured here are 143 trays with 128 of the images.

Internet auctions seem to reflect the type of trays that exist in each decade. The 1980s are characterized by a wide variety of trays covering many different areas. Many do not have famous images and most were not made in great quantity. The number of 1980s trays found in an auction at least once is 108, or *seventy percent* of identified trays. But the number of auctions reviewed is 539, lower than the 1970s. Sixty-three percent of the trays placed in auction were successfully sold. Buyers should note that in auctions for recent trays (1970s-1990s) over fifty percent of the sales receive only *one* bid!

Please refer to the comments in the Introduction, pages 9-10, to review information on Dollar Values shown in the captions.

1980s (Unspecified Year)

The lack of information on many of the trays from this decade produces a group of twenty-two that have been listed in the 1980s but with no specific year within the decade, more trays of this type than all the other decades combined. Seventeen trays with thirteen images are pictured in this section.

Fifteen reproductions include five from earlier trays. Three different trays (two pictured) reproduce *The Coca-Cola Girl*, 1910, plus a 1914 *Betty* and the only known reproduction of *Girl with Wind in Hair*, 1950.

Ten trays are reproduced from a wide variety of ads. They include a 1910 ad, *The Gibson Girl*; two trays from 1911 *Duster Girl* ads; a woman from a c.1940s ad on an Italian tray; a c.1908 soda fountain scene on a tray with a bamboo bottom; and the 1922 *Four Seasons* festoon. A festoon is a type of sign that usually has several sections and is hung across a wall or displayed in a window. *Four Seasons* has five sections and shows women in activities from all the seasons. It is one of the most reproduced ads on trays.

A rectangle tray and a small irregular size tip tray both contain the same picture of a woman with a glass. The image is poorly done (even ugly?). But, the trays *do* resemble the celebrity *Marion Davies*, from a distributor calendar dated 1919. The extended fingers and the hair are a match! This image was also reproduced on a round tray (not pictured).

Two plastic logo trays, one U.S. and one that is *probably* Scandinavian, are in a bottle cap shape. Also in the group is the first of four *Canadian Safe Driving Award* trays that will be identified in this decade. Not pictured are a *St. Johns, Newfoundland* plant opening commemorative, another logo tray, and a stainless steel tray with a small centered image advertised as issued in Belgium.

Name: The Coca-Cola Girl; **Issued:** 1980s
Comments: Reproduction of 1910 tray, by Hamilton King, repro signed; **Shape:** Large Rectangle; **Size:** 13.5" x 18.5"; **Story:** —;
Country: US; **Mfr/Dist:** —; **Border/Edge:** Yellow, red trim; **Quantity:** —;
Courtesy of John E. Peterson.
$ Value, References: est $20-$30 (x)
$ Value, Internet Auctions: $5 (for info only); **# Sales:** 1

Name: The Coca-Cola Girl;
Issued: 1980s
Comments: Reproduction of 1910 tray, by Hamilton King, repro signed; **Shape:** Std Rectangle; **Size:** 10.5" x 13.25"; **Story:** —; **Country:** Italy; **Mfr/Dist:** —; **Border/Edge:** Yellow; **Quantity:** —.
$ Value, References: est $10-$15 (x)
$ Value, Internet Auctions: —; **# Sales:** —

Name: Gibson Girl *or* 1910 Girl; **Issued:** 1980s
Comments: Reproduction of 1910 ad; **Shape:** Deep Round; **Size:** 12.25" dia. x 1.5" depth; **Story:** —; **Country:** US; **Mfr/Dist:** —; **Border/Edge:** Brown; **Quantity:** —; *Courtesy of John E. Peterson.*
$ Value, References: est $15-$30 (x)
$ Value, Internet Auctions: $36 (for info only); **# Sales:** 1

Name: Betty *or* Betty Girl; **Issued:** 1980s
Comments: Reproduction of 1914 tray; **Shape:** Deep Round; **Size:** 12.5" dia. x 1.5" depth; **Story:** —; **Country:** US; **Mfr/Dist:** —; **Border/Edge:** Dark blue with trim; **Quantity:** —; *Courtesy of John E. Peterson.*
$ Value, References: est $10-$15 (x)
$ Value, Internet Auctions: —; **# Sales:** —

Name: Duster Girl *or* Motor Girl; **Issued:** 1980s
Comments: Reproduction of 1911 ad; **Shape:** Std Rectangle; **Size:** 10.5" x 13.25"; **Story:** —; **Country:** US; **Mfr/Dist:** —; **Border/Edge:** Red; **Quantity:** —.
$ Value, References: est $5-$20 (4,x)
$ Value, Internet Auctions: —; **# Sales:** —

Name: Girl with Wind in Hair *or* Girl with Red Hair; **Issued:** 1980s
Comments: Reproduction of 1950 tray, by Haddon Sundblom. Colors are not as rich and sharp as original; **Shape:** Std Rectangle; **Size:** 10.5" x 13.25"; **Story:** —; **Country:** US; **Mfr/Dist:** —; **Border/Edge:** Red, silver edge; **Quantity:** —; *Courtesy of John E. Peterson.*
$ Value, References: est $25-$45 (x)
$ Value, Internet Auctions: —; **# Sales:** —

Name: Duster Girl *or* Motor Girl; **Issued:** 1980s
Comments: Reproduction of 1911 ad, *Drink Coca-Cola* on bottom border; **Shape:** Flat Rectangle; **Size:** 11" x 15.75"; **Story:** —; **Country:** US; **Mfr/Dist:** —; **Border/Edge:** Red; **Quantity:** —.
$ Value, References: est $5-$20 (x)
$ Value, Internet Auctions: —; **# Sales:** —

Name: Four Seasons; **Issued:** 1980s
Comments: Reproduction of 1922 festoon, only time reproduced without a black background; **Shape:** Large Rectangle; **Size:** 12.75" x 16.5"; **Story:** —; **Country:** US; **Mfr/Dist:** —; **Border/Edge:** Red; **Quantity:** —; *Courtesy of John E. Peterson.*
$ Value, References: est $10-$20 (x)
$ Value, Internet Auctions: —; **# Sales:** —

Name: Girl with Glass; **Issued:** 1980s
Comments: A poor quality image with thin metal. However, it appears to be a reproduction of a 1919 distributor calendar featuring the movie star *Marion Davies*. The hair and extended fingers are the same as the calendar image. The same picture is also on a round tray and a tip tray; **Shape:** Large Rectangle; **Size:** 11.125" x 15.75"; **Story:** —; **Country:** US; **Mfr/Dist:** —; **Border/Edge:** Red; **Quantity:** —; *Courtesy of John E. Peterson.*
$ Value, References: est $5-$10 (x)
$ Value, Internet Auctions: —; **# Sales:** —

Name: Girl with Glass; **Issued:** 1980s
Comments: A poor quality image with thin metal. However, it appears to be a reproduction of a 1919 distributor calendar featuring the movie star *Marion Davies*. The hair and extended fingers are the same as the calendar image. The same picture is also on a large rectangle tray and a round tray; **Shape:** Small Rectangle; **Size:** 6.25" x 7.75"; **Story:** —; **Country:** US; **Mfr/Dist:** —; **Border/Edge:** Red; **Quantity:** —.
$ Value, References: est $5-$10 (x)
$ Value, Internet Auctions: —; **# Sales:** —

Name: Refreshing; **Issued:** 1980s
Comments: Reproduction of c.1940s ad, woman in veiled hat; **Shape:** Deep Round; **Size:** 13.75" dia. x 1.75" depth; **Story:** —; **Country:** Italy; **Mfr/Dist:** —; **Border/Edge:** Brown with trim; **Quantity:** —; *Courtesy of John E. Peterson.*
$ Value, References: est $10-$25 (x)
$ Value, Internet Auctions: —; **# Sales:** —

Name: Soda Fountain; **Issued:** 1980s
Comments: Reproduction of c.1908 Massengale Agency ad (cropped), tray has a bamboo backing; **Shape:** Round; **Size:** 13.25" dia. x .75" depth; **Story:** —; **Country:** US; **Mfr/Dist:** —; **Border/Edge:** —; **Quantity:** —; *Courtesy of John E. Peterson.*
$ Value, References: est $15-$25 (x)
$ Value, Internet Auctions: —; **# Sales:** —

Name: Bottle Cap; **Issued:** 1980s
Comments: Shaped as a bottle cap, plastic, with Dynamic Ribbon II which began use in 1986; **Shape:** Round; **Size:** 12" dia. x 1.75" depth; **Story:** —; **Country:** US; **Mfr/Dist:** —; **Border/Edge:** Red; **Quantity:** —; *Courtesy of John E. Peterson.*
$ Value, References: est $10-$20 (x)
$ Value, Internet Auctions: —# **Sales:** —

Name: Bottle Cap, Snesbee; **Issued:** 1980s
Comments: The largest round tray identified, shaped as a bottle cap, plastic. The tray word *Drik* is not German, and *Drikk* is Norwegian. This tray is likely from some part of Scandinavia. The meaning of *Snesbee* is not known; **Shape:** Large Deep Round; **Size:** 17.0" x 1.875" depth; **Story:** —; **Country:** *est* Scandinavia; **Mfr/Dist:** —; **Border/Edge:** Red; **Quantity:** —; *Courtesy of John E. Peterson.*
$ Value, References: est $15-$35 (x)
$ Value, Internet Auctions: —
 # Sales: —

Name: Woman in Blue Dress at a Window; **Issued:** 1980s
Comments: Woman in blue dress, Coke logo in bottom border. Words on the dress: *I love children very much. Sometimes I wonder why I love them this much. Children are lovely.* **Shape:** Large Rectangle; **Size:** 11.75" x 16.25"; **Story:** —; **Country:** US; **Mfr/Dist:** —; **Border/Edge:** Brown; **Quantity:** —; *Courtesy of John E. Peterson.*
$ Value, References: est $15-$35 (x)
$ Value, Internet Auctions: —; **# Sales:** —

Name: Safe Driving Award; **Issued:** 1980s
Comments: Awarded to bottler employees, graphics are a small collage of bottling operations, plastic; **Shape:** Flat Round; **Size:** 13.0" dia. x .25" depth; **Story:** Yes; **Country:** Canada (English); **Mfr/Dist:** —; **Border/Edge:** Cream; **Quantity:** —; *Courtesy of John E. Peterson.*
$ Value, References: est $20-$40 (x)
$ Value, Internet Auctions: $22 (for info only); **# Sales:** 1

1980

Two very attractive trays are the last in the group of c.1980s trays. One ad reproduction of young girls at a ballet rehearsal, also c.1980s, commemorates the 100th Anniversary of the *Esso Oil Company*. No year appears on the tray. It should be a simple task to figure out the year that this major company was founded. Right! Various business references indicate that Standard Oil was founded in 1882. In 1888, one part of the company, Standard Oil of New Jersey, acquired a company to market oil in the British Isles. *That* company was the predecessor of Esso, a German company, acquired two years later, etc. etc. So, the tray has been placed in the 1980s.

The last tray has a mysterious and beautiful image, *Woman in Blue Dress at a Window*. A Coke logo is in the bottom border but no other information is found *anywhere* on the tray. This tray and the *Esso* commemorative tray are perfect examples of the best and, for collectors, less than the best of trays of this decade! Here are two beautiful trays with unique images but no date or any identifying information.

This group of thirteen has four different types of commemorative trays. Eleven of the trays are pictured.

Three trays commemorate the 60th Anniversary of the Coca-Cola bottler in Vancouver. A 1920 picture of the city and a 1980 aerial view of the city and surrounding waters are two of the most attractive trays of this decade. The third is the only known reproduction of *The Golfer Girl*, originally issued in 1920, the year this bottler began operations. These three trays are the first in a series of 1980s Vancouver trays. (A series being two or more trays created around a similar theme or location.)

Name: Girls at Ballet **Issued:** 1980s
Comments: Reproduction of c.1980s ad, commemorates 100th Anniversary of Esso Oil Company, *Coke Presents Refreshment Time*; **Shape:** Oval; **Size:** 11.75" x 14.5"; **Story:** Yes; **Country:** US; **Mfr/Dist:** —; **Border/Edge:** Red; **Quantity:** —; *Courtesy of John E. Peterson.*
$ Value, References: est $15-$25 (x)
$ Value, Internet Auctions: —; **# Sales:** —

Name: Picture of Vancouver, c.1920; **Issued:** 1980
Comments: Commemorative of 60th Anniversary of Vancouver bottler, # one of series, beautiful color tones in an old picture of the city; **Shape:** Std Rectangle; **Size:** 10.5" x 13.25"; **Story:** Yes; **Country:** Canada (French); **Mfr/Dist:** —; **Border/Edge:** Brown; **Quantity:** —.
$ Value, References: est $10-$20 (x)
$ Value, Internet Auctions: —; **# Sales:** —

Name: Vancouver Today; **Issued:** 1980
Comments: Commemorative of 60th Anniversary of Vancouver bottler, # two of series, city and harbor pictured from the air; **Shape:** Std Rectangle; **Size:** 10.5" x 13.25"; **Story:** Yes; **Country:** Canada (French); **Mfr/Dist:** —; **Border/Edge:** Dark Blue; **Quantity:** —.
$ Value, References: $7-$15 (3,6,x)
$ Value, Internet Auctions: $8 (for info only); **# Sales:** 1

Name: Euclid Beach, Baseball; **Issued:** 1980
Comments: Commemorative of 75th Anniversary of Cleveland, Ohio bottler, features Napoleon Lajoe; **Shape:** Std Rectangle; **Size:** 10.5" x 13.25"; **Story:** Yes; **Country:** US; **Mfr/Dist:** —; **Border/Edge:** Black; **Quantity:** —; *Courtesy of John E. Peterson.*
$ Value, References: est $10-$30 (3,x)
$ Value, Internet Auctions: $18; **# Sales:** 5

Name: Golfer Girl *or* Garden Girl; **Issued:** 1980
Comments: Reproduction of 1920 tray for commemorative of 60th Anniversary of Vancouver bottler, # three of series, the only known reproduction of the tray; **Shape:** Std Rectangle;
Size: 10.5" x 13.25"; **Story:** Yes; **Country:** Canada (French); **Mfr/Dist:** —; **Border/Edge:** Green, gold edge; **Quantity:** —; *Courtesy of John E. Peterson.*
$ Value, References: est $10-$25 (x)
$ Value, Internet Auctions: $10 (for info only); **# Sales:** 1

Name: Bottle 5¢; **Issued:** 1980
Comments: Back of tray. Reproduction of 1903 tray, commemorative of 75th Anniversary, Jackson, Tennessee bottler; **Shape:** Round; **Size:** 12.5"; **Story:** Yes; **Country:** US; **Mfr/Dist:** —; **Border/Edge:** Yellow; **Quantity:** est 8,000, individually numbered.
$ Value, References: $8-$20 (3,6,x)
$ Value, Internet Auctions: —; **# Sales:** —

Three additional bottler 75th Anniversary trays include Houston and Cleveland, with local images; the third, from Jackson, Tennessee, reproduces the 1903 *Bottle 5¢* tray. Two customer commemoratives are a 1923 *Flapper Girl* reproduction used for the 25th Anniversary of Coke and McDonalds in Canada, and an antique car at a gas pump for the 100th Anniversary of Canada's largest oil company, Imperial Oil (not pictured). Esso acquired Imperial Oil in 1898.

Only four of the forty-six Santa ad reproduction trays are commemoratives. The first of fourteen Santa trays from the 1980s again uses the 1963 ad, *Dear Santa*. This Canadian tray commemorates the 25th Anniversary of Santa Village in Bracebridge, Ontario Canada, (advertised as halfway to the North Pole). A sports commemorative tray, *Normandeau Cup* (not pictured) features the 75th Anniversary of this Alberta, Canada horse show.

Name: Houston, Texas Bottling Plant; **Issued:** 1980
Comments: Commemorative of 75th Anniversary of Houston, Texas bottler, picture of facility; **Shape:** Std Rectangle; **Size:** 10.5" x 13.25"; **Story:** Yes; **Country:** US; **Mfr/Dist:** —; **Border/Edge:** Green with ten Coke bottles around border; **Quantity:** —; *Courtesy of John E. Peterson.*
$ Value, References: $10-$25 (3,4,x)
$ Value, Internet Auctions: $16 (for info only); **# Sales:** 1

Name: Flapper Girl; **Issued:** 1980
Comments: Reproduction of 1923 tray, commemorative of customer. Tray words: *25th Anniversary, May 6-14, 1980 – Toronto, Ontario Canada presented by Coca-Cola, Ltd. To Commemorate McDonald's 25th Anniversary;* **Shape:** Std Rectangle; **Size:** 10.5" x 13.25"; **Story:** Yes; **Country:** Canada (English); **Mfr/Dist:** —; **Border/Edge:** Brown; **Quantity:** —; *Courtesy of John E. Peterson.*
$ Value, References: est $20-$60 (8,x)
$ Value, Internet Auctions: $10 (for info only); **# Sales:** 2

Name: Dear Santa *or* Santa at Chimney; **Issued:** 1980
Comments: Reproduction of 1963 Santa ad by Haddon Sundblom, commemorates 25th Anniversary of Santa Village at Bracebridge, Ontario; **Shape:** Std Rectangle;
Size: 10.5" x 13.25"; **Story:** Border; **Country:** Canada (English); **Mfr/Dist:** —;
Border/Edge: Green; **Quantity:** —.
$ Value, References: est $12-$25 (x)
$ Value, Internet Auctions: $5 (for info only); **# Sales:** 1

Three c.1980 trays include a 1981 Canadian calendar, a glass bottomed tray, and a round plastic product tray from Chile, *Tore Vedve*.

Name: Calendar, 1981;
Issued: 1980
Comments: Eight ad reproductions and a calendar;
Shape: Large Rectangle;
Size: 13.5" x 18.5"; **Story:** —
; **Country:** Canada (French);
Mfr/Dist: —; **Border/Edge:**
Black; **Quantity:** —.
$ Value, References: est
$10-$20 (3,x)
$ Value, Internet Auctions:
$8; **# Sales:** 4

Name: Tore Vedve; **Issued:** c.1980
Comments: Side view of tray showing Coca-Cola logos around the side. Tray face is red, no graphics. Plastic, acquired from Chile; **Shape:** Deep Round; **Size:** 13.5" dia. x 1.5" depth; **Story:** —; **Country:** Chile; **Mfr/Dist:** —; **Border/Edge:** Red;
Quantity: —; *Courtesy of John E. Peterson.*
$ Value, References: est $15-$25 (x)
$ Value, Internet Auctions: —; **# Sales:** —

1981

Eighteen trays are listed from 1981; sixteen are pictured. As a comparison, note that the entire decade from 1930-1939 had a total tray count of seventeen.

Eight commemorative trays for the year include one sports theme, one bottler anniversary, the only identified commemorative tray for a specific person in a bottler organization, two new bottling plant openings, a dam (not pictured), and the first two trays identified that commemorate *Coca-Cola Collectors* events.

Name: How 'bout them dawgs?; **Issued:** 1981
Comments: Commemorates sports event, the 1980 National Football Champions,
Georgia Bulldogs; **Shape:** Large Rectangle; **Size:** 13.5" x 18.5"; **Story:** Yes; **Country:** US;
Mfr/Dist: —; **Border/Edge:** Black; **Quantity:** —.
$ Value, References: $5-$15 (3,6,x)
$ Value, Internet Auctions: $10; **# Sales:** 4

Name: Delicious and Refreshing; **Issued:** c.1980
Comments: Glass face, bamboo base and handles; **Shape:** Std Rectangle;
Size: 10.5" x 13.25"; **Story:** —; **Country:** US; **Mfr/Dist:** —; **Border/
Edge:** —; **Quantity:** —; *Courtesy of John E. Peterson.*
$ Value, References: est $15-$25 (x)
$ Value, Internet Auctions: $10; **# Sales:** 3

Name: Relieves Fatigue; **Issued:** 1981
Comments: Reproduction of 1907 tray, commemorative of 75th Anniversary of Tullahoma, Tennessee bottler, back of tray relates how 125,000 servicemen at Camp Forest were served by the bottler during World War II; **Shape:** Large Deep Oval; **Size:** 12.5" x 15.5"; **Story:** Yes; **Country:** US; **Mfr/Dist:** —; **Border/Edge:** Brown; **Quantity:** 10,000; *Courtesy of Ann Poppenheimer Sherrod and Dave Sherrod, Pop's Mail Order Collectibles.*
$ Value, References: $5-$20 (3,6,x)
$ Value, Internet Auctions: —; **# Sales:** —

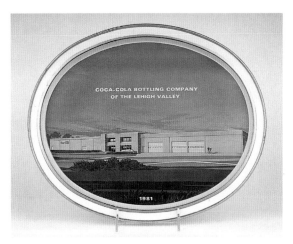

Name: Lehigh Valley; **Issued:** 1981
Comments: Commemorative of new facility for *The Bottling Company of Lehigh Valley*, artist rendition of new plant; **Shape:** Oval; **Size:** 11.25" x 14.5"; **Story:** —; **Country:** US; **Mfr/Dist:** Fabcraft; **Border/Edge:** White, gold edge; **Quantity:** —; *Courtesy of John E. Peterson.*
$ Value, References: $5-$20 (2,3,7,x)
$ Value, Internet Auctions: —; **# Sales:** —

Name: Springtime in Atlanta; **Issued:** 1981
Comments: First identified commemorative of Coca-Cola Collectors event, Atlanta, Georgia. Collage of Candler, Pemberton, and early Coca-Cola items; **Shape:** Std Rectangle; **Size:** 10.5" x 13.25"; **Story:** Yes; **Country:** US; **Mfr/Dist:** —; **Border/Edge:** Red, yellow edge; **Quantity:** est 2,000.
$ Value, References: $5-$25 (3,4,x)
$ Value, Internet Auctions: $22 (for info only); **# Sales:** 1

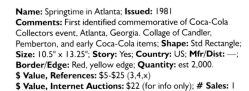

Name: James Carlen, Cooksville, Tennessee; **Issued:** 1981
Comments: Commemorates *Fifty Years of Service*, drawing of the Cooksville Coca-Cola bottling plant and picture of Mr. Carlen; **Shape:** Small Rectangle; **Size:** 8.75" x 14.5"; **Story:** Yes; **Country:** US; **Mfr/Dist:** —; **Border/Edge:** Dark Green; **Quantity:** —; *Courtesy of John E. Peterson.*
$ Value, References: est $5-$20 (x)
$ Value, Internet Auctions: —; **# Sales:** —

Name: Regina Saskatchewan; **Issued:** 1981
Comments: Commemorative of new facility. Bottler serves 159,000 people, in operation sixty years. Artist rendition of plant, two children, and fields of wheat; **Shape:** Std Rectangle; **Size:** 10.5" x 13.25"; **Story:** —; **Country:** Canada (English); **Mfr/Dist:** —; **Border/Edge:** Orange, gold edge; **Quantity:** —; *Courtesy of John E. Peterson.*
$ Value, References: est $10-$20 (x)
$ Value, Internet Auctions: $30 (for info only); **# Sales:** 1

Name: Exhilaration; **Issued:** 1981
Comments: Commemorative of 7th National Convention, Coca-Cola Collectors, Kansas City, Missouri; **Shape:** Large Deep Oval; **Size:** 12.5" x 15.5"; **Story:** Yes; **Country:** US; **Mfr/Dist:** —; **Border/Edge:** Black, gold words; **Quantity:** 1,500.
$ Value, References: $10-$25 (3,8,x) **$ Value, Internet Auctions:** —; **# Sales:** —

Seven ad reproductions for the year include three of Norman Rockwell's calendars from 1932, 1934, and 1935, and a 1922 *Four Seasons*. *1927 Calendar Girl* (not pictured) is third in the series of eight commemorative Italian trays; *1914 Syrup Label* reproduces a label from a five gallon keg of Coca-Cola syrup; and a 1953 Santa ad, *The Pause that Refreshes,* completes the ad reproductions. This Santa tray is the *first* to use an ad other than *Dear Santa* from 1963 and is the first identified tray to be distributed by Markatron.

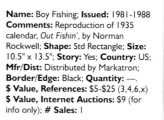

Name: Boy Fishing; **Issued:** 1981-1988
Comments: Reproduction of 1935 calendar, *Out Fishin',* by Norman Rockwell; **Shape:** Std Rectangle; **Size:** 10.5" x 13.5"; **Story:** Yes; **Country:** US; **Mfr/Dist:** Distributed by Markatron; **Border/Edge:** Black; **Quantity:** —.
$ Value, References: $5-$25 (3,4,6,x)
$ Value, Internet Auctions: $9 (for info only); **# Sales:** 1

Name: The Old Oaken Bucket; **Issued:** 1981
Comments: Reproduction of 1932 calendar, by Norman Rockwell; **Shape:** Std Rectangle; **Size:** 10.5" x 13.5"; **Story:** Yes; **Country:** US; **Mfr/Dist:** —; **Border/Edge:** Black; **Quantity:** —.
$ Value, References: $5-$15 (3,4,x)
$ Value, Internet Auctions: $23 (for info only); **# Sales:** 2

Name: Four Seasons; **Issued:** 1981
Comments: Reproduction of 1922 festoon; **Shape:** Large Deep Oval; **Size:** 12.5" x 15.5"; **Story:** Rim; **Country:** US; **Mfr/Dist:** Distributed by Markatron; **Border/Edge:** Yellow; **Quantity:** —.
$ Value, References: $5-$15 (3,4,x)
$ Value, Internet Auctions: $6 (for info only); **# Sales:** 1

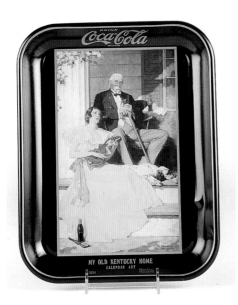

Name: Old Kentucky Home; **Issued:** 1981
Comments: Reproduction of 1934 calendar, *Carry Me Back to Old Virginny,* by Norman Rockwell; **Shape:** Std Rectangle; **Size:** 10.5" x 13.5"; **Story:** Yes; **Country:** US; **Mfr/Dist:** —; **Border/Edge:** Black, gold edge; **Quantity:** —. **$ Value, References:** $5-$25 (3,4,x)
$ Value, Internet Auctions: —; **# Sales:** —

Name: Syrup Label; **Issued:** c.1981
Comments: Reproduction of c.1914 syrup label for five gallon keg of syrup; **Shape:** Flat Round; **Size:** 12.5"; **Story:** —; **Country:** US; **Mfr/Dist:** —; **Border/Edge:** Red, cola bean trim; **Quantity:** —.
$ Value, References: $5-$10 (3,4,6,x)
$ Value, Internet Auctions: $8; **# Sales:** 5

Name: The Pause that Refreshes;
Issued: 1981
Comments: Reproduction of 1953 ad, by Haddon Sundblom. Santa in chair being served Coke by two children;
Shape: Std Rectangle;
Size: 10.5" x 13.25"; **Story:** —;
Country: US; **Mfr/Dist:** Distributed by Markatron; **Border/Edge:** Black, holiday trim; **Quantity:** —.
$ Value, References: $5-$15 (3,4,x)
$ Value, Internet Auctions: $14; **# Sales:** 3

Peabody Hotel is the first of six wonderful trays in a series by the Memphis bottler. A logo tray, in dark black, is made of a hard plastic material called phenolic. A Canadian tray, *1982 Calendar,* completes the 1981 group.

Name: 1982 Calendar; **Issued:** c.1981
Comments: Reproduction of six ads and a calendar for 1982; **Shape:** Std Rectangle; **Size:** 10.5" x 13.25"; **Story:** —; **Country:** Canada (English); **Mfr/Dist:** —; **Border/Edge:** Black; **Quantity:** —.
$ Value, References: $10-$25 (3,6,x)
$ Value, Internet Auctions: $7; **# Sales:** 5

1982

In 1982 the number of identified trays increases to twenty-one. All are pictured in this section.

One logo tray features *Coca-Cola is it!*, a slogan introduced in 1982. Four additional trays use Coke in this slogan. One is an oval with colorful hot air balloons and another, with wooden handles, pictures a can of Coke in ice. Markatron distributed both. Two Canadian trays have the same image in English and French versions (*Y'a juste Coke!*).

Name: Peabody Hotel, Memphis, Tennessee; **Issued:** 1981
Comments: Commemorative of restoration of hotel first opened in 1925, # one in series of trays by Memphis bottler; **Shape:** Std Rectangle; **Size:** 10.5" x 13.25"; **Story:** Yes; **Country:** US; **Mfr/Dist:** —; **Border/Edge:** Grape; **Quantity:** —.
$ Value, References: est $5-$20 (3,x)
$ Value, Internet Auctions: $13 (for info only); **# Sales:** 1

Name: Enjoy Coca-Cola, by Courac®; **Issued:** 1981
Comments: Black plastic-like material called phenolic, sticker on back reads: *Courac serving pieces are cherished gifts because of their variety and beauty of design. Hand inlaid by master craftsmen, shells, coins, woods and metals are fused into satin black phenolic. They are impervious to alcohol and boiling water. Wash with soap and water;* **Shape:** Small Rectangle; **Size:** 9.75" x 12.75"; **Story:** Yes; **Country:** US; **Mfr/Dist:** Courac, distributed by Markatron; **Border/Edge:** Black; **Quantity:** —.
$ Value, References: est $20-$40 (x)
$ Value, Internet Auctions: —; **# Sales:** —

Name: Coca-Cola is it!; **Issued:** 1982
Comments: Trink Coca-Cola, could also serve as a trivet, dated from year slogan first introduced; **Shape:** Square; **Size:** 7"; **Story:** —; **Country:** Germany; **Mfr/Dist:** Ornamold; **Border/Edge:** Red; **Quantity:** —; *Courtesy of John E. Peterson.*
$ Value, References: est $8-$20 (x)
$ Value, Internet Auctions: —; **# Sales:** —

Name: Coke is it!; **Issued:** 1982
Comments: Hot air balloons, similar to 1981 Coke Collector Commemorative tray; **Shape:** Large Deep Oval; **Size:** 12.5" x 15.5"; **Story:** —;
Country: US; **Mfr/Dist:** Distributed by Markatron;
Border/Edge: Red; **Quantity:** —.
$ Value, References: $10-$20 (3,4,x)
$ Value, Internet Auctions: —; **# Sales:** —

Name: Y'a juste Coke!; **Issued:** 1982
Comments: French Canadian version of Kim at Christmas (identified on rim), hair flying and holding a bottle of Coke; **Shape:** Large Deep Oval; **Size:** 12.5" x 15.5"; **Story:** Rim; **Country:** Canada (French);
Mfr/Dist: —; **Border/Edge:** Red, gold stripe; **Quantity:** —;
Courtesy of John E. Peterson.
$ Value, References: est $10-$20 (x)
$ Value, Internet Auctions: $5 (for info only); **# Sales:** 1

Event commemoratives include an attractive picture of *Branton, Manitoba* during its Centennial and the *1982 World's Fair, Knoxville Tennessee*, also found shrink-wrapped with a coupon booklet. Customer commemoratives are a second *McDonalds* (the only customer with a second tray); *Red River Co-op*, a Limited Edition from a Canadian supermarket group; and *Piggly Wiggly*, second in the Memphis series.

Four additional commemoratives include a reproduction of *Relieves Fatigue, 1907*, and a collage of local scenes from *Hawaii*, both bottler anniversary trays. A Limited Edition of 750 copies commemorates a new Florida bottling plant, *Pembroke Pines*. Finally, *Sprite Boy*, a 1951 ad, commemorates Coca-Cola Collectors at their 8th annual convention. This tray uses *Silhouette Girl* in the border, its only use on a tray since *Skater Girl, 1941*. *Silhouette Girl* is a logo still used by the Coca-Cola Collectors Club.

Name: Coke is it!; **Issued:** 1982
Comments: Coke can in crushed ice, tray has handles; **Shape:** Std Rectangle;
Size: 10.5" x 13.25" plus 1.0" each side for handles; **Story:** —; **Country:** US;
Mfr/Dist: Distributed by Markatron;
Border/Edge: Black, blue corner trim; **Quantity:** —.
$ Value, References: est $10-$20 (3,x)
$ Value, Internet Auctions: —; **# Sales:** —

Name: Coke is it!; **Issued:** 1982
Comments: Kim at Christmas (identified on rim), hair flying and holding a bottle of Coke; **Shape:** Large Deep Oval; **Size:** 12.5" x 15.5";
Story: Rim; **Country:** Canada (English); **Mfr/Dist:** —; **Border/Edge:** Red, gold stripe; **Quantity:** —; *Courtesy of John E. Peterson.*
$ Value, References: est $10-$20 (x)
$ Value, Internet Auctions: —; **# Sales:** —

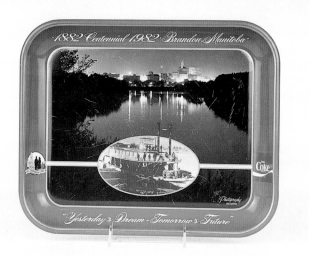

Name: Branton, Manitoba Centennial; **Issued:** 1982
Comments: Commemorative of event, *Yesterday's Dream, Tomorrow's Future*, picture of city and riverboat; **Shape:** Std Rectangle; **Size:** 10.5" x 13.25"; **Story:** Yes;
Country: Canada (English); **Mfr/Dist:** —; **Border/Edge:** Brown; **Quantity:** —.
$ Value, References: $5-$15 (3,6,x)
$ Value, Internet Auctions: —; **# Sales:** —

Name: The 1982 World's Fair, with coupon book; **Issued:** 1982
Comments: The tray was packaged with a coupon book good for several activities in the Knoxville area.
$ Value, References: est $15-$25 (with coupon book) (x)
$ Value, Internet Auctions: —;
 # Sales: —

Name: The 1982 World's Fair; **Issued:** 1982
Comments: Commemorative of event, *The World's Fair, Knoxville, Tennessee*, artist rendition of fairgrounds; **Shape:** Round; **Size:** 12.5"; **Story:** Yes; **Country:** US; **Mfr/Dist:** —; **Border/Edge:** Red; **Quantity:** —.
$ Value, References: $5-$10 (3,4,6,x)
$ Value, Internet Auctions: $7; **# Sales:** 9

Name: Piggly-Wiggly, the Original American Supermarket; **Issued:** 1982
Comments: Commemorative of customer, HQ move to Memphis, collage of founder, logo, and shopping, by Keith Kohler, # two in series of trays from Memphis bottler; **Shape:** Std Rectangle; **Size:** 10.5" x 13.25"; **Story:** Yes; **Country:** —; **Mfr/Dist:** —; **Border/Edge:** Gray; **Quantity:** —.
$ Value, References: est $30-$65 (x)
$ Value, Internet Auctions: —; **# Sales:** —

Name: McDonald's Convention; **Issued:** 1982
Comments: Commemorative of customer, second tray for *McDonald's*, owner-operator convention in San Francisco. Collage of skyline, six San Francisco attractions and McDonald's founder, by Keats Petree; **Shape:** Large Rectangle; **Size:** 13.5" x 18.5"; **Story:** Yes; **Country:** US; **Mfr/Dist:** —; **Border/Edge:** White, gold edge; **Quantity:** —; *Courtesy of John E. Peterson.*
$ Value, References: est $50-$100 (3,x)
$ Value, Internet Auctions: $45 (for info only); **# Sales:** 1

Name: Relieves Fatigue;
Issued: 1982
Comments: Reproduction of 1907 tray, commemorative of 75th Anniversary, Corinth, Mississippi bottler; **Shape:** Std Rectangle; **Size:** 10.5" x 13.25"; **Story:** Yes; **Country:** US; **Mfr/Dist:** —; **Border/Edge:** Maroon; **Quantity:** 10,000.
$ Value, References: est $8-$20 (6,x)
$ Value, Internet Auctions: —; **# Sales:** —

Name: Relieves Fatigue; **Issued:** 1982
Comments: Back of Corinth, Mississippi tray.

Name: Red River Co-op; **Issued:** 1982
Comments: Commemorative of customer, a grocery co-op in Winnipeg, Manitoba, picture of building and trucks; **Shape:** Std Rectangle; **Size:** 10.5" x 13.25"; **Story:** Yes; **Country:** Canada (English); **Mfr/Dist:** —; **Border/Edge:** Red; **Quantity:** —.
$ Value, References: $10-$20 (3,6,x)
$ Value, Internet Auctions: $7 (for info only); **# Sales:** 1

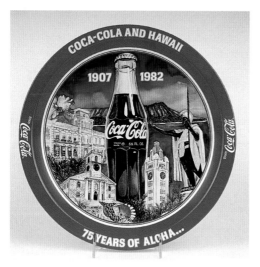

Name: Hawaii 75th Anniversary; **Issued:** 1982
Comments: Commemorative of 75th Anniversary, Hawaii bottler, collage of local scenes; **Shape:** Round; **Size:** 12.5"; **Story:** Yes; **Country:** US; **Mfr/Dist:** —; **Border/Edge:** Red; **Quantity:** —.
$ Value, References: est $5-$15 (3,x)
$ Value, Internet Auctions: $17; **# Sales:** 9

Three 1982 Mexican trays are listed, each in a different shape with graphics but no images. Additional tray reproductions include *Party Girl*, 1925, the fourth tray in the Italian series of eight; and *The Coca-Cola Girl*, 1910, in a round tray with grooves on the face of the tray. These trays were packaged with twelve cans of Coca-Cola as a promotional offering.

Additional trays with ad reproductions are *The Village Blacksmith*, from the 1933 calendar by Frederick Stanley, and a c.1982 reproduction of *Santa with Elves, A Merry Christmas*, from a 1960 ad.

Name: Disfrute; **Issued:** 1982
Comments: Logo tray, white graphics on red; **Shape:** Large Rectangle; **Size:** 13.5" x 18.5"; **Story:** —; **Country:** Mexico; **Mfr/Dist:** —; **Border/Edge:** White; **Quantity:** —; *Courtesy of John E. Peterson.*
$ Value, References: est $10-$25 (x)
$ Value, Internet Auctions: —; **# Sales:** —

Name: Pembroke Pines; **Issued:** 1982
Comments: Commemorative of new bottling plant in Miami, Florida area, picture of c.1915 antique truck, produced in very limited volumes; **Shape:** Std Rectangle; **Size:** 10.5" x 13.25"; **Story:** Yes; **Country:** US; **Mfr/Dist:** —; **Border/Edge:** Red, gold edge; **Quantity:** 750; *Courtesy of Ann Poppenheimer Sherrod and Dave Sherrod, Pop's Mail Order Collectibles.*
$ Value, References: $90-$200 (3,6,8,x)
$ Value, Internet Auctions: $110 (for info only); **# Sales:** 1

Name: Disfrute; **Issued:** 1982
Comments: Logo tray, large graphics with white Coca-Cola script on red; **Shape:** Deep Round; **Size:** 13.5" dia. x 1.5" depth; **Story:** —; **Country:** Mexico; **Mfr/Dist:** —; **Border/Edge:** Red; **Quantity:** —; *Courtesy of John E. Peterson.*
$ Value, References: est $20-$40 (x)
$ Value, Internet Auctions: —; **# Sales:** —

Name: Sprite Boy; **Issued:** 1982
Comments: Reproduction of 1951 ad, by Haddon Sundblom, commemorative of 8th National Convention, Coca-Cola Collectors, Nashville, Tennessee; **Shape:** Std Rectangle; **Size:** 10.5" x 13.25"; **Story:** Yes; **Country:** US; **Mfr/Dist:** —; **Border/Edge:** Red, gold stripe, Silhouette Girl logo in border; **Quantity:** 2,000.
$ Value, References: $50-$100 (3,4,8,x)
$ Value, Internet Auctions: $44; **# Sales:** 3

Name: Disfruta; **Issued:** 1982
Comments: Logo tray, white graphics on red, sloping sides; **Shape:** Large Rectangle; **Size:** 11.875" x 15.875"; **Story:** —; **Country:** Mexico; **Mfr/Dist:** —; **Border/Edge:** Red; **Quantity:** —; *Courtesy of John E. Peterson.*
$ Value, References: est $15-$25 (x)
$ Value, Internet Auctions: —; **# Sales:** —

Name: Party Girl *or* Girl at Party;
Issued: 1982
Comments: Reproduction of 1925 tray, next in series of Italian trays to commemorate fifty years of bottling in Italy; **Shape:** Std Rectangle; **Size:** 10.5" x 13.25"; **Story:** Yes; **Country:** Italy; **Mfr/Dist:** —; **Border/Edge:** Verdi Oliva (olive green), with trim; **Quantity:** —; *Courtesy of John E. Peterson.*
$ Value, References: est $25-$70 (x)
$ Value, Internet Auctions: $19 (for info only); **# Sales:** 2

Name: A Merry Christmas; **Issued:** c.1982
Comments: Reproduction of 1960 ad, by Haddon Sundblom, *Coke is it!*; **Shape:** Std Rectangle; **Size:** 10.5" x 13.25"; **Story:** —; **Country:** US; **Mfr/Dist:** Distributed by Markatron; **Border/Edge:** Green, no trim; **Quantity:** —.
$ Value, References: est $10-$20 (x)
$ Value, Internet Auctions: $13; **# Sales:** 3

1983

Ten 1983 trays are listed and all have pictures in this section.

Beale Street is third in the Memphis series of trays, and commemorates that street's history of music. *Enjoy Coca-Cola* and *Diet Coke* are similar trays that both feature products and have backgrounds of a *wet look*. *Antique Truck* was for the 9th Coca-Cola Collectors convention, and *Antique Delivery Wagon* commemorates The Kroger Company. Two tray reproductions are *Autumn Girl*, 1922, and *Flapper Girl*, 1923.

For the first time, multiple trays with Santa Claus ad reproductions are issued in one year. Three are listed, including *A Merry Christmas*, the same image as the 1982 reproduction but this time with colorful holiday border trim. *Thanks for the Pause* is from a 1938 image and *Good Boys and Girls* is the first of *five* trays to reproduce this 1951 ad.

Name: The Coca-Cola Girl;
Issued: 1982
Comments: Reproduction of 1910 tray, by Hamilton King, not signed, packaged with twelve cans as a promotion, face of tray grooved to stabilize cans; **Shape:** Deep Round; **Size:** 12.75" dia. x .75" depth; **Story:** —; **Country:** Italy; **Mfr/Dist:** Manufactured in Hong Kong; **Border/Edge:** Red, circles of flowers as trim; **Quantity:** —.
$ Value, References: est $10-$25 (x)
$ Value, Internet Auctions: $8 (for info only); **# Sales:** 1

Name: The Village Blacksmith; **Issued:** 1982
Comments: Reproduction of 1933 calendar, by Frederick Stanley; **Shape:** Large Flat Oval; **Size:** 14.25" x 17.25"; **Story:** Yes; **Country:** US; **Mfr/Dist:** Distributed by Markatron; **Border/Edge:** Black, red edge, yellow trim; **Quantity:** —.
$ Value, References: $5-$15 (3,6,x)
$ Value, Internet Auctions: —; **# Sales:** —

Name: Beale Street; **Issued:** c.1983
Comments: Commemorative of place. Trumpeter and other street scenes, # three in series of trays by Memphis bottler; **Shape:** Std Rectangle; **Size:** 10.5" x 13.25"; **Story:** Yes; **Country:** US; **Mfr/Dist:** —; **Border/Edge:** Red; **Quantity:** —.
$ Value, References: $8-$25 (3,6,x)
$ Value, Internet Auctions: $11; **# Sales:** 7

Name: Enjoy Coca-Cola; **Issued:** 1983
Comments: Background has wet look;
Shape: Std Rectangle; **Size:** 10.5" x
13.25"; **Story:** —; **Country:** US; **Mfr/
Dist:** Ohio Art Company; **Border/
Edge:** Amber, wet look; **Quantity:** —.
$ Value, References: $10-$20 (3,4,x)
$ Value, Internet Auctions: $13; **#
Sales:** 6

Name: Antique Delivery Wagon; **Issued:** 1983
Comments: Commemorative of customer, 100th Anniversary Kroger Corporation,
by C. Don Engor; **Shape:** Small Oval; **Size:** 8.0" x 11.0"; **Story:** Yes; **Country:** US;
Mfr/Dist: Fabcraft; **Border/Edge:** White, gold edge; **Quantity:** —.
$ Value, References: $5-$10 (3,6,x)
$ Value, Internet Auctions: $12; **# Sales:** 11

Name: Diet Coke; **Issued:** 1983
Comments: Hand pouring Diet Coke into glass, product introduced
during 1982, beads of water in background create wet look;
Shape: Std Rectangle; **Size:** 10.5" x 13.25"; **Story:** —; **Country:**
Canada (English); **Mfr/Dist:** Ohio Art Company; **Border/Edge:** Gray,
beads of water; **Quantity:** —.
$ Value, References: $8-$20 (3,4,6,x)
$ Value, Internet Auctions: $18; **# Sales:** 5

Name: Flapper Girl; **Issued:** 1983
Comments: Reproduction of 1923
tray; **Shape:** Large Deep Oval;
Size: 12.5" x 15.5"; **Story:** —;
Country: US; **Mfr/Dist:** Ohio
Art Company; **Border/Edge:**
Brown; **Quantity:** —;
Courtesy of John E. Peterson.
$ Value, References: est $8-
$15; (x)
$ Value, Internet Auctions:
—; **# Sales:** —

Name: Antique Truck; **Issued:** 1983
Comments: Commemorative of 9th National Convention, Coca-
Cola Collectors, Washington, DC, artist rendition of antique truck
and US Capitol; **Shape:** Flat Round; **Size:** 12.0"; **Story:** Yes;
Country: US; **Mfr/Dist:** —; **Border/Edge:** Green;
Quantity: 2,000.
$ Value, References: $5-$15 (3,4,6,x)
$ Value, Internet Auctions: $10 (for info only); **# Sales:** 1

Name: Autumn Girl *or* Navy Girl; **Issued:** 1983
Comments: Reproduction of 1922 tray;
Shape: Long Rectangle; **Size:** 8.5" x 19.0";
Story: —; **Country:** US; **Mfr/Dist:** Ohio Art
Company; **Border/Edge:** Green, gold stripe;
Quantity: —.
$ Value, References: est $10-$15 (6,x)
$ Value, Internet Auctions: —; **# Sales:** —

Name: A Merry Christmas;
Issued: c.1982-1983
Comments: Reproduction of 1960 ad, by Haddon Sundblom, *Coke is it!*; **Shape:** Std Rectangle; **Size:** 10.5" x 13.25"; **Story:** —; **Country:** US; **Mfr/Dist:** Distributed by Markatron; **Border/Edge:** Red and yellow, holiday trim; **Quantity:** —.
$ Value, References: est $10-$20 (3,x)
$ Value, Internet Auctions: $19; **# Sales:** 3

Eleven trays are identified for 1984 and bring the total listed for the 1980s so far to ninety-five. Nine of the eleven are pictured here.

The Memphis series adds three trays, with *The Memphis Chicks*, a popular, local, minor-league baseball team; *Special Train*; and a city collage called *Memphis, A Good Place To Be*. *Zanesville Y-Bridge*, a painting by the artist Leslie Cope, is the first in a series of trays from Zanesville, Ohio with images of historic transportation sites in this Midwestern area. *Zanesville Y-Bridge* was also for a bottler 75th Anniversary.

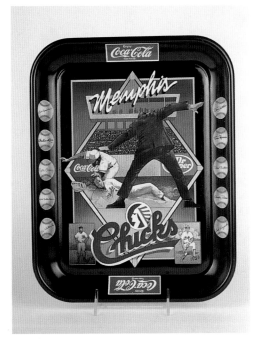

Name: Memphis Chicks; **Issued:** 1984
Comments: Commemorative of Minor League team, collage of the team, umpire and other scenes, # four in series of trays by Memphis bottler; **Shape:** Std Rectangle; **Size:** 10.5" x 13.25"; **Story:** Yes; **Country:** US; **Mfr/Dist:** —; **Border/Edge:** Black; **Quantity:** —.
$ Value, References: $5-$15 (3,6,x)
$ Value, Internet Auctions: $11; **# Sales:** 6

Name: Thanks for the Pause; **Issued:** 1983
Comments: Reproduction of 1938 ad, Santa in chair with arm around a child, by Haddon Sundblom; **Shape:** Std Rectangle; **Size:** 10.5" x 13.25"; **Story:** —; **Country:** US; **Mfr/Dist:** Ohio Art Company; **Border/Edge:** Green with trim; **Quantity:** —.
$ Value, References: $8-$20 (3,4,6,x)
$ Value, Internet Auctions: $12; **# Sales:** 4

Name: Good Boys and Girls; **Issued:** 1983
Comments: Reproduction of 1951 ad, by Haddon Sundblom; **Shape:** Std Rectangle; **Size:** 10.5" x 13.25"; **Story:** —; **Country:** US; **Mfr/Dist:** —; **Border/Edge:** Green with trim; **Quantity:** —.
$ Value, References: est $15-$20 (3,x)
$ Value, Internet Auctions: $9; **# Sales:** 9

Name: Special Train; **Issued:** 1984
Comments: Commemorative of restored train, artist rendition of engine and cars, # five in series of trays by Memphis bottler; **Shape:** Std Rectangle; **Size:** 10.5" x 13.25"; **Story:** Yes; **Country:** US; **Mfr/Dist:** —; **Border/Edge:** Red; **Quantity:** —.
$ Value, References: $5-$10 (3,6,x)
$ Value, Internet Auctions: $14; **# Sales:** 7

Name: A Good Place To Be; **Issued:** 1984
Comments: Commemorative of place, collage of twenty-three city attractions, # six in series of trays by Memphis bottler; **Shape:** Large Rectangle; **Size:** 13.5" x 18.5"; **Story:** Yes; **Country:** US; **Mfr/Dist:** —; **Border/Edge:** White, gold edge; **Quantity:** —.
$ Value, References: $8-$15 (3,6,x)
$ Value, Internet Auctions: $7; **# Sales:** 5

Kids in Front of a Grocery Store is a French Canadian tray. A reproduction of *Summer Girl*, 1921 (not pictured) is next in the series of eight Italian trays commemorating the anniversary of Coke in Italy. Finally, a large rectangle logo tray with graphics and a white border was originally packaged with a set of six glasses.

Name: Covered Wagon; **Issued:** 1984
Comments: Commemorative of 10th National Convention, Coca-Cola Collectors, Sacramento, California; back of tray shows year and location of all Coca-Cola Collector conventions; **Shape:** Small oval; **Size:** 8.5" x 11.0"; **Story:** Yes; **Country:** US; **Mfr/Dist:** —; **Border/Edge:** White, gold edge; **Quantity:** 1,600.
$ Value, References: $5-$15 (3,6,x)
$ Value, Internet Auctions: $12 (for info only); **# Sales:** 2

Name: Zanesville Y-Bridge; **Issued:** 1984
Comments: Commemorative of 75th Anniversary, Zanesville, Ohio bottler, original art by Leslie Cope, new bridge opened in year of anniversary, #one in series of trays by Zanesville bottler; **Shape:** Std Rectangle; **Size:** 10.5" x 13.25"; **Story:** Yes; **Country:** US; **Mfr/Dist:** —; **Border/Edge:** Gold; **Quantity:** 5,000.
$ Value, References: est $20-$45 (3,x)
$ Value, Internet Auctions: $17; **# Sales:** 3

Name: Big Bear Supermarket; **Issued:** 1984
Comments: Reproduction of 1935 ad, *It will refresh you too*, by Haddon Sundblom, commemorative of 50th Anniversary of customer; **Shape:** Large Rectangle; **Size:** 13.5" x 18.5"; **Story:** Yes; **Country:** US; **Mfr/Dist:** —; **Border/Edge:** Gold; **Quantity:** —.
$ Value, References: est $10-$20 (3,x)
$ Value, Internet Auctions: $12 (for info only); **# Sales:** 2

Additional commemorative trays include *Covered Wagon* for the 10th Coca-Cola Collectors Convention and *Big Bear*, a 1935 Santa ad that is the only identified Santa reproduction commemorating a customer's anniversary. *Four Seasons*, 1922, is again reproduced, this time for a bottler anniversary and plant opening (not pictured). A *1984 Olympics* tray lists 117 U.S. Olympic records through 1980 on the back of the tray.

Name: Kids in Front of a Grocery Store; **Issued:** 1984
Comments: Original art by *Mathews*; **Shape:** Std Rectangle; **Size:**
10.5" x 13.25"; **Story:** —; **Country:** Canada (French); **Mfr/Dist:**
—; **Border/Edge:** Gold; **Quantity:** —.
$ Value, References: $10-$20 (3,6,x)
$ Value, Internet Auctions: $8; **# Sales:** 4

Name: USA Olympics; **Issued:** 1984
Comments: Commemorative of Olympic Games, 117 event records
through 1980 on back of tray; **Shape:** Large Deep Oval; **Size:** 12.5"
x 15.5"; **Story:** Yes; **Country:** US; **Mfr/Dist:** Distributed by
Markatron; **Border/Edge:** Red, black stripe; **Quantity:** —.
$ Value, References: est $15-$25 (3,x)
$ Value, Internet Auctions: $8; **# Sales:** 3

Name: Coca-Cola; **Issued:** 1984
Comments: Logo tray, white graphics on red, originally packaged with six
glasses; **Shape:** Large Rectangle; **Size:** 13.5" x 18.5"; **Story:** —; **Country:** US;
Mfr/Dist: —; **Border/Edge:** White; **Quantity:** —.
$ Value, References: est $15-$25 (x)
$ Value, Internet Auctions: $21 (for info only); **# Sales:** 1

1985

The number of issued trays licensed by Coke for distribution
through retail sales continues to grow. These trays, at least in the 1980s,
are mostly reproductions. The licensed tray is *not* usually a commemorative, a product ad, a logo tray, or part of a bottler sponsored series,
though exceptions can be found. Some licensed trays may have originally been part of a promotion by The Coca-Cola Company or a customer. Eleven trays are identified from 1985 and all are pictured in this
section.

One tray and three ad reproduction trays were all also licensed for
sale. A reproduction of *Hilda with The Roses*, 1901, follows its previous
use on the 1975 *Nashville* commemorative. The ad reproductions are
Duster Girls, 1912; *Atlantic City Girl*, 1918; and an early collage of models
from ads of 1927, 1930, and 1936.

Name: USA Olympics; **Issued:** 1984
Comments: Back of tray showing the records of Olympic athletes.

Another licensed tray is a collage of over thirty items of Coca-Cola memorabilia, *Through All the Years*, created by Sandra K. Porter. *Through All the Years* will become the licensed tray with the highest quantity produced and, in fact, is the top selling licensed image of this thirty-year period from the 1970s to the end of the century.

Name: Hilda with The Roses; **Issued:** c.1985-1988
Comments: Reproduction of 1901 tray; **Shape:** Large Rectangle; **Size:** 13.5" x 18.5"; **Story:** —; **Country:** US; **Mfr/Dist:** Distributed by Markatron; **Border/Edge:** Black; **Quantity:** est 15,000.
$ Value, References: $7-$12 (3,6,x)
$ Value, Internet Auctions: $10 (for info only); **# Sales:** 2

Name: Duster Girls; **Issued:** c.1985-1989
Comments: Reproduction of 1912 ad; **Shape:** Large Deep Oval; **Size:** 12.5" x 15.5"; **Story:** —; **Country:** US; **Mfr/Dist:** Distributed by Markatron; **Border/Edge:** Black; **Quantity:** est 10,000.
$ Value, References: $5-$15 (3,4,6,x)
$ Value, Internet Auctions: $8 (for info only); **# Sales:** 2

Name: Calendar Girls; **Issued:** c.1985-1988
Comments: Collage, reproduction of models from ads of 1927, 1930 (two), and 1936; **Shape:** Deep Round; **Size:** 13.5" dia. x 1.5" depth; **Story:** —; **Country:** US; **Mfr/Dist:** Distributed by Markatron; **Border/Edge:** Black; **Quantity:** est 7,000.
$ Value, References: $5-$15 (3,6,x)
$ Value, Internet Auctions: $8; **# Sales:** 5

Name: Through All The Years; **Issued:** 1985-1988
Comments: Title is same as 1936 Coca-Cola 50th Anniversary theme, and was used in 1939 advertising that featured vintage ads. Tray has collage of more than thirty Coke Memorabilia items, by Sandra K. Porter. No tray information on back, reissued 1990, becomes the most popular licensed image ever; **Shape:** Std Rectangle; **Size:** 10.5" x 13.25"; **Story:** —; **Country:** US; **Mfr/Dist:** Ohio Art Company; **Border/Edge:** Black; **Quantity:** see 1990 tray.
$ Value, References: $5-$40 (3,8,x)
$ Value, Internet Auctions: $10; **# Sales:** 8

Name: Atlantic City Girl; **Issued:** c.1985
Comments: Reproduction of 1918 ad, woman in period bathing suit, first horizontal image on a long rectangle shape; **Shape:** Long Rectangle; **Size:** 8.5" x 19.0"; **Story:** Yes; **Country:** US; **Mfr/Dist:** —; **Border/Edge:** Black; **Quantity:** —.
$ Value, References: est $5-$15 (3,x)
$ Value, Internet Auctions: $10 (for info only); **# Sales:** 2

84

Three Canadian trays include *Diet Coke* with a futuristic space image; a Coke can in ice called *Taste of the Year*; and *Safe Driving Award*, a tray given to employees of bottlers. Four such *Awards* trays are listed throughout the decade.

A March Coke Collector event in Ohio is commemorated with a plastic tray. *Hoover Dam* commemorates the 50th Anniversary of this monumental achievement. It is a familiar but striking image. The second tray in Leslie Cope's series from Zanesville, Ohio shows *The Headly Inn*.

Name: Ohio Winterfest;
Issued: 1985
Comments: Commemorative of a Coke Collector Event, white graphics; **Shape:** Deep Round; **Size:** 13.5" dia. x 1.5" depth; **Story:** Yes; **Country:** US; **Mfr/Dist:** —; **Border/Edge:** Red; **Quantity:** —; *Courtesy of John E. Peterson.*
$ Value, References: est $15-$25 (x)
$ Value, Internet Auctions: —; **# Sales:** —

Name: Diet Coke and Globe;
Issued: 1985
Comments: A bottle and the world in white wire design on black;
Shape: Std Rectangle; **Size:** 10.5" x 13.25"; **Story:** —; **Country:** Canada (French); **Mfr/Dist:** —; **Border/Edge:** Black; **Quantity:** —.
$ Value, References: $10-$20 (3,6,x)
$ Value, Internet Auctions: $12; **# Sales:** 8

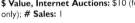

Name: Hoover Dam; **Issued:** 1985
Comments: Commemorative of 50th Anniversary of this wonder, great picture; **Shape:** Std Rectangle; **Size:** 10.5" x 13.25"; **Story:** Yes; **Country:** US; **Mfr/Dist:** —; **Border/Edge:** Silver; **Quantity:** —.
$ Value, References: est $12-$30 (3,6,x)
$ Value, Internet Auctions: $10; **# Sales:** 5

Name: The Taste of the Year; **Issued:** 1985
Comments: A can in ice, with graphics;
Shape: Std Rectangle; **Size:** 10.5" x 13.25";
Story: Yes; **Country:** Canada (English);
Mfr/Dist: —; **Border/Edge:** Black;
Quantity: —.
$ Value, References: est $15-$25 (x)
$ Value, Internet Auctions: $10 (for info only); **# Sales:** 1

Name: Safe Driving Award; **Issued:** c.1985
Comments: Awarded to employees for safe driving, pictures a car and truck; **Shape:** Small Rectangle; **Size:** 8.75" x 14.5"; **Story:** Yes; **Country:** Canada (English); **Mfr/Dist:** —; **Border/Edge:** Blue; **Quantity:** —; *Courtesy of John E. Peterson.*
$ Value, References: est $10-$20 (x)
$ Value, Internet Auctions: $16 (for info only); **# Sales:** 1

Name: The Headly Inn, Zanesville, Ohio; **Issued:** 1985
Comments: Original art by Leslie Cope. The Inn was a stop on the National Road, # two in series of trays by Zanesville bottler; **Shape:** Std Rectangle;
Size: 10.5" x 13.25"; **Story:** Yes; **Country:** US; **Mfr/Dist:** —; **Border/Edge:** Gold; **Quantity:** —.
$ Value, References: est $20-$45 (3,x)
$ Value, Internet Auctions: $15 (for info only); **# Sales:** 1

1986

Fifteen trays are identified and pictured in 1986, the 100th Anniversary of the beginning of The Coca-Cola Company. This year does not yield an abundance of centennial commemorative trays but it does have four.

The centennial commemorative trays are a 1923 *Flapper Girl* reproduction tray from Italy, the sixth in this series; a Canadian tray *1886-1986*; a U.S. tray that ties the Coke centennial and the 1986 anniversary of the Statue of Liberty into the centennial celebration of a resort hotel in Arkansas; and *Celebration of the Century*, a detailed tray with fifty-five small pictures of Coke Memorabilia.

Name: Flapper Girl; **Issued:** 1986
Comments: Reproduction of 1923 tray. Another in the series of trays commemorating fifty years of Coca-Cola bottling in Italy, also commemorates 100th Anniversary of the Coca-Cola Company; **Shape:** Std Rectangle; **Size:** 10.5" x 13.25"; **Story:** Yes; **Country:** Italy; **Mfr/Dist:** —; **Border/Edge:** Turchese o Magenta (turquoise and magenta), white trim; **Quantity:** —; *Courtesy of John E. Peterson.*
$ Value, References: est $15-$35 (x)
$ Value, Internet Auctions: $10 (for info only); **# Sales:** 1

Name: Statue, Crescent, and Coke; **Issued:** 1986
Comments: Commemorates 100th Anniversary of The Coca-Cola Company, the Statue of Liberty and (mostly) the Crescent Hotel in Arkansas, pictures of each; **Shape:** Std Rectangle; **Size:** 10.5" x 13.25"; **Story:** Yes; **Country:** US; **Mfr/Dist:** —; **Border/Edge:** Gray; **Quantity:** —.
$ Value, References: $8-$20 (3,6,x)
$ Value, Internet Auctions: $8; **# Sales:** 6

Name: Celebration of the Century; **Issued:** 1986
Comments: Commemorates 100th Anniversary of The Coca-Cola Company, tray contains fifty-five images (calendars and ads have the most) and eighteen paragraphs of text commenting on The Company. Larger text reads: *Great Taste is Timeless. It's been a century of great taste. And it's just the beginning.*; **Shape:** Large Rectangle; **Size:** 13.5" x 18.5"; **Story:** Yes; **Country:** US; **Mfr/Dist:** —; **Border/Edge:** Black; **Quantity:** —; *Courtesy of John E. Peterson.*
$ Value, References: est $12-$25 (x)
$ Value, Internet Auctions: $13 (for info only); **# Sales:** 1

Name: 1886-1986; **Issued:** 1986
Comments: Commemorates 100th Anniversary of The Coca-Cola Company, from Canada; **Shape:** Std Rectangle; **Size:** 10.5" x 13.25"; **Story:** Yes; **Country:** Canada (English); **Mfr/Dist:** —; **Border/Edge:** Black; **Quantity:** —.
$ Value, References: $8-$15 (3,6,x)
$ Value, Internet Auctions: $9; **# Sales:** 5

Although the rate and number of commemorative trays has generally been decreasing, this year provides an additional eight in addition to the centennial trays. A bright city scene is on the *City of Palms* tray from the bottler in Ft. Myers, Florida, and a Coke Collectors commemorative is also from Florida. Two attractive trays from the Vancouver bottler celebrate *Expo '86*. Two additional Canadian *Safe Driving Awards* trays are listed and a German tray with *Trink* commemorates the 1986 World Cup Soccer matches in Mexico. Finally, *NAC ShoWest '86* is from the association for people that own and run concessions selling Coke and popcorn in movie theaters.

Name: Expo Fireworks; **Issued:** 1986
Comments: Commemorative of event in Vancouver, BC., pictures fireworks at night. Another attractive image from the Vancouver bottler; **Shape:** Std Rectangle; **Size:** 10.5" x 13.25"; **Story:** Yes; **Country:** Canada (French); **Mfr/Dist:** —; **Border/Edge:** Dark Blue; **Quantity:** —.
$ Value, References: $5-$15 (3,6,x)
$ Value, Internet Auctions: $12; **# Sales:** 11

Name: City of Palms; **Issued:** 1986
Comments: Commemorative of 75th Anniversary, Ft. Myers, Florida bottler, artist rendition of city scene; **Shape:** Std Rectangle; **Size:** 10.5" x 13.25"; **Story:** Yes; **Country:** US; **Mfr/Dist:** —; **Border/Edge:** White, red stripe; **Quantity:** —.
$ Value, References: est $10-$20 (3,x)
$ Value, Internet Auctions: $13 (for info only); **# Sales:** 1

Name: Expo Map; **Issued:** 1986
Comments: Commemorative of event in Vancouver, BC., pictures a map of Vancouver in the style of the artist Steinberg with his map of a *New Yorker's View of the World*. Another attractive image from the Vancouver bottler; **Shape:** Std Rectangle; **Size:** 10.5" x 13.25"; **Story:** Yes; **Country:** Canada (French); **Mfr/Dist:** —; **Border/Edge:** Silver; **Quantity:** —.
$ Value, References: $5-$15 (3,6,x)
$ Value, Internet Auctions: $7; **# Sales:** 3

Name: Twelfth Annual Winter Antiques Festival; **Issued:** 1986
Comments: Commemorative of event in Zephyrhills, Florida, pictures tanks, cars, and a park; **Shape:** Large Rectangle; **Size:** 13.5" x 18.5"; **Story:** Yes; **Country:** US; **Mfr/Dist:** —; **Border/Edge:** Maroon; **Quantity:** —; *Courtesy of John E. Peterson.*
$ Value, References: est $20-$30 (3,x)
$ Value, Internet Auctions: —; **# Sales:** —

Name: Driver Safety Achievement; **Issued:** 1986
Comments: Commemorative for Safe Driving in 1987, awarded to employees of bottler, pictures seven trucks. Bottom border: *Safe Driving Award*; **Shape:** Std Rectangle; **Size:** 10.5" x 13.25"; **Story:** Yes; **Country:** Canada (English); **Mfr/Dist:** —; **Border/Edge:** Black; **Quantity:** —.
$ Value, References: est $15-$30 (x)
$ Value, Internet Auctions: —; **# Sales:** —

Name: Driver Safety Achievement; **Issued:** 1986
Comments: Commemorative for Safe Driving, awarded to employees of bottler, pictures c.1915 Chevy Truck. Tray has a section used to record the name of the winner. Bottom border: *Safe Driving Award*; **Shape:** Std Rectangle; **Size:** 10.5" x 13.25"; **Story:** Yes; **Country:** Canada (English); **Mfr/Dist:** —; **Border/Edge:** Brown; **Quantity:** —.
$ Value, References: est $15-$30 (3,x)
$ Value, Internet Auctions: $22; **# Sales:** 3

Two product trays include another German tray similar to the World Cup, and *Snowcap*, a Canadian tray with bottle caps from five Coke products. One Santa tray reproduces a 1964 ad. This ad is one of the last by Haddon Sundblom.

Name: Zeit für Coca-Cola; **Issued:** 1986
Comments: Logo tray, logo repeated four times around outside border, similar look to 1986 World Cup tray, plastic; **Shape:** Deep Round; **Size:** 13.5" dia. x 1.5" depth; **Story:** —; **Country:** Germany; **Mfr/Dist:** —; **Border/Edge:** Red; **Quantity:** —; *Courtesy of John E. Peterson.*
$ Value, References: est $10-$20 (x)
$ Value, Internet Auctions: —; **# Sales:** —

Name: Trink, World Cup Soccer; **Issued:** 1986
Comments: Commemorative of Sports Event, held in Mexico, *offizielles Erffrishschung syetranh der Fuzball- Weltmoisterschaff*, plastic; **Shape:** Deep Round; **Size:** 11.5" dia. x 1.25" depth; **Story:** Yes; **Country:** Germany; **Mfr/Dist:** —; **Border/Edge:** Red; **Quantity:** —; *Courtesy of John E. Peterson.*
$ Value, References: est $15-$30 (x)
$ Value, Internet Auctions: —; **# Sales:** —

Name: Zeit für Coca-Cola; **Issued:** 1986
Comments: Side view of tray, showing logos on outside border.

Name: NAC, ShoWest '86; **Issued:** 1986
Comments: Commemorative from convention of National Association of Concessionaires, the folks who sell us popcorn and Coke at the movies; **Shape:** Deep Round; **Size:** 13.25" dia. x 1.5" depth; **Story:** Yes; **Country:** US; **Mfr/Dist:** —; **Border/Edge:** Red; **Quantity:** —; *Courtesy of John E. Peterson.*
$ Value, References: est $15-$30 (x)
$ Value, Internet Auctions: —; **# Sales:** —

Name: Snowcap; **Issued:** 1986
Comments: Product tray, pictures snow and bottle caps from Coke, Coke Classic, Diet Coke, Sprite, and Diet Sprite, shown in larger-than-life or super-realism style; **Shape:** Std Rectangle; **Size:** 10.5" x 13.25"; **Story:** —; **Country:** Canada (English); **Mfr/Dist:** —; **Border/Edge:** Silver; **Quantity:** —.
$ Value, References: est $20-$40 (x)
$ Value, Internet Auctions: —; **# Sales:** —

Name: Things go better . . . ; **Issued:** 1986
Comments: Reproduction of 1964 ad, by Haddon Sundblom, only reproduction of this ad image; **Shape:** Std Rectangle; **Size:** 10.5" x 13.25"; **Story:** —; **Country:** US; **Mfr/Dist:** Ohio Art Company;
Border/Edge: Red; **Quantity:** —.
$ Value, References: $12-$20 (3,6,x)
$ Value, Internet Auctions: $16; **# Sales:** 8

1987

Fifteen 1987 trays are identified and pictured. In 1987, *Trademark Marketing, International* begins to appear on licensed trays as the distributor. This Atlanta company has the commendable practice of printing details about the tray image on the *back*. Details include information about the origin of the image, the year issued, and, for some Limited Editions, the quantity manufactured. Many licensed trays are sold as new for more than one year. This practice is certainly *not* new (refer to *Bottle 5¢, Menu Girl,* and other earlier trays).

Twelve licensed trays include one tray reproduction, the 1899 *Hilda with The Pen.* Only one tray has been reproduced from the 1908 calendar, *Lady in Red.* This image has a note on a table that reads *Good to the Last Drop.* The slogan didn't last long for Coca-Cola, but another caffeine drink eventually made pretty good use of it. A colorful 1948 reproduction of Santa with a big bag of toys is titled *Hospitality.* Both *Lady in Red* and *Hospitality* are in large oval shapes. This Santa tray is the first to vary from a rectangle shape.

Touring Car, a 1924 ad reproduction, was also issued as a lap tray. Other reproductions include a cropped image of *Constance,* the 1917 calendar; *Girls at the Seashore,* the 1918 calendar; two versions of a c.1923 ad; and a c.1930s festoon. *Sea Captain,* reproduced from a 1936 image by N. C. Wyeth, was a calendar during the year that The Coca-Cola Company celebrated its 50th Anniversary. Another reproduction of *The Village Blacksmith,* 1933, completes the group.

Name: Lady in Red; **Issued:** 1987-1992, 1995-1998
Comments: Reproduction of 1908 Calendar, note reads: *Good to the Last Drop;*
Shape: Large Deep Oval; **Size:** 12.5" x 15.5"; **Story:** Yes; **Country:** US; **Mfr/Dist:** Distributed by Trademark Marketing; **Border/Edge:** Black;
Quantity: 45,200.
$ Value, References: $5-$20 (3,6,x)
$ Value, Internet Auctions: $11; **# Sales:** 8

Name: 1899 Hilda **Issued:** 1987-1990, 1994-1997
Comments: Reproduction of 1899 tray, *Hilda with The Pen,* the only identified repro; **Shape:** Round; **Size:** 12.5"; **Story:** —; **Country:** US; **Mfr/Dist:** Ohio Art Company; **Border/Edge:** Black, flower trim; **Quantity:** 13,500.
$ Value, References: $5-$15 (3,6,x)
$ Value, Internet Auctions: $7; **# Sales:** 5

Name: Hospitality; **Issued:** 1987-1991
Comments: Reproduction of 1948 ad, by Haddon Sundblom; **Shape:** Large Deep Oval; **Size:** 12.5" x 15.5"; **Story:** —; **Country:** US; **Mfr/Dist:** Ohio Art Company; **Border/Edge:** Red; **Quantity:** 8,200.
$ Value, References: $8-$20 (3,6,x)
$ Value, Internet Auctions: $6; **# Sales:** 11

Name: Girls at the Seashore;
Issued: 1987-1991
Comments: Reproduction of
1918 calendar, pictured is the
standing girl on the right;
Shape: Deep Round; **Size:**
13.5"; **Story:** —; **Country:**
US; **Mfr/Dist:** Ohio Art
Company; **Border/Edge:**
Red; **Quantity:** 21,650.
$ Value, References: $5-
$20 (3,6,x)
$ Value, Internet Auctions:
$6.50; **# Sales:** 10

Name: Touring Car; **Issued:** 1987-1993
Comments: Reproduction of 1924 ad, the right panel of a panoramic poster;
Shape: Large Rectangle; **Size:** 13.5" x 18.5"; **Story:** Yes; **Country:** US; **Mfr/Dist:**
Ohio Art Company; **Border/Edge:** Red; **Quantity:** 64,500.
$ Value, References: est $5-$15 (3,x)
$ Value, Internet Auctions: $9; **# Sales:** 6

Name: Touring Car, Laptop Tray; **Issued:** 1987
Comments: Reproduction of 1924 ad, the right panel of a panoramic
poster, another release of the tray made with lighter metal and
attached folding aluminum legs; **Shape:** Large Rectangle; **Size:** 13.5" x
18.5"; **Story:** Yes; **Country:** US; **Mfr/Dist:** Ohio Art Company;
Border/Edge: Red; **Quantity:** —.
$ Value, References: est $5-$15 (x)
$ Value, Internet Auctions: $7; **# Sales:** 6

Name: Lady with Mums *or* Thirst Knows no Time nor Season;
Issued: 1987
Comments: Reproduction of c.1923 ad; **Shape:** Std Rectangle; **Size:**
10.5" x 13.25"; **Story:** —; **Country:** US; **Mfr/Dist:** —; **Border/Edge:**
Black; **Quantity:** —; *Courtesy of Ann Poppenheimer Sherrod and Dave
Sherrod, Pop's Mail Order Collectibles.*
$ Value, References: $5-$15 (3,6,x)
$ Value, Internet Auctions: $6 (for info only); **# Sales:** 2

Name: Constance *or* Girl at
Tennis Match; **Issued:** 1987
Comments: Reproduction of
1917 calendar, *Constance* is
holding a parasol; **Shape:** Deep
Round; **Size:** 13.0" dia. x 1.875"
depth; **Story:** —; **Country:**
Mexico; **Mfr/Dist:** —; **Border/
Edge:** Red; **Quantity:** —;
Courtesy of John E. Peterson.
$ Value, References: est $10-
$20; (x)
$ Value, Internet Auctions:
—; **# Sales:** —

Name: Lady with Mums *or* Thirst
Knows no Time nor Season;
Issued: 1987
Comments: Reproduction of c.1923
ad, acrylic material; **Shape:** Std
Rectangle; **Size:** 10.5" x 14.0";
Story: Yes; **Country:** US; **Mfr/Dist:**
mfr in Japan, distributed by The
Heirloom Collection; **Border/Edge:**
Black; **Quantity:** —.
$ Value, References: est $10-$20
(x)
$ Value, Internet Auctions: —;
 # Sales: —

Name: Lady with Pansies; **Issued:** 1987-1989
Comments: Reproduction of c.1930s festoon; **Shape:** Long Rectangle; **Size:** 8.5" x 19.0";
Story: —; **Country:** US; **Mfr/Dist:** —, **Border/Edge:** Black; **Quantity:** 6,500;
Courtesy of John E. Peterson.
$ Value, References: est $5-$10 (3,x)
$ Value, Internet Auctions: —; **# Sales:** —

An attractive 1987 Canadian tray was issued to commemorate the 1988 *Calgary Winter Olympic Games*. Fifteen Olympic posters are shown in the border. Two Italian trays include a reproduction of the 1923 *Flapper Girl* and *Mondo Bottilliz*, a 1956 ad with a hand, a bottle, and a world globe as background.

Name: XV Winter Olympics, Calgary Winter Games; **Issued:** 1987
Comments: Commemorative for the 1988 Olympic Games, current poster and fourteen posters of past games on tray; **Shape:** Std Rectangle; **Size:** 10.5" x 13.25"; **Story:** Yes; **Country:** Canada (French); **Mfr/Dist:** —; **Border/Edge:** Silver; **Quantity:** —.
$ Value, References: $15-$30 (3,6,x)
$ Value, Internet Auctions: $19;
 # Sales: 3

Name: Sea Captain; **Issued:** 1987-1991, 1994-1997
Comments: Reproduction of 1936 calendar, by N.C. Wyeth, originally issued as calendar for 50th Anniversary of The Coca-Cola Company; **Shape:** Small Flat Rectangle; **Size:** 10.5" x 14.0"; **Story:** Yes; **Country:** US; **Mfr/Dist:** Ohio Art Company; **Border/Edge:** Black; **Quantity:** 46,100.
$ Value, References: $5-$10 (3,6,x)
$ Value, Internet Auctions: $14 (for info only); **# Sales:** 2

Name: Flapper Girl; **Issued:** 1987
Comments: Reproduction of 1923 tray; **Shape:** Round; **Size:** 12.0"; **Story:** —; **Country:** Italy; **Mfr/Dist:** —; **Border/Edge:** Green; **Quantity:** —; *Courtesy of John E. Peterson.*
$ Value, References: est $10-$20 (x)
$ Value, Internet Auctions: —; **# Sales:** —

Name: The Village Blacksmith; **Issued:** 1987-1990
Comments: Reproduction of 1933 calendar, by Frederick Stanley; **Shape:** Std Rectangle; **Size:** 10.5" x 13.25"; **Story:** Yes; **Country:** US; **Mfr/Dist:** Ohio Art Company; **Border/Edge:** Red; **Quantity:** 18,100.
$ Value, References: $5-$15 (3,6,x)
$ Value, Internet Auctions: $9; **# Sales:** 3

Name: Mondo Bottilliz; **Issued:** 1987
Comments: Reproduction of 1956 ad, *Hand with Bottle and World, Friendliest Drink on Earth*, seventh in the series of trays commemorating fifty years of bottling in Italy; **Shape:** Small Rectangle; **Size:** 8.0" x 11.0"; **Story:** —; **Country:** Italy; **Mfr/Dist:** —; **Border/Edge:** Red, Azuro (Blue) stripe; **Quantity:** —; *Courtesy of Ann Poppenheimer Sherrod and Dave Sherrod, Pop's Mail Order Collectibles.*
$ Value, References: est $15-$25 (6,x)
$ Value, Internet Auctions: —; **# Sales:** —

1988

Seven trays, the lowest number of the decade, are identified from 1988. Six of the trays are pictured here.

Three of the 1988 trays are *The B&O Railroad Train and Station*, the third Zanesville tray by Leslie Cope; *Coke and 7-11, Can't Beat the Feeling*, a baseball theme; and another *1988 Olympic Games* tray promoting the Calgary Winter Games as well as the Summer Games from Seoul, Korea. The large image on the tray is the same collage found on *U.S. Olympic Records* in 1984. Not pictured is a bottler tray reproduced from a 1912 ad, *Duster Girls*.

Name: Olympics - Calgary and Seoul; **Issued:** 1988
Comments: Commemorative of Winter and Summer Games, same large logo as 1984 Olympic tray; **Shape:** Large Rectangle; **Size:** 13.5" x 18.5"; **Story:** —; **Country:** Canada (French); **Mfr/Dist:** Distributed by Markatron; **Border/Edge:** Silver, with thirty-six posters around the border; **Quantity:** —.
$ Value, References: est $10-$25 (x)
$ Value, Internet Auctions: —; **# Sales:** —

Name: The B&O Railroad Station, Zanesville, Ohio; **Issued:** 1988
Comments: Original art by Leslie Cope, # three in series of trays from Zanesville bottler; **Shape:** Std Rectangle; **Size:** 10.5" x 13.25"; **Story:** Yes; **Country:** US; **Mfr/Dist:** —; **Border/Edge:** Gold, brown edge; **Quantity:** —; *Courtesy of John E. Peterson.*
$ Value, References: $15-$30 (3,6,x)
$ Value, Internet Auctions: —; **# Sales:** —

A round Italian tray is one of two reproductions of *The Hamilton King Girl, 1913*. And, the first round shape in Santa trays is a reproduction of a 1961 Santa ad.

The last 1988 tray is *Boy and Dog*, from a 1937 painting by N. C. Wyeth. It is the eighth and last in the series of Italian trays issued since 1977 commemorating fifty years of Coke bottling in Italy. During research for this book, the Wyeth image was the *first* of the series to be identified. When translated, the Italian detail on the back of the tray provided clues to the identification of the other trays in this series.

Name: The Hamilton King Girl; **Issued:** 1988
Comments: Reproduction of 1913 tray; **Shape:** Deep Round; **Size:** 13.25" dia. x 1.5" depth; **Story:** —; **Country:** Italy; **Mfr/Dist:** —; **Border/Edge:** Red, flower trim; **Quantity:** —.
$ Value, References: est $15-$25 (6,x)
$ Value, Internet Auctions: $9 (for info only); **# Sales:** 1

Name: Can't Beat the Feeling; **Issued:** c.1988
Comments: Commemorative to customer, 7-11 Stores, Official Drink of Summer, baseball scene; **Shape:** Flat Rectangle; **Size:** 11.0" x 15.0"; **Story:** —; **Country:** US; **Mfr/Dist:** —; **Border/Edge:** Red; **Quantity:** —.
$ Value, References: est $5-$25 (3,x)
$ Value, Internet Auctions: —; **# Sales:** —

Name: When Friends Drop In;
Issued: 1988-1989, 1994-1996
Comments: Reproduction of 1961 ad, by Haddon Sundblom;
Shape: Round; **Size:** 12.25";
Story: Yes; **Country:** US; **Mfr/ Dist:** Ohio Art Company;
Border/Edge: Red, green edge;
Quantity: 46,000.
$ Value, References: $5-$15 (3,6,x)
$ Value, Internet Auctions: $10 (for info only); **# Sales:** 1

Twelve 1989 trays, all pictured, complete the review of 155 trays identified from the 1980s. This last group is typical of the variety and attractiveness of trays from this decade.

Leslie Cope paintings are issued in another two Zanesville trays. *Market House* is the fourth with local scenes of early transportation sites. *Holiday, Zanesville, Ohio* is a Limited Edition that pictures small images of the first four trays in the series.

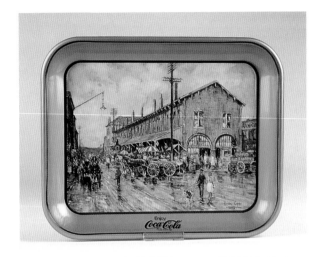

Name: Boy and Dog *or* Fishin' Hole;
Issued: 1988
Comments: Reproduction of 1937 calendar, by N.C. Wyeth, last in the series of eight trays by the Italian bottler to commemorate the 50th Anniversary of Coca-Cola bottling in Italy, other trays in series listed on back; **Shape:** Std Rectangle; **Size:** 10.5" x 13.25"; **Story:** Yes; **Country:** Italy; **Mfr/Dist:** —; **Border/Edge:** Green; **Quantity:** —; *Courtesy of Ann Poppenheimer Sherrod and Dave Sherrod, Pop's Mail Order Collectibles.*
$ Value, References: est $15-$35 (6,x)
$ Value, Internet Auctions: $22 (for info only); **# Sales:** 1

Name: Market House, Zanesville, Ohio; **Issued:** 1989
Comments: Original art by Leslie Cope, # four in series of trays by Zanesville bottler; **Shape:** Std Rectangle; **Size:** 10.5" x 13.25"; **Story:** Yes; **Country:** US; **Mfr/Dist:** —; **Border/Edge:** Gold, brown stripe; **Quantity:** —.
$ Value, References: est $20-$35 (3,x)
$ Value, Internet Auctions: —; **# Sales:** —

Name: Boy and Dog *or* Fishin' Hole;
Issued: 1988
Comments: Back of tray with details on the other seven commemorative trays, in Italian of course. The first paragraph, roughly translated, reads: *In 1977, on the occasion of the 50th anniversary of the Italian Coca-Cola Industry. From its conception, the commemorative tray was an operation to recover (sic. Reproduce) old ad campaigns . . .*

Name: Holiday, Zanesville, Ohio; **Issued:** 1989
Comments: Tray pictures small images of first four trays in the series of trays by Zanesville bottler, all original art by Leslie Cope; **Shape:** Large Deep Oval; **Size:** 12.0" x 15.5"; **Story:** Yes; **Country:** US **Mfr/Dist:** —; **Border/Edge:** Green; **Quantity:** 3,000; *Courtesy of John E. Peterson.*
$ Value, References: est $10-$20 (x)
$ Value, Internet Auctions: —; **# Sales:** —

Four commemorative trays are listed. *Touring Car*, a 1924 ad reproduction (first reproduced in 1987), is issued this year for the 75th Anniversary of the York, Pennsylvania bottler. As noted earlier, the first franchised bottler in Chattanooga, Tennessee issued no 75th Anniversary tray, but an *80th Anniversary* tray was issued in 1979. This year, two *90th Anniversary* Chattanooga trays feature a *1929 Painted Truck* on one and the *Crown Bottling Machine* on the other. A commemorative tray for the *15th Coca-Cola Collectors Convention* shows the Anaheim, California bottling plant.

Name: Anaheim, California Bottling Plant; **Issued:** 1989
Comments: Commemorative of 15th National Convention, Coca-Cola Collectors, Anaheim, California; **Shape:** Std Rectangle; **Size:** 10.5" x 13.25"; **Story:** Yes; **Country:** US; **Mfr/Dist:** —; **Border/Edge:** Black; **Quantity:** est 2,000.
$ Value, References: est $10-$15 (3,x)
$ Value, Internet Auctions: $6 (for info only); **# Sales:** 2

Name: Touring Car; **Issued:** 1989
Comments: Reproduction of a 1924 ad, the right panel of a panoramic poster. Originally issued in 1987, issued here as a commemorative of the 75th Anniversary, York, Pennsylvania bottler; **Shape:** Large Standard; **Size:** 13.5" x 18.5"; **Story:** Yes; **Country:** US; **Mfr/Dist:** Ohio Art Company; **Border/Edge:** Red; **Quantity:** —; *Courtesy of John E. Peterson.*
$ Value, References: est $10-$20 (x)
$ Value, Internet Auctions: —; **# Sales:** —

Six ad reproductions complete the trays for 1989 and the decade. All six are licensed for sale. *Soda Fountain*, c.1908, was popular, with over fifty thousand trays produced. A 1907 ad, *Baseball*, has a ballpark crowd scene. Finally, a record four Santa ads, from 1936, 1951, 1958, and 1963, are reproduced. The 1963 ad has now been reproduced for the fifth time, but is still a best seller.

Name: Antique Truck, c.1929; **Issued:** 1989
Comments: Commemorative of 90th Anniversary, Chattanooga, Tennessee bottler. Tray reads: *Coca-Cola Truck Painting, 1929*; **Shape:** Std Rectangle; **Size:** 10.5" x 13.25"; **Story:** Yes; **Country:** US; **Mfr/Dist:** —; **Border/Edge:** Green; **Quantity:** 5,000; *Courtesy of John E. Peterson.*
$ Value, References: est $15-$30 (3,x)
$ Value, Internet Auctions: —; **# Sales:** —

Name: Crown Bottling Machine; **Issued:** 1989
Comments: Commemorative of 90th Anniversary, Chattanooga, Tennessee bottler. The back information notes that the *Crown Bottling Machine was the first piece of equipment at the first franchised bottler*; **Shape:** Std Rectangle; **Size:** 10.5" x 13.25"; **Story:** Yes; **Country:** US; **Mfr/Dist:** —; **Border/Edge:** Gold; **Quantity:** 5,000; *Courtesy of John E. Peterson.*
$ Value, References: est $10-$20 (3,x)
$ Value, Internet Auctions: —; **# Sales:** —

Name: Soda Fountain; **Issued:** 1989-1995
Comments: Reproduction of c.1908 ad by the Massengale Agency; **Shape:** Large Standard; **Size:** 13.5" x 18.5"; **Story:** Yes; **Country:** US; **Mfr/Dist:** Ohio Art Company; **Border/Edge:** Blue; **Quantity:** 50,500.
$ Value, References: est $5-$10 (3,x)
$ Value, Internet Auctions: $6 (for info only); **# Sales:** 1

Name: Good Boys and Girls;
Issued: 1989
Comments: Reproduction of 1951 ad, by Haddon Sundblom; **Shape:** Large Rectangle; **Size:** 13.5" x 18.5"; **Story:** —; **Country:** US; **Mfr/Dist:** —; **Border/Edge:** Green with trim; **Quantity:** —.
$ Value, References: est $7-$15 (x)
$ Value, Internet Auctions: —; **# Sales:** —

Name: Baseball; **Issued:** 1989-1995
Comments: Reproduction of 1907 ad by the Massengale Agency, scene in the stands at a baseball game; **Shape:** Std Rectangle; **Size:** 10.5" x 13.25"; **Story:** Yes; **Country:** US; **Mfr/Dist:** Ohio Art Company; **Border/Edge:** Red; **Quantity:** 35,000.
$ Value, References: est $10-$20 (3,6,x)
$ Value, Internet Auctions: —; **# Sales:** —

Name: Santa with Deer;
Issued: 1989-1991
Comments: Reproduction of 1958 ad, *The Pause that Refreshes*, by Haddon Sundblom; **Shape:** Std Rectangle; **Size:** 10.5" x 13.25"; **Story:** Yes; **Country:** US; **Mfr/Dist:** Ohio Art Company; **Border/Edge:** Green; **Quantity:** 19,000.
$ Value, References: $5-15 (3,6,x)
$ Value, Internet Auctions: $7; **# Sales:** 3

Name: Can't Beat the Feeling; **Issued:** 1989
Comments: Reproduction of 1936 ad, *Old Santa says, Me too*, Santa under the tree with toys, by Haddon Sundblom; **Shape:** Small Flat Rectangle; **Size:** 10.5" x 14.0";
Story: —; **Country:** US; **Mfr/Dist:** —; **Border/Edge:** Red; **Quantity:** —.
$ Value, References: est $7-$15 (x)
$ Value, Internet Auctions: —; **# Sales:** —

Name: Dear Santa *or* Santa at Chimney;
Issued: 1989-1990, 1996-1998
Comments: Reproduction of 1963 ad, by Haddon Sundblom;
Shape: Std Rectangle; **Size:** 10.5" x 13.25"; **Story:** Yes;
Country: US; **Mfr/Dist:** Ohio Art Company, distributed by Trademark Marketing; **Border/Edge:** Green with trim;
Quantity: 58,000.
$ Value, References: est $5-$15 (6,x)
$ Value, Internet Auctions: $10; **# Sales:** 5

## Chapter Six

It's Signature Time
(Ad Reproductions, Too),
1990-1999

The last decade of the century contains the 100th anniversary of the first identified Coca-Cola serving tray. In these ten years more trays are found than in any other decade and the total of 175 trays is fifteen percent more than the 1980s. It took from the first tray in 1897 all the way to *1975* to record the same number of trays as have been identified in the 1990s! Pictured in this chapter are 167 trays, or ninety-five percent of those identified, containing 152 of the 158 images.

Over eighty percent of the 1990s trays were licensed for retail sale. Six reproductions of earlier trays are found and at least *ninety* trays reproduce ads, including twenty-nine Santa Claus trays.

The fact that a tray is licensed by The Coca-Cola Company and sold through various retail channels does not mean that it should or should not be considered a collectible, or that a tray will or will not increase in value over time. Many of the recent licensed trays are of excellent quality and contain wonderful reproductions of earlier images as well as original pictures. An important consideration to keep in mind is that licensed trays have generally been produced in *lower* quantities than many of the classic trays. After being offered for sale as new for a few years they become less available, just as trays of past years become harder to find over time.

About forty trays create a new type of 1990s tray: a variation on a previous theme. The trays are created from works by specific artists and include Coke images in the picture. These trays are noted as *The Signature Series*.

Artists, starting early in the century, produced works for The Coca-Cola Company that contained Coke images and that were used as advertising items. As we have seen, many works of these artists were also featured on trays. Fred Mizen, Frederick Stanley, N.C. Wyeth, Hayden Hayden, Norman Rockwell, and, of course, Haddon Sundblom are just some of the artists who created wonderful images from the early 1900s through the 1960s. Many of these pictures were simple, focused, and representative of the times. They featured people in happy scenes.

The *new* group of artists include Pamela C. Renfroe, Jeanne Mack, Jim Harrison, John Sandridge, Sandra K. Porter, and others. With the exception of the *Last Smiles* series by John Sandridge, most of the other works are scenes of rural life, a landscape, or a collage. Most don't feature a person and most are not scenes of *today* but rather are from the same general time period as the classic images. Many of the pictures in *The Signature Series* have also been distributed on coasters, playing cards, calendars, and other items, just as in the past. Of course, as previously mentioned, the difference is that then the bottler paid for most of the items and distributed them to customers. Today the licensed distributors pay the Company and individual consumers buy the items from retailers.

Whether or not the recent trays will, over time, be desirable collectibles that grow in value is something that future collector books will have to record. But it certainly is a good possibility!

Internet auctions for trays of the 1990s total 1,855! Over *seventy-eight* percent of the identified trays from the 1990s were seen in an auction at least once. Especially for auctions of trays from the last few years, the selling process seems to be . . . *if it is listed enough times it will sell*. The rate of successful sales versus total auctions is the lowest for *any* decade, with a rate of about one sale for every four trays placed in an auction.

The data recorded on recent trays indicate that, at least on the days reviewed, a tray can regularly be seen in ten to fifteen auctions without a sale. On the other hand, over 450 trays from the 1990s *were* documented as sold.

Auctions were recorded from seventy specific days over ten months. The number of recent trays that were auctioned, and the sales rate, remained fairly consistent over this time. From extrapolating the data it can be estimated that about *2400* trays from the 1990s will be sold in eBay auctions during the current year (the year 2000).

1990s (Unspecified Year)

Seven trays, all pictured, are listed as 1990s trays but without a specific year of issue. All are international trays.

Italy has two polar bear trays with scenes of bear family life in *Pesca una paison con gustin* and *Provu sur emozione*. Another Italian tray is a small plastic rectangle tray that reproduces the 1904 calendar, *Lillian Nordica with Sign*.

Three ad reproductions from 1936, 1937, and the 1940s are identified on trays for distribution in Argentina that were manufactured in Italy. And, the tradition of trays and ads featuring a beautiful woman on a beach is continued in a tray from the Coca-Cola bottler in Thailand.

Name: Pesca una paison con gustin; **Issued:** 1990s
Comments: Polar bears ice fishing; **Shape:** Large Rectangle; **Size:** 11.25" x 15.25"; **Story:** —; **Country:** Italy; **Mfr/Dist:** —; **Border/Edge:** Red; **Quantity:** —; *Courtesy of John E. Peterson.*
$ Value, References: est $20-$40 (x)
$ Value, Internet Auctions: —; **# Sales:** —

Name: Provu un emozione; **Issued:** 1990s
Comments: Polar bear with two cubs in
back pack; **Shape:** Large Rectangle; **Size:**
11.25" x 15.25"; **Story:** —; **Country:** Italy;
Mfr/Dist: —; **Border/Edge:** Red;
Quantity: —; *Courtesy of John E. Peterson.*
$ Value, References: est $20-$40 (x)
$ Value, Internet Auctions: —;
 # Sales: —

Name: Mother and Daughter at the Soda Fountain; **Issued:** 1990s
Comments: Reproduction of 1937 ad, tray © information in
Spanish; **Shape:** Deep Round; **Size:** 13.125" dia. x 1.5" depth;
Story: —; **Country:** Argentina; **Mfr/Dist:** Italy, for Argentina;
Border/Edge: Red with white/gold trim; **Quantity:** —;
Courtesy of John E. Peterson.
$ Value, References: est $25-$35 (x)
$ Value, Internet Auctions: —; **# Sales:** —

Name: Lillian Nordica with Sign; **Issued:** 1990s
Comments: Reproduction of 1904 calendar, plastic;
Shape: Small Rectangle; **Size:** 9.75" x 12.0"; **Story:** —;
Country: Italy; **Mfr/Dist:** —; **Border/Edge:** Picture
extends into border; **Quantity:** —;
Courtesy of John E. Peterson.
$ Value, References: est $10-$20 (x)
$ Value, Internet Auctions: —; **# Sales:** —

Name: Circus Scene; **Issued:** 1990s
Comments: Reproduction of 1936 ad, clown, showgirl, circus
dog, tray © information in Spanish; **Shape:** Deep Round; **Size:**
13.125" dia. x 1.5" depth; **Story:** —; **Country:** Argentina; **Mfr/
Dist:** Italy, for Argentina; **Border/Edge:** Red with white/gold
trim; **Quantity:** —; *Courtesy of John E. Peterson.*
$ Value, References: est $25-$35 (x)
$ Value, Internet Auctions: —; **# Sales:** —

Name: Hospitality; **Issued:** 1990s
Comments: Reproduction of 1940s ad, two couples reaching for Coke
in a refrigerator, tray © information in Spanish; **Shape:** Deep Round;
Size: 13.125" dia. x 1.5" depth; **Story:** —; **Country:** Argentina; **Mfr/
Dist:** Italy, for Argentina; **Border/Edge:** Red with white/gold trim;
Quantity: —; *Courtesy of John E. Peterson.*
$ Value, References: est $25-$35 (x)
$ Value, Internet Auctions: —; **# Sales:** —

Name: Beach Girl with Red Hair; **Issued:** 1990s
Comments: Thai wording, bottler *Haad Thip Company*; **Shape:**
Round; **Size:** 12.0"; **Story:** —; **Country:** Thailand; **Mfr/Dist:** —;
Border/Edge: Red; **Quantity:** —; *Courtesy of John E. Peterson.*
$ Value, References: est $10-$20 (x)
$ Value, Internet Auctions: —; **# Sales:** —

1990

Two long rectangle shapes are the first of a new series of trays and are among eight trays identified from 1990. Seven are reproductions of earlier ads. All eight trays are pictured.

The tray series that begins in 1990 has the theme *Refreshed. Drive Refreshed* and *Play Refreshed* ads from 1950 and 1951, both by noted artists, start the series.

Court Day, a 1921 ad reproduction, portrays small town life in the heartland of America. Another reproduction is *Touring Car*, 1924, originally issued in 1987. This version commemorates an IGA store but curiously does not mention its location. Completing the group are ad reproductions from 1922 and 1930, and a reproduction of a 1947 Santa ad.

The last tray from 1990 is a re-issue of 1985's *Through All the Years*. The tray pictures a collage of over thirty Coke Memorabilia items and is the best selling licensed tray ever. The new tray, distributed by Trademark Marketing, International, now has information about the image and the artist, Sandra K. Porter, printed on the back. It christens *The Signature Series* of licensed trays.

Name: Court Day; **Issued:** 1990-1992 **Comments:** Reproduction of 1921 ad, small town courtyard, much detail, same (unknown) artist as 1991 tray *Circus Has Come to Town*; **Shape:** Std Rectangle; **Size:** 10.5" x 13.25"; **Story:** Yes; **Country:** US; **Mfr/Dist:** Ohio Art Company, distributed by Trademark Marketing; **Border/Edge:** Red; **Quantity:** 4,000. **$ Value, References:** $5-$20 (3,6,x) **$ Value, Internet Auctions:** —; **# Sales:** —

Name: Touring Car; **Issued:** 1990 **Comments:** Reproduction of 1924 ad, right panel of a panoramic poster. First issued in 1987, commemorative of customer 35th Anniversary, *Bob's IGA*, location unknown; **Shape:** Large Rectangle; **Size:** 13.5" x 18.5"; **Story:** Yes; **Country:** US; **Mfr/Dist:** —; **Border/Edge:** Red; **Quantity:** —. **$ Value, References:** est $5-$15 (x) **$ Value, Internet Auctions:** —; **# Sales:** —

Name: Drive Refreshed; **Issued:** 1990-1995 **Comments:** Reproduction of 1950 ad, yellow roadster, by Gil Elvgren, # one in series of *Refreshed* tray reproductions; **Shape:** Long Rectangle; **Size:** 8.5" x 19.0"; **Story:** Yes; **Country:** US; **Mfr/Dist:** Ohio Art Company; **Border/Edge:** Red; **Quantity:** 53,000. **$ Value, References:** est $5-$12 (3,x) **$ Value, Internet Auctions:** $13; **# Sales:** 3

Name: To Play Refreshed; **Issued:** 1990-1993 **Comments:** Reproduction of 1951 ad, by Haddon Sundblom, woman in bathing suit, # two in series of *Refreshed* tray reproductions; **Shape:** Long Rectangle; **Size:** 8.5" x 19.0"; **Story:** Yes; **Country:** US; **Mfr/Dist:** Ohio Art Company; **Border/Edge:** Red; **Quantity:** 24,000. **$ Value, References:** $5-$12 (3,6,x) **$ Value, Internet Auctions:** —; **# Sales:** —

Name: Four Seasons; **Issued:** 1990 **Comments:** Reproduction of 1922 festoon; **Shape:** Small Rectangle; **Size:** 9.0" x 14.5"; **Story:** Yes; **Country:** US; **Mfr/Dist:** Ohio Art Company; **Border/Edge:** Black; **Quantity:** 63,000. **$ Value, References:** $5-$12 (3,6,x) **$ Value, Internet Auctions:** $9; **# Sales:** 5

Name: 7 Million a Day; **Issued:** 1990-1992
Comments: Reproduction of c.1930 ad; **Shape:** Large Rectangle;
Size: 13.5" x 18.5"; **Story:** Yes; **Country:** US; **Mfr/Dist:** Ohio Art
Company; **Border/Edge:** Red; **Quantity:** 8,000; *Courtesy of Ann
Poppenheimer Sherrod and Dave Sherrod, Pop's Mail Order Collectibles.*
$ Value, References: $5-$15 (3,6,x)
$ Value, Internet Auctions: $10 (for info only); **# Sales:** 2

In 1991, sixteen identified trays include the only sports commemorative of the decade. All sixteen trays and images are pictured. Seven of these trays feature works by Haddon Sundblom and six reflect themes during and just after the years of World War II.

Circus Has Come to Town, a 1920 ad reproduction, is a scene picturing small town activities, similar to *Court Day*, 1990. A third tray in the *Refreshed* series is a reproduction of Haddon Sundblom's 1950 ad named *Travel Refreshed*. Versions are shown with and without the Coke button sign.

Tray reproductions include *Summer Girl*, 1921 and a reproduction of *Barefoot Boy*, Norman Rockwell's 1931 calendar and tray. *Summer Girl* is also on a customer commemorative tray of a Kroger Supermarket opening.

The *1992 Olympics, Barcelona*, as with the 1988 *Calgary Olympics* tray, features past Olympic posters in the border.

Name: Busy Man's Pause; **Issued:** 1990-1991
Comments: Reproduction of 1947 ad,
Hospitality, Santa with toy bunny, by Haddon
Sundblom; **Shape:** Large Rectangle; **Size:**
13.5" x 18.5"; **Story:** Yes; **Country:** US; **Mfr/
Dist:** Ohio Art Company; **Border/Edge:**
Green with red ribbon trim;
Quantity: 11,000.
$ Value, References: $8-$15 (3,6,x)
$ Value, Internet Auctions: $13 (for info
only); **# Sales:** 2

Name: Circus Has Come to Town;
Issued: 1991-1994
Comments: Reproduction of 1920
ad, tent, elephants, same (unknown)
artist as 1990 tray *Court Day*; **Shape:**
Std Rectangle; **Size:** 10.5" x 13.25";
Story: Yes; **Country:** US; **Mfr/Dist:**
Ohio Art Company; **Border/Edge:**
Red; **Quantity:** 4,000.
$ Value, References: $8-$20 (3,6,x)
$ Value, Internet Auctions: —;
 # Sales: —

Name: Travel Refreshed; **Issued:** 1991-1998
Comments: Reproduction of 1950 ad, cowboy on horse without Coke
button sign, by Haddon Sundblom, # three in series of *Refreshed* tray
reproductions; **Shape:** Long Rectangle; **Size:** 8.5" x 19.0"; **Story:** —;
Country: US; **Mfr/Dist:** Ohio Art Company, distributed by Trademark
Marketing; **Border/Edge:** Red; **Quantity:** —; *Courtesy of John E. Peterson.*
$ Value, References: est $15-$30 (x)
$ Value, Internet Auctions: —; **# Sales:** —

Name: Through The Years; **Issued:** 1990-1997 (reissue of 1985 tray)
Comments: Back of tray with artist information and announcement of new series.
Collage image on front, by Sandra K. Porter. First in new *Signature Series* of trays becomes
largest selling licensed image; **Shape:** Std Rectangle; **Size:** 10.5" x 13.25"; **Story:** Yes;
Country: US; **Mfr/Dist:** Ohio Art Company, distributed by Trademark Marketing;
Border/Edge: Black; **Quantity:** 200,000 (includes sales of 1985 issue);
Courtesy of John E. Peterson.
$ Value, References: est $8-$20 (x)
$ Value, Internet Auctions: $5 (for info only); **# Sales:** 2

Name: Travel Refreshed; **Issued:** 1991-1998
Comments: Reproduction of 1950 ad, cowboy on horse with Coke button sign, by
Haddon Sundblom, # three in series of *Refreshed* tray reproductions; **Shape:** Long
Rectangle; **Size:** 8.5" x 19.0"; **Story:** —; **Country:** US; **Mfr/Dist:** Ohio Art
Company, distributed by Trademark Marketing; **Border/Edge:** Red;
Quantity: 22,000.
$ Value, References: $8-$20 (3,6,x)
$ Value, Internet Auctions: $6; **# Sales:** 4

Name: Barefoot Boy, Boy with Dog, *or* The Rockwell Tray; **Issued:** c.1991-1995 **Comments:** Reproduction of 1931 tray, by Norman Rockwell; **Shape:** Small Flat Rectangle; **Size:** 10.5" x 14.0"; **Story:** Yes; **Country:** US; **Mfr/Dist:** Ohio Art Company, distributed by Trademark Marketing; **Border/Edge:** Red; **Quantity:** 38,500.
$ Value, References: $8-$20 (3,6,x)
$ Value, Internet Auctions: $7; **# Sales:** 7

Name: 1992 Olympic Games, Barcelona; **Issued:** 1991 **Comments:** Commemorative of Summer Olympic Games, collage, twenty-one Olympic posters; **Shape:** Std Rectangle; **Size:** 10.5" x 13.25"; **Story:** Yes; **Country:** US; **Mfr/Dist:** —; **Border/Edge:** Red; **Quantity:** —.
$ Value, References: est $8-$20 (3,x)
$ Value, Internet Auctions: —; **# Sales:** —

An additional nine ad reproduction trays from 1991 include an attractive large oval tray, *1912 Calendar Girl*, third of Hamilton King's four calendars to be reproduced. Four ads from the 1940s reflect America during and after World War II. Two, from 1944 and 1945, are by Haddon Sundblom. The original 1945 ad is also shown below. The other two trays reproduce 1943 and 1948 ads. Three Santa trays include two from a c.1943 ad with a World War II war bond theme, and a 1960 image of Santa resting with his elves.

The last ad reproduction tray of this year is very attractive. Two women in 1920s beach attire are leaning on a wooden boat. This image reproduces a 1924 window display but the blue and pink color splashes in the tray's top half have been added in the reproduction. Tray details state that a company in Paris, France distributed the tray, making it the only *European* French tray identified in this book.

Name: Summer Girl *or* Baseball Girl; **Issued:** 1991-1997 **Comments:** Reproduction of 1921 tray; **Shape:** Small Rectangle; **Size:** 9.0" x 14.5"; **Story:** Yes; **Country:** US; **Mfr/Dist:** Ohio Art Company; **Border/Edge:** Blue; **Quantity:** 17,500; *Courtesy of Ann Poppenheimer Sherrod and Dave Sherrod, Pop's Mail Order Collectibles.*
$ Value, References: $8-$20 (3,6,x)
$ Value, Internet Auctions: $12; **# Sales:** 5

Name: Summer Girl *or* Baseball Girl; **Issued:** 1991 **Comments:** Reproduction of 1921 tray, commemorative of customer, Kroger Company new store opening, historical area of Savannah, Georgia; **Shape:** Small Rectangle; **Size:** 9.0" x 14.5"; **Story:** Yes; **Country:** US; **Mfr/Dist:** Ohio Art Company; **Border/Edge:** Blue; **Quantity:** 2,000.
$ Value, References: est $8-$20 (x)
$ Value, Internet Auctions: —; **# Sales:** —

Name: 1912 Calendar Girl; **Issued:** 1991-1996 **Comments:** Reproduction of 1912 calendar, by Hamilton King; **Shape:** Large Deep Oval; **Size:** 12.5" x 15.5"; **Story:** Yes; **Country:** US; **Mfr/Dist:** Ohio Art Company, distributed by Trademark Marketing; **Border/Edge:** Dark Blue; **Quantity:** 27,000.
$ Value, References: est $6-$15 (3,x)
$ Value, Internet Auctions: —; **# Sales:** —

Name: He's Coming Home Tomorrow; **Issued:** 1991-1997 **Comments:** Reproduction of 1944 ad, near the end of World War II, taking loose bottles of Coke home in a wagon since materials restrictions eliminated cartons, by Haddon Sundblom; **Shape:** Small Flat Rectangle; **Size:** 10.5" x 14.0"; **Story:** Yes; **Country:** US; **Mfr/Dist:** Ohio Art Company, distributed by Trademark Marketing; **Border/ Edge:** Green; **Quantity:** 54,000. **$ Value, References:** $5-$15 (3,6,x) **$ Value, Internet Auctions:** $8; **# Sales:** 5

Name: Welcome; **Issued:** 1991-1997 **Comments:** Reproduction of 1943 ad, uniformed man talking with a woman, still wartime; **Shape:** Long Rectangle; **Size:** 8.5" x 19.0"; **Story:** Yes; **Country:** US; **Mfr/Dist:** Ohio Art Company, distributed by Trademark Marketing; **Border/Edge:** Pink; **Quantity:** 37,000. **$ Value, References:** $8-$15 (3,6,x) **$ Value, Internet Auctions:** $8; **# Sales:** 3

Name: Have a Coke; **Issued:** 1991-1998 **Comments:** Reproduction of 1948 ad, couple at a cooler; **Shape:** Large Rectangle; **Size:** 13.5" x 18.5"; **Story:** Yes; **Country:** US; **Mfr/Dist:** Ohio Art Company, distributed by Trademark Marketing; **Border/Edge:** Red; **Quantity:** 66,000. **$ Value, References:** $8-$15 (3,6,x) **$ Value, Internet Auctions:** $9 (for info only); **# Sales:** 2

Name: The Family; **Issued:** 1991-1997 **Comments:** Reproduction of 1945 ad, return from World War II, by Haddon Sundblom; **Shape:** Round; **Size:** 12.5"; **Story:** —; **Country:** US; **Mfr/Dist:** Ohio Art Company, distributed by Trademark Marketing; **Border/Edge:** Maroon; **Quantity:** 10,000. **$ Value, References:** $8-$15 (3,6,x) **$ Value, Internet Auctions:** $10 (for info only); **# Sales:** 1

Name: The Family; **Issued:** 1991-1997 **Comments:** December, 1945 ad, *National Geographic Magazine.* One of only two Decembers in about thirty years in which a Haddon Sundblom Santa ad was not in the December issue of *National Geographic* (but at least the replacement ad was also by Haddon Sundblom).

Name: Wherever I Go; **Issued:** 1991-1996 **Comments:** Reproduction of c.1943 ad, war bonds in Santa's bag, by Haddon Sundblom; **Shape:** Small Flat Rectangle; **Size:** 10.5" x 14.0"; **Story:** Yes; **Country:** US; **Mfr/Dist:** Ohio Art Company, distributed by Trademark Marketing; **Border/ Edge:** Red; **Quantity:** 29,000. **$ Value, References:** $8-$15 (3,6,x) **$ Value, Internet Auctions:** $6.50 (for info only); **# Sales:** 2

Name: Santa Around the World;
Issued: 1991-1996
Comments: Reproduction of
c.1943 ad *Wherever I Go*, by
Haddon Sundblom, variation on
the ad; **Shape:** Round; **Size:**
12.0"; **Story:** Yes; **Country:** US;
Mfr/Dist: Ohio Art Company,
distributed by Trademark
Marketing; **Border/Edge:** Red;
Quantity: 13,500.
$ Value, References: $8-$15
(3,6,x)
$ Value, Internet Auctions: —;
 # Sales: —

Italian Small Rectangle Trays, c.1992-1995

This four-year period lists twenty-five identified Italian trays. A few
were possibly manufactured in Italy and distributed in other European
countries. Questions on date and country arise since almost no identification appears on the trays except for a small logo of the Italian manufacturer and an occasional change in language in the Coke logo. The
trays are certainly among the most unique and attractive of the thirty-
year, post-classics period!

Twenty-four of these trays are all in the same shape and size. Reference materials indicate that most were issued as promotions. Twelve
cans of Coke fit into the tray, which has small grooves on the face to
help stabilize the cans. The whole package was shrink-wrapped. Twenty-
two of the twenty-five identified trays are pictured in this section.

Three trays in this group are at the top of the unique list. Each
image is an outdoor scene that results in an *'Absolut-ly'* recognizable
outline of a Coke bottle in a rock formation, a waterfall, and the wake of
a sailboat. Quite a group of fun images!

Name: Rock Formation;
Issued: c.1992-1995
Comments: Rock formation with
opening formed in the shape of a Coke
bottle. *'Absolut-ly'* a great image;
Shape: Small Rectangle; **Size:** 8.0" x
11.0" x 1.0"; **Story:** —; **Country:** Italy;
Mfr/Dist: Scatolificio Lecchese;
Border/Edge: Green; **Quantity:** —;
*Courtesy of Ann Poppenheimer Sherrod
and Dave Sherrod, Pop's Mail Order
Collectibles.*
$ Value, References: est $12-$30
(6,x)
$ Value, Internet Auctions: —;
 # Sales: —

Name: A Merry Christmas; **Issued:** 1991-1997
Comments: Reproduction of 1960 ad, Santa resting in chair, elves helping,
by Haddon Sundblom; **Shape:** Flat Rectangle; **Size:** 11.0" x 15.0"; **Story:**
Yes; **Country:** US; **Mfr/Dist:** Ohio Art Company, distributed by Trademark
Marketing; **Border/Edge:** Red; **Quantity:** 16,000.
$ Value, References: $8-$15 (3,6,x)
$ Value, Internet Auctions: $9 (for info only); **# Sales:** 2

Name: Waterfall; **Issued:** c.1992-1995
Comments: Waterfall is in shape of
Coke bottle and surrounded by trees.
'Absolut-ly' a great image; **Shape:** Small
Rectangle; **Size:** 8.0" x 11.0" x 1.0";
Story: —; **Country:** Italy; **Mfr/Dist:**
Scatolificio Lecchese; **Border/Edge:**
Orange; **Quantity:** —; *Courtesy of John
E. Peterson.*
$ Value, References: est $12-$30
(6,x)
$ Value, Internet Auctions: —; **#
Sales:** —

Name: Swimsuit Girls; **Issued:** 1991
Comments: Reproduction of 1924 ad,
window display, two women leaning
against wooden boats. Pink and blue
splashes on top half of tray are not from
original image; **Shape:** Large Rectangle;
Size: 12.5" x 16.5"; **Story:** —; **Country:**
France; **Mfr/Dist:** Marketed (Distributed)
by Virogan gtor, Paris, France; **Border/
Edge:** Blue; **Quantity:** —; *Courtesy of
John E. Peterson.*
$ Value, References: est $15-$35 (x)
$ Value, Internet Auctions: —;
 # Sales: —

Name: Boat with Wake; **Issued:** c.1992-1995
Comments: Sailboat creates wake in the shape of a Coke bottle. '*Absolut-ly*' a great image; **Shape:** Small Rectangle; **Size:** 8.0" x 11.0" x 1.0"; **Story:** —; **Country:** Italy; **Mfr/Dist:** Scatolificio Lecchese; **Border/Edge:** Red; **Quantity:** —; *Courtesy of Ann Poppenheimer Sherrod and Dave Sherrod, Pop's Mail Order Collectibles.*
$ Value, References: est $12-$30 (6,x)
$ Value, Internet Auctions: —; **# Sales:** —

Name: 1900 Calendar; **Issued:** c.1992-1995
Comments: Reproduction of 1900 calendar, *Hilda with The Glass*, all months printed on first sheet, # two in series of three trays; **Shape:** Small Rectangle; **Size:** 8.0" x 11.0" x 1.0"; **Story:** Yes; **Country:** Italy; **Mfr/Dist:** Scatolificio Lecchese; **Border/Edge:** Silver; **Quantity:** —; *Courtesy of John E. Peterson.*
$ Value, References: est $12-$30 (6,x)
$ Value, Internet Auctions: —;
 # Sales: —

Name: 1901 Calendar; **Issued:** c.1992-1995
Comments: Reproduction of 1901 calendar, *Girl with Pansies*, # three in series of three trays; **Shape:** Small Rectangle; **Size:** 8.0" x 11.0" x 1.0"; **Story:** Yes; **Country:** Italy; **Mfr/Dist:** Scatolificio Lecchese; **Border/Edge:** Maroon, silver stripe; **Quantity:** —; *Courtesy of John E. Peterson.*
$ Value, References: est $12-$30 (6,x)
$ Value, Internet Auctions: —;
 # Sales: —

Another interesting group has three trays that each reproduce a calendar, but in a different way. These trays not only reproduce the *image* from the original calendar but also show the total detail of the full sheet, including the pad. The 1891 calendar, *Young Girl with Tennis Racquet*, advertises Asa Candler and Company. It is thought to be a reproduction of the first calendar ever used as advertising by The Coca-Cola Company. The dark circle at the top of the calendar is a grommet hole. The second calendar, *1900 Hilda Clark with Glass*, is a different look since all twelve months are displayed around the image instead of in a calendar pad. The third calendar, from 1901, is *Girl with Pansies*. It was an additional calendar for that year when the most familiar calendar and tray image was *Hilda with The Roses*.

Nineteen trays are reproductions of earlier trays or ads. Two reproduce Sundblom's *Sprite Boy* from 1941 and 1946 ads. Six trays (four pictured) are colorful, familiar images of the 1930s and 1940s: *Girl in a White Bathing Suit* is from a 1938 ad; *Female Aviator*, 1941, *Couple with a Snowman*, 1942, and *Winter Girl*, 1948, were all on the calendar of that year. Ads not pictured are *Out Fishin'* from Rockwell's 1935 calendar, and *Drink Coca-Cola*, 1901. Tray reproductions are *Flapper Girl*, 1923, and *Barefoot Boy*, 1931, in a standard rectangle shape (not pictured).

The remaining nine are reproductions of Santa ads. One is the first tray that blends images from more than one ad. The picture combines Santa's face from a 1962 ad, his hand and arm from *Good Boys and Girls*, 1951, and a polar bear from what is probably a TV ad but which has not been identified from any tray. Two trays use only small parts of the Santa image from 1935 and 1962 ads. The remaining six have more complete reproductions of ads, which are all from the 1940s and 1950s.

Name: 1891 Calendar; **Issued:** c.1992-1995
Comments: Reproduction of 1891 calendar, probably first calendar issued by The Coca-Cola Company. Note lack of familiar Coca-Cola script, # one in series of three trays; **Shape:** Small Rectangle; **Size:** 8.0" x 11.0" x 1.0"; **Story:** Yes; **Country:** Italy; **Mfr/Dist:** Scatolificio Lecchese; **Border/Edge:** Teal, silver stripe; **Quantity:** —; *Courtesy of John E. Peterson.*
$ Value, References: est $12-$30 (6,x)
$ Value, Internet Auctions: —; **# Sales:** —

Name: Sprite Boy with Bottle; **Issued:** c.1992-1995
Comments: Reproduction of 1941 ad, by Haddon Sundblom; **Shape:** Small Rectangle; **Size:** 8.0" x 11.0" x 1.0"; **Story:** —; **Country:** Italy; **Mfr/Dist:** Scatolificio Lecchese; **Border/Edge:** Red; **Quantity:** —; *Courtesy of Ann Poppenheimer Sherrod and Dave Sherrod, Pop's Mail Order Collectibles.*
$ Value, References: est $12-$30 (6,x)
$ Value, Internet Auctions: $13 (for info only); **# Sales:** 1

Name: Sprite Boy with Carton;
Issued: c.1992-1995
Comments: Reproduction of
1946 ad, by Haddon Sundblom;
Shape: Small Rectangle; **Size:**
8.0" x 11.0" x 1.0"; **Story:** —;
Country: Italy; **Mfr/Dist:**
Scatolificio Lecchese; **Border/
Edge:** Red; **Quantity:** —;
*Courtesy of Ann Poppenheimer
Sherrod and Dave Sherrod, Pop's
Mail Order Collectibles.*
$ Value, References: est $12-
$30 (6,x)
$ Value, Internet Auctions: —;
 # Sales: —

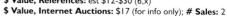

Name: Female Aviator; **Issued:** c.1992-1995
Comments: Reproduction of 1941 calendar, US, March/April
page, *Your Thirst Takes Wings*. Skater Girl was featured image on
calendar; **Shape:** Small Rectangle; **Size:** 8.0" x 11.0" x 1.0";
Story: —; **Country:** Italy; **Mfr/Dist:** Scatolificio Lecchese;
Border/Edge: Red; **Quantity:** —; *Courtesy of Ann Poppenheimer
Sherrod and Dave Sherrod, Pop's Mail Order Collectibles.*
$ Value, References: est $12-$30 (6,x)
$ Value, Internet Auctions: $17 (for info only); **# Sales:** 2

Name: Sprite Boy with Carton; **Issued:** c.1992-1995
Comments: Tray pictured with twelve cans as it would have been
before being shrink-wrapped for sale.

Name: Couple with Snowman; **Issued:** c.1992-1995
Comments: Reproduction of 1942 calendar, US,
January/February page, *Thirst knows no Season*. Tray
Coke logo has word *trademark* in Polish; **Shape:**
Small Rectangle; **Size:** 8.0" x 11.0" x 1.0"; **Story:** —;
Country: Italy; **Mfr/Dist:** Scatolificio Lecchese,
distributed into Europe, probably Poland;
Border/Edge: Red; **Quantity:** —; *Courtesy of Ann
Poppenheimer Sherrod and Dave Sherrod,
Pop's Mail Order Collectible.*
$ Value, References: est $12-$30 (6,x)
$ Value, Internet Auctions: $14 (for info only);
 # Sales: 1

Name: Girl in White Bathing Suit; **Issued:** c.1992-1995
Comments: Reproduction of 1938 ad, original photo by Snyder and
Black; **Shape:** Small Rectangle; **Size:** 8.0" x 11.0" x 1.0"; **Story:** —;
Country: Italy; **Mfr/Dist:** Scatolificio Lecchese; **Border/Edge:** Red;
Quantity: —; *Courtesy of Ann Poppenheimer Sherrod and Dave Sherrod,
Pop's Mail Order Collectibles.*
$ Value, References: est $12-$30 (6,x)
$ Value, Internet Auctions: $7 (for info only); **# Sales:** 1

Name: Winter Girl; **Issued:** c.1992-1995
Comments: Reproduction of 1948
calendar, US, January/February page,
woman in coat and gloves with bottle of
Coke; **Shape:** Small Rectangle; **Size:** 8.0"
x 11.0" x 1.0"; **Story:** —; **Country:** Italy;
Mfr/Dist: Scatolificio Lecchese; **Border/
Edge:** Red; **Quantity:** —; *Courtesy of
Ann Poppenheimer Sherrod and Dave
Sherrod, Pop's Mail Order Collectible.*
$ Value, References: est $12-$30 (6,x)
$ Value, Internet Auctions: $12 (for
info only); **# Sales:** 1

Name: Flapper Girl;
Issued: c.1992-1995
Comments: Reproduction of 1923 tray; **Shape:** Small Rectangle; **Size:** 8.0" x 11.0" x 1.0"; **Story:** —; **Country:** Italy; **Mfr/Dist:** Fran Bosisio-Parisi-Commo (Bottler?); **Border/Edge:** Green; **Quantity:** —; *Courtesy of John E. Peterson.*
$ Value, References: est $12-$30 (6,x)
$ Value, Internet Auctions: —;
 # Sales: —

Name: And the same for you; **Issued:** c.1992-1995
Comments: Reproduction of 1962 Santa ad, face only, by Haddon Sundblom; **Shape:** Small Rectangle; **Size:** 8.0" x 11.0" x 1.0"; **Story:** —; **Country:** Italy; **Mfr/Dist:** Scatolificio Lecchese; **Border/Edge:** Red; **Quantity:** —; *Courtesy of Ann Poppenheimer Sherrod and Dave Sherrod, Pop's Mail Order Collectible.*
$ Value, References: est $12-$30 (6,x)
$ Value, Internet Auctions: —; **# Sales:** —

Name: Santa and Polar Bear; **Issued:** c.1992-1995
Comments: Reproduction of multiple ads. Santa's face is reproduced from 1962 ad, arm and hand with bottle is from 1951 ad, originals by Haddon Sundblom. Polar bear is from a c.1990s TV ad, specific tray or image not identified; **Shape:** Small Rectangle; **Size:** 8.0" x 11.0" x 1.0"; **Story:** —; **Country:** Italy; **Mfr/Dist:** Scatolificio Lecchese; **Border/Edge:** Red; **Quantity:** —; *Courtesy of Ann Poppenheimer Sherrod and Dave Sherrod, Pop's Mail Order Collectible.*
$ Value, References: est $12-$30 (6,x)
$ Value, Internet Auctions: —; **# Sales:** —

Name: Wherever I Go; **Issued:** c.1992-1995
Comments: Reproduction (with variation) of c.1943 ad, Santa's bag has all toys and no war bonds, by Haddon Sundblom; **Shape:** Small Rectangle; **Size:** 8.0" x 11.0" x 1.0"; **Story:** —; **Country:** Italy; **Mfr/Dist:** Scatolificio Lecchese; **Border/Edge:** Gold; **Quantity:** —; *Courtesy of John E. Peterson.*
$ Value, References: est $12-$30 (6,x)
$ Value, Internet Auctions: —; **# Sales:** —

Name: Santa, Refreshing Times; **Issued:** c.1992-1995
Comments: Reproduction of top part of 1935 ad, by Haddon Sundblom. In the original ad, Santa is on top of a ladder. A wreath has been added to the reproduction; **Shape:** Small Rectangle; **Size:** 8.0" x 11.0" x 1.0"; **Story:** —; **Country:** Italy; **Mfr/Dist:** Scatolificio Lecchese; **Border/Edge:** Red; **Quantity:** —; *Courtesy of John E. Peterson.*
$ Value, References: est $12-$30 (6,x)
$ Value, Internet Auctions: $6 (for info only); **# Sales:** 1

Name: Hospitality;
Issued: c.1992-1995
Comments: Reproduction of 1948 ad, Santa making toys, by Haddon Sundblom; **Shape:** Small Rectangle; **Size:** 8.0" x 11.0" x 1.0"; **Story:** —; **Country:** Italy; **Mfr/Dist:** Scatolificio Lecchese; **Border/Edge:** Green; **Quantity:** —; *Courtesy of Ann Poppenheimer Sherrod and Dave Sherrod, Pop's Mail Order Collectible.*
$ Value, References: est $12-$30 (6,x)
$ Value, Internet Auctions: —; **# Sales:** —

Name: Travel Refreshed;
Issued: c.1992-1995
Comments: Reproduction
of 1949 ad, Santa drinking
Coke, by Haddon Sundblom;
Shape: Small Rectangle;
Size: 8.0" x 11.0" x 1.0";
Story: —; **Country:** Italy;
Mfr/Dist: Scatolificio
Lecchese; **Border/Edge:**
Green; **Quantity:** —;
Courtesy of John E. Peterson.
$ Value, References: est
$12-$30 (6,x)
**$ Value, Internet
Auctions:** $10 (for info
only); **# Sales:** 1

Name: Refreshing Surprise; **Issued:** c.1992-1995
Comments: Reproduction of 1959 ad, by
Haddon Sundblom; **Shape:** Small Rectangle;
Size: 8.0" x 11.0" x 1.0"; **Story:** —; **Country:**
Italy; **Mfr/Dist:** Scatolificio Lecchese;
Border/Edge: Blue; **Quantity:** —;
Courtesy of John E. Peterson.
$ Value, References: est $12-$30 (6,x)
$ Value, Internet Auctions: $16 (for info only);
 # Sales: 1

Name: Good Boys and Girls;
Issued: c.1992-1995
Comments: Reproduction of
1951 ad, by Haddon
Sundblom; **Shape:** Small
Rectangle; **Size:** 8.0" x 11.0"
x 1.0"; **Story:** —; **Country:**
Italy; **Mfr/Dist:** Scatolificio
Lecchese; **Border/Edge:**
Red; **Quantity:** —.
$ Value, References: est
$12-$30 (6,x)
**$ Value, Internet
Auctions:** $7 (for info only);
 # Sales: 1

1992

Licensed reproductions of ads are thirteen of the fifteen 1992
trays. Fourteen are pictured here.

Cape Canaveral Lift-Off is a striking image with dramatic morning
sunlight. The tray was issued for the 18th Coca-Cola Collectors Convention in Orlando, Florida.

The last Zanesville tray by the artist Leslie Cope is titled *Dresden
Village*.

Name: Cape Canaveral Lift-Off; **Issued:** 1992
Comments: Commemorative of 18th National Convention, Coca-Cola Collectors,
Orlando, Florida; **Shape:** Std Rectangle; **Size:** 10.5" x 13.25"; **Story:** Yes; **Country:** US;
Mfr/Dist: —; **Border/Edge:** Silver; **Quantity:** —.
$ Value, References: est $25-$60 (3,x)
$ Value, Internet Auctions: $20; **# Sales:** 4

Name: Refreshing Surprise;
Issued: c.1992-1995
Comments: Reproduction of
1959 ad, by Haddon
Sundblom; **Shape:** Small
Rectangle; **Size:** 8.0" x 11.0" x
1.0"; **Story:** —; **Country:**
Italy; **Mfr/Dist:** Scatolificio
Lecchese; **Border/Edge:** Red;
Quantity: —.
$ Value, References: est $12-
$30 (6,x)
$ Value, Internet Auctions:
$16 (for info only); **# Sales:** 1

Name: Be Really Refreshed; **Issued:** 1992-1997
Comments: Reproduction of 1958 ad, baseball player and umpire; **Shape:** Small Flat Rectangle; **Size:** 10.5" x 14.0"; **Story:** Yes; **Country:** US; **Mfr/Dist:** Ohio Art Company, distributed by Trademark Marketing; **Border/Edge:** Red; **Quantity:** 37,000.
$ Value, References: $8-$15 (3,6,x)
$ Value, Internet Auctions: $15 (for info only); **# Sales:** 1

Name: Dresden Village, Zanesville, Ohio; **Issued:** 1992
Comments: Original painting by Leslie Cope, last in series of trays by Zanesville bottler. The only tray in the series to deviate from picturing transportation scenes around Zanesville. **Shape:** Std Rectangle; **Size:** 10.5" x 13.25"; **Story:** Yes; **Country:** US; **Mfr/Dist:** —; **Border/Edge:** Blue; **Quantity:** —.
$ Value, References: $15-$30 (3,6,x)
$ Value, Internet Auctions: —; **# Sales:** —

Ad reproductions include one from 1942 picturing America during World War II, similar to the six from 1991. Two trays reproduce ads with baseball themes and one, in the *Refreshed* series, uses a Haddon Sundblom ad, *Play Refreshed*.

Additional ads include one from each of the first four decades of the century: a coupon, two women (with the original ad shown), a 1926 Halloween scene, and a c.1930s ad with a large glass (not pictured).

Four Santa ads are reproduced in four different shapes. *Travel Refreshed*, 1949, is the only Santa ad that actually shows Santa Claus drinking a Coke.

Finally, the cover of a 1937 German Coke Magazine is reproduced.

Name: Pause for Coke; **Issued:** 1992-1997
Comments: Reproduction of 1948 ad, baseball player and fan; **Shape:** Small Flat Rectangle; **Size:** 10.5" x 14.0"; **Story:** Yes; **Country:** US; **Mfr/Dist:** Ohio Art Company, distributed by Trademark Marketing; **Border/Edge:** Red; **Quantity:** 16,000.
$ Value, References: est $8-$15 (x)
$ Value, Internet Auctions: —; **# Sales:** —

Name: Howdy Friend; **Issued:** 1992-1996
Comments: Reproduction of 1942 ad, pictures soldier on a hot day; **Shape:** Flat Rectangle; **Size:** 11.0" x 15.0"; **Story:** Yes; **Country:** US; **Mfr/Dist:** Ohio Art Company, distributed by Trademark Marketing; **Border/Edge:** Red; **Quantity:** 12,000.
$ Value, References: $8-$15 (3,6,x)
$ Value, Internet Auctions: $12 (for info only); **# Sales:** 2

Name: Play Refreshed; **Issued:** 1992-1997
Comments: Reproduction of 1950 ad, by Haddon Sundblom, # four in series of *Refreshed* tray reproductions; **Shape:** Long Rectangle; **Size:** 8.5" x 19.0"; **Story:** Yes; **Country:** US; **Mfr/Dist:** Ohio Art Company, distributed by Trademark Marketing; **Border/Edge:** Red; **Quantity:** 14,000.
$ Value, References: $8-$15 (3,6,x)
$ Value, Internet Auctions: $10 (for info only); **# Sales:** 1

Name: Ask at the Soda Fountain; **Issued:** 1992-1997
Comments: Reproduction of c.1900 ad/coupon; **Shape:** Small
Rectangle; **Size:** 9.0" x 14.5"; **Story:** Yes; **Country:** US; **Mfr/
Dist:** Ohio Art Company, distributed by Trademark Marketing;
Border/Edge: Green; **Quantity:** 16,000; *Courtesy of Trademark
Marketing International, Barbara Brim.*
$ Value, References: $6-$12 (3,6,x)
$ Value, Internet Auctions: $6 (for info only); **# Sales:** 2

Name: What's Really Good Finds its Way;
Issued: 1992-1997
Comments: Reproduction of 1926 ad,
Halloween theme; **Shape:** Small Flat
Rectangle; **Size:** 10.5" x 14.0"; **Story:** Yes;
Country: US; **Mfr/Dist:** Ohio Art
Company, distributed by Trademark
Marketing; **Border/Edge:** Black;
Quantity: 9,000.
$ Value, References: $8-$15 (3,6,x)
$ Value, Internet Auctions: $6 (for info
only); **# Sales:** 2

Name: Supremely Satisfying;
Issued: 1992-1997
Comments: Reproduction of 1914
ad, two women drinking Coke;
Shape: Small Rectangle; **Size:** 9.0"
x 14.5"; **Story:** Yes; **Country:** US;
Mfr/Dist: Ohio Art Company,
distributed by Trademark
Marketing; **Border/Edge:** Black;
Quantity: 5,500.
$ Value, References: est $8-$15
(3,x)
$ Value, Internet Auctions: $7
(for info only); **# Sales:** 1

Name: Season's Greetings; **Issued:** 1992-1998
Comments: Reproduction of 1942 ad, *That Extra Something! They
Remembered Me*, by Haddon Sundblom; **Shape:** Std Rectangle;
Size: 10.5" x 13.25"; **Story:** Yes; **Country:** US; **Mfr/Dist:** Ohio
Art Company, distributed by Trademark Marketing;
Border/Edge: Green; **Quantity:** 19,550.
$ Value, References: $8-$15 (3,6,x)
$ Value, Internet Auctions: $5 (for info only); **# Sales:** 1

Name: Supremely Satisfying;
Issued: 1992-1997
Comments: 1914 ad,
unknown magazine.
Reproduced for this tray.

Name: They Knew What I Wanted; **Issued:** 1992-1999
Comments: Reproduction of 1945 ad, end of WWII, theme is *return*, by
Haddon Sundblom; **Shape:** Long Rectangle; **Size:** 8.5" x 19.0"; **Story:** Yes;
Country: US; **Mfr/Dist:** Ohio Art Company, distributed by Trademark
Marketing; **Border/Edge:** Red; **Quantity:** 20,000.
$ Value, References: $8-$15 (3,6,x)
$ Value, Internet Auctions: $6 (for info only); **# Sales:** 2

Name: Santa; **Issued:** 1992-1997
Comments: Reproduction of 1949 ad, *Travel Refreshed*, by Haddon Sundblom. The entire ad includes Sprite Boy and reindeer. Only ad with Santa drinking from bottle; **Shape:** Round; **Size:** 12.5"; **Story:** Yes; **Country:** US; **Mfr/Dist:** Ohio Art Company, distributed by Trademark Marketing; **Border/Edge:** Green, gold edge; **Quantity:** 11,500.
$ Value, References: $7-$15 (3,6,x)
$ Value, Internet Auctions: $9 (for info only); **# Sales:** 1

1993

This year has trays from a variety of categories. Sixteen trays are identified and pictured.

Three commemoratives include the 75th year of bottling in *Coatesville, Pennsylvania*. An award winning, cheerful 1945 ad is reproduced for an Atlanta Coke Collectors meeting. And the third, a Canadian tray, commemorates the *National Strawberry Festival* from Portage La Prairie in Manitoba.

Name: Bottling Works; **Issued:** 1993
Comments: Commemorative of 75th Anniversary, Coatesville, Pennsylvania bottler, picture of antique truck and (second) bottling plant, 1923; **Shape:** Std Rectangle; **Size:** 10.5" x 13.25"; **Story:** Yes; **Country:** US; **Mfr/Dist:** —; **Border/Edge:** Black; **Quantity:** —; *Courtesy of John E. Peterson.*
$ Value, References: est $10-$25 (3,x)
$ Value, Internet Auctions: $15 (for info only); **# Sales:** 2

Name: For Sparkling Holidays; **Issued:** 1992
Comments: Reproduction of 1953 ad, Santa and elves in workshop, by Haddon Sundblom; **Shape:** Flat Rectangle; **Size:** 11.0" x 15.0"; **Story:** —; **Country:** US; **Mfr/Dist:** —; **Border/Edge:** Green; **Quantity:** —.
$ Value, References: est $8-$15 (6,x)
$ Value, Internet Auctions: $10 (for info only); **# Sales:** 1

Name: Blue Lady; **Issued:** 1992-1997
Comments: Reproduction, cover of 1937 German magazine; **Shape:** Round; **Size:** 12.5"; **Story:** Yes; **Country:** US; **Mfr/Dist:** Ohio Art Company, distributed by Trademark Marketing; **Border/Edge:** Blue; **Quantity:** 5,500.
$ Value, References: est $10-$20 (x)
$ Value, Internet Auctions: $8 (for info only); **# Sales:** 2

Name: Everything is Coming Up Springtime; **Issued:** 1993
Comments: Reproduction of 1945 ad, *Why Grow Thirsty*, by Haddon Sundblom. The ad won awards in 1945. Commemorative of 10th Anniversary, Atlanta Coca-Cola Collectors Event; **Shape:** Std Rectangle; **Size:** 10.5" x 13.25"; **Story:** Yes; **Country:** US; **Mfr/Dist:** —; **Border/Edge:** White; **Quantity:** est 2,000.
$ Value, References: $8-$20 (3,6,x)
$ Value, Internet Auctions: $11 (for info only); **# Sales:** 2

Name: Strawberry Festival, at Portage La Prairie; **Issued:** 1993
Comments: Commemorative of event, *Canada's National Strawberry Festival* in Manitoba. The tray pictures the largest drive-by replica of a Coke can. Another interesting tray from Brandon, Manitoba bottler; **Shape:** Std Rectangle; **Size:** 10.5" x 13.25"; **Story:** Yes; **Country:** Canada (French); **Mfr/Dist:** Ohio Art Company; **Border/Edge:** Green; **Quantity:** —; *Courtesy of John E. Peterson.*
$ Value, References: est $8-$20 (x)
$ Value, Internet Auctions: —; **# Sales:** —

Name: Boys on the Curb; **Issued:** 1993-1997
Comments: Reproduction of 1935 ad, by Haddon Sundblom; **Shape:** Small Flat Rectangle; **Size:** 9.0" x 14.5'; **Story:** Yes; **Country:** US; **Mfr/Dist:** Ohio Art Company, distributed by Trademark Marketing; **Border/Edge:** Red; **Quantity:** 21,000; *Courtesy of Ann Poppenheimer Sherrod and Dave Sherrod, Pop's Mail Order Collectible.*
$ Value, References: $8-$15 (3,6,x)
$ Value, Internet Auctions: —; **# Sales:** —

Seven 1993 trays are ad reproductions. They include a c.1930s newspaper ad; one ad each from the 1930s, 1940s, 1950s, and 1960s; the first U.S. tray reproducing images from a TV ad; and one Santa ad.

Name: Whaddya' Know?; **Issued:** 1993-1998
Comments: Reproduction c.1930s ad, black and white newspaper style, crossroads scene, by Frank Godwin; **Shape:** Std Rectangle; **Size:** 10.5" x 13.25"; **Story:** Yes; **Country:** US; **Mfr/Dist:** Ohio Art Company, distributed by Trademark Marketing; **Border/Edge:** Black; **Quantity:** 7,500.
$ Value, References: $8-$15 (3,6,x)
$ Value, Internet Auctions: $5 (for info only); **# Sales:** 2

Name: Work Refreshed; **Issued:** 1993-1997
Comments: Reproduction of 1941 ad, hand with bottle and factory whistle, by Charles E. Heizerling; **Shape:** Small Flat Rectangle; **Size:** 10.5" x 14.0"; **Story:** Yes; **Country:** US; **Mfr/Dist:** Ohio Art Company, distributed by Trademark Marketing; **Border/Edge:** Red; **Quantity:** 14,500.
$ Value, References: est $8-$15 (3,x)
$ Value, Internet Auctions: $6 (for info only); **# Sales:** 1

Name: Reflections in the Mirror;
Issued: 1993-1998
Comments: Reproduction of
1950 ad, mirror reflects person
drinking Coke, by Hananiah
Harari; **Shape:** Std Rectangle;
Size: 10.5" x 13.25"; **Story:** Yes;
Country: US; **Mfr/Dist:** Ohio Art
Company, distributed by
Trademark Marketing; **Border/
Edge:** Green; **Quantity:** 24,500.
$ Value, References: $8-$15
(3,6,x)
$ Value, Internet Auctions: $6
(for info only); **# Sales:** 2

Name: My Gift for Thirst; **Issued:** 1993
Comments: Reproduction of 1952 ad, vertical, . . .
and now the gift for thirst . . . Christmas morning, by
Haddon Sundblom; **Shape:** Large Deep Oval; **Size:**
12.5" x 15.5"; **Story:** Yes; **Country:** US; **Mfr/Dist:**
Ohio Art Company, distributed by Trademark
Marketing; **Border/Edge:** Red; **Quantity:** 16,500.
$ Value, References: $10-$20 (3,6,x)
$ Value, Internet Auctions: $5 (for info only); **#
Sales:** 1

Name: Always Coca-Cola;
Issued: 1993
Comments: Reproduction of
logo, c.1990; **Shape:** Deep
Round; **Size:** 13.5" dia. x 1.5"
depth; **Story:** Yes; **Country:**
US; **Mfr/Dist:** Ohio Art
Company; **Border/Edge:** Red;
Quantity: —; *Courtesy of John
E. Peterson.*
$ Value, References: $20-$40
(3,6,x)
$ Value, Internet Auctions:
—; **# Sales:** —

Another group of polar bears is found on a 1993 tray, and the year
also brings four trays that are probably better named *snack trays* instead
of serving trays. Are they trays? They're metal, 10.0" in diameter, and
have 2.5" sloping sides. They are probably fairly difficult to use for serving Coke but could hold peanuts or potato chips on the side. Pictures
on these trays are cropped from 1917 and 1918 calendars and a 1918
ad.

The last identified 1993 tray is the first of what will total thirteen
trays in the 1990s from paintings by Pamela C. Renfroe. The back of the
tray states that the rural store pictured on the tray is the second in the
series. Actually, the *tray* is the second in *The Signature Series* but the *first*
by Pamela Renfroe. As mentioned, pictures in *The Signature Series* also
appear on coasters, calendars, playing cards, change trays, and many
other items.

Name: Always Cool;
Issued: 1993-current
Comments: Reproduction of
c.1992 ad for TV, bear is
watching Aurora Borealis;
Shape: Std Rectangle; **Size:**
10.5" x 13.25"; **Story:** Yes;
Country: US; **Mfr/Dist:** Ohio
Art Company, distributed by
Trademark Marketing; **Border/
Edge:** Red; **Quantity:** 74,000.
$ Value, References: $8-$15
(3,6,x)
$ Value, Internet Auctions:
$8.50; **# Sales:** 7

Name: Eleven Polar Bears; **Issued:** 1993
Comments: Group of eleven bears, ten with Coke,
seven with scarves, watching Aurora Borealis; **Shape:**
Flat Round; **Size:** 12.0"; **Story:** —; **Country:** US;
Mfr/Dist: Mfr in China, distributed by AMG Trading;
Border/Edge: Red; **Quantity:** —.
$ Value, References: est $7-$12 (x)
$ Value, Internet Auctions: —; **# Sales:** —

Name: Constance; **Issued:** c.1993
Comments: Reproduction of 1917 calendar; **Shape:** Snack Tray, Round; **Size:** 10.5" dia. x 2.5" depth, sloping sides; **Story:** —; **Country:** US; **Mfr/Dist:** The Tin Box Company; **Border/Edge:** Blue, four logos, white trim; **Quantity:** —.
$ Value, References: est $5-$12 (x)
$ Value, Internet Auctions: —; **# Sales:** —

Name: Atlantic City Girl; **Issued:** c.1993
Comments: Reproduction of 1918 ad, pictures woman leaning back on beach chair; **Shape:** Snack Tray, Round; **Size:** 10.5" dia. x 2.5" depth, sloping sides; **Story:** —; **Country:** US; **Mfr/Dist:** The Tin Box Company; **Border/Edge:** Green, four logos, white trim; **Quantity:** —.
$ Value, References: est $5-$12 (x)
$ Value, Internet Auctions: —;**# Sales:** —

Name: Girls at the Seashore; **Issued:** c.1993
Comments: Reproduction of 1918 calendar, pictures woman kneeling on left in original image; **Shape:** Snack Tray, Round; **Size:** 10.5" dia. x 2.5" depth, sloping sides; **Story:** —; **Country:** US; **Mfr/Dist:** The Tin Box Company; **Border/Edge:** Red, four logos, white trim; **Quantity:** —.
$ Value, References: est $5-$12 (x)
$ Value, Internet Auctions: —; **# Sales:** —

Name: The Pause that Refreshes, Smith's Grocery Store; **Issued:** 1993-1995
Comments: Original painting, by Pamela C. Renfroe, # one from artist, # two in *Signature Series*; **Shape:** Large Rectangle; **Size:** 13.5" x 18.5"; **Story:** Yes; **Country:** US; **Mfr/Dist:** Ohio Art Company, distributed by Trademark Marketing; **Border/Edge:** Black; **Quantity:** 59,500.
$ Value, References: $8-$18 (3,6,x)
$ Value, Internet Auctions: —; **# Sales:** —

1994

Eleven of twelve 1994 trays are pictured here. All but one was licensed for retail distribution.

Eight ad reproductions include a 1907 ad with Uncle Sam, a 1952 calendar image (non-Santa) by Haddon Sundblom, a 1951 product ad, and two Santa images. Two trays reproduce scenes from the 1990s *Polar Bear* TV ads (one pictured).

Name: Girls at the Seashore; **Issued:** c.1993
Comments: Reproduction of 1918 calendar, pictures woman standing on right in original image; **Shape:** Snack Tray, Round; **Size:** 10.5" dia. x 2.5" depth, sloping sides; **Story:** —; **Country:** US; **Mfr/Dist:** The Tin Box Company; **Border/Edge:** Red, four logos, white trim; **Quantity:** —.
$ Value, References: est $5-$12 (x)
$ Value, Internet Auctions: —; **# Sales:** —

Name: Keep Cool;
Issued: 1994-1997
Comments: Reproduction of 1907 ad, *The Great National Drink*, couple with Uncle Sam; **Shape:** Flat Rectangle; **Size:** 11.0" x 15.0"; **Story:** —; **Country:** US; **Mfr/Dist:** Ohio Art Company, distributed by Trademark Marketing; **Border/Edge:** Red; **Quantity:** 5,000; *Courtesy of Trademark Marketing International, Barbara Brim.*
$ Value, References: est $10-$20 (3,x)
$ Value, Internet Auctions: —; **# Sales:** —

Name: Girls Softball Team; **Issued:** 1994-1997
Comments: Reproduction of 1952 calendar, US, May/June page, *Play Refreshed,* by Haddon Sundblom; **Shape:** Round; **Size:** 13.0"; **Story:** Yes; **Country:** US; **Mfr/Dist:** Ohio Art Company, distributed by Trademark Marketing; **Border/Edge:** Red, blue stripe; **Quantity:** 23,500; *Courtesy of Trademark Marketing International, Barbara Brim.*
$ Value, References: est $8-$18 (3,x)
$ Value, Internet Auctions: —; **# Sales:** —

Name: Season's Greetings; **Issued:** 1994
Comments: Reproduction of 1962 ad, Santa playing with toys, by Haddon Sundblom; **Shape:** Large Rectangle; **Size:** 13.5" x 18.5";
Story: Yes; **Country:** US; **Mfr/Dist:** —;
Border/Edge: Green; **Quantity:** —.
$ Value, References: $8-$20 (3,6,x)
$ Value, Internet Auctions: —; **# Sales:** —

Name: Coca-Cola with Bottle; **Issued:** 1994-1998
Comments: Reproduction of 1951 button sign; **Shape:** Deep Round; **Size:** 13.5" dia. x 1.5" depth; **Story:** Yes; **Country:** US; **Mfr/Dist:** Ohio Art Company, distributed by Trademark Marketing;
Border/Edge: Red; **Quantity:** 55,000.
$ Value, References: $8-$18 (3,6,x)
$ Value, Internet Auctions: $6; **# Sales:** 3

Name: Good Boys and Girls; **Issued:** c.1994
Comments: Reproduction of 1951 ad, by Haddon Sundblom; **Shape:** Cookie Tray, Round; **Size:** 13.125"; **Story:** —; **Country:** US; **Mfr/Dist:** Tinware by AMG Trading; **Border/Edge:** Red, green, gold holiday trim; **Quantity:** —.
$ Value, References: est $8-$15 (x)
$ Value, Internet Auctions: —; **# Sales:** —

Name: Skiing Polar Bear; **Issued:** 1994
Comments: Polar bear on skis; **Shape:** Round; **Size:** 12.0"; **Story:** —; **Country:** US; **Mfr/Dist:** Mfr in China, distributed by Cavanaugh; **Border/Edge:** Red; **Quantity:** —.
$ Value, References: est $7-$15 (3,x)
$ Value, Internet Auctions: —; **# Sales:** —

The *Biedenharn Candy Company* of Vicksburg, Mississippi issued an 85th Anniversary tray in 1979. In 1994 it became the first location to commemorate *one hundred years* of Coca-Cola bottling with a tray that is a collage of twenty images. This tray is the last one identified to commemorate a bottler anniversary.

Four identified *Signature Series* trays include the second tray by Pamela C. Renfroe and three from new artists. Jeanne Mack has paintings issued on two trays and John Sandridge has the first in his *Just Smiles* series.

Name: Thrift Mercantile; **Issued:** 1994-1998 **Comments:** Original painting, Tennessee store with Coke sign, by Jeanne Mack, # one from artist; **Shape:** Std Rectangle; **Size:** 10.5" x 13.25"; **Story:** Yes; **Country:** US; **Mfr/Dist:** Ohio Art Company, distributed by Trademark Marketing; **Border/Edge:** Red; **Quantity:** 27,000.
$ Value, References: $8-$18 (3,6,x)
$ Value, Internet Auctions: $11; **# Sales:** 3

Name: Biedenharn Candy Company; **Issued:** 1994 **Comments:** Commemorative of 100th Anniversary, Biedenharn Candy Company, Vicksburg, Mississippi, the first bottler. Collage, twenty Coca-Cola items, by Cynthia Day Neely. Last identified bottler commemorative; **Shape:** Small Flat Rectangle; **Size:** 11.0" x 15.0"; **Story:** Yes; **Country:** US; **Mfr/Dist:** —; **Border/Edge:** Red; **Quantity:** —.
$ Value, References: est $10-$20 (x)
$ Value, Internet Auctions: —; **# Sales:** —

Name: Cat in Window; **Issued:** 1994-1998 **Comments:** Original painting, by Jeanne Mack, # two from artist; **Shape:** Large Rectangle; **Size:** 13.5" x 18.5"; **Story:** Yes; **Country:** US; **Mfr/Dist:** Ohio Art Company, distributed by Trademark Marketing; **Border/Edge:** Green; **Quantity:** 16,000.
$ Value, References: $8-$15 (3,6,x)
$ Value, Internet Auctions: $8; **# Sales:** 3

Name: Sign of Good Taste; **Issued:** 1994-1998
Comments: Original painting, diner with Coke truck and Corvette, by Pamela C. Renfroe, # two from artist; **Shape:** Std Rectangle; **Size:** 10.5" x 13.25"; **Story:** Yes; **Country:** US; **Mfr/Dist:** Ohio Art Company, distributed by Trademark Marketing; **Border/Edge:** Blue; **Quantity:** 44,000.
$ Value, References: $8-$20 (3,6,x)
$ Value, Internet Auctions: $9 (for info only); **# Sales:** 2

Name: Winning Smiles; **Issued:** 1994-1998 **Comments:** Original painting, two children playing checkers, by John Sandridge, *Just Smiles Series*, # one from artist; **Shape:** Std Rectangle; **Size:** 10.5" x 13.25"; **Story:** Yes; **Country:** US; **Mfr/Dist:** Ohio Art Company, distributed by Trademark Marketing; **Border/Edge:** Black, gold edge; **Quantity:** 27,000.
$ Value, References: $8-$20 (3,6,x)
$ Value, Internet Auctions: $8 (for info only); **# Sales:** 2

1995

The first year of the decade's second half has a comparatively low number of identified trays. Eleven are listed with ten pictured. All eleven are licensed for distribution.

The last identified long rectangle tray of the *Refreshed* series is *Shop Refreshed*, from a 1948 ad. And, after the great success of the 1990 reissued collage *Through The Years*, a second collage, in 1995, is titled *Sign Art*. This tray groups eleven Coca-Cola signs and coupons and had the second highest sales volume of any licensed tray. A small tray titled *Atlanta, You Can't Beat the Feeling* is not pictured. It may have been part of a promotion for the 1996 Olympic Games. A clever 1958 ad titled *Family Drive-In* is reproduced and also shown with the original magazine ad. Two Santa trays reproduce 1938 and 1953 ads.

Name: Family Drive-In; **Issued:** 1995-1998 **Comments:** Reproduction of 1958 ad, two ladies in Thunderbird, by George Hughes; **Shape:** Std Rectangle; **Size:** 10.5" x 13.5"; **Story:** Yes; **Country:** US; **Mfr/Dist:** Ohio Art Company, distributed by Trademark Marketing; **Border/Edge:** Black; **Quantity:** 14,500. **$ Value, References:** est $8-$15 (3,x) **$ Value, Internet Auctions:** —; **# Sales:** —

Name: Shop Refreshed; **Issued:** 1995-1998 **Comments:** Reproduction of 1948 ad, last in series of *Refreshed* tray reproductions; **Shape:** Long Rectangle; **Size:** 8.5" x 19.0"; **Story:** Yes; **Country:** US; **Mfr/Dist:** Ohio Art Company, distributed by Trademark Marketing; **Border/Edge:** Yellow; **Quantity:** 5,500. **$ Value, References:** $8-$15 (3,6,x) **$ Value, Internet Auctions:** —; **# Sales:** —

Name: Family Drive-In; **Issued:** 1995-1998 **Comments:** April, 1958 ad, *National Geographic Magazine.* Reproduced for tray.

Name: Sign Art; **Issued:** 1995-1998 **Comments:** Collage of eleven tin and cardboard signs and coupons, dating from 1902-1960. Key to items on back of tray; **Shape:** Long Rectangle; **Size:** 8.5" x 19.0"; **Story:** Yes; **Country:** US; **Mfr/Dist:** Ohio Art Company, distributed by Trademark Marketing; **Border/Edge:** Black; **Quantity:** 89,500. **$ Value, References:** $7-$14 (3,6,x) **$ Value, Internet Auctions:** $12; **# Sales:** 6

Name: Thanks for the Pause that Refreshes; **Issued:** 1995-1996 **Comments:** Reproduction of 1938 ad, Santa in chair with arm around child, by Haddon Sundblom; **Shape:** Small Deep Oval; **Size:** 8.5" x 11.0"; **Story:** Yes; **Country:** US; **Mfr/Dist:** Independent Can Company, distributed by Trademark Marketing; **Border/Edge:** Red; **Quantity:** 8,000. **$ Value, References:** $7-$15 (3,6,x) **$ Value, Internet Auctions:** —; **# Sales:** —

Name: The Pause that Refreshes; **Issued:** 1995
Comments: Reproduction of 1953 ad, Santa in a chair, two children serving him Coke, by Haddon Sundblom; **Shape:** Round; **Size:** 12.0"; **Story:** —; **Country:** US; **Mfr/Dist:** Mfr in China, distributed by Cavanaugh; **Border/Edge:** Red; **Quantity:** —;
Courtesy of John E. Peterson.
$ Value, References: est $7-$15 (x)
$ Value, Internet Auctions: —; **# Sales:** —

Name: Drink Coca-Cola, Jacob's Pharmacy, Atlanta, GA; **Issued:** 1995-current
Comments: Original painting, pictures c.1902 building where Coke first served, by Pamela C. Renfroe, # four from artist; **Shape:** Large Rectangle; **Size:** 13.5" x 18.5"; **Story:** Yes; **Country:** US; **Mfr/Dist:** Ohio Art Company, distributed by Trademark Marketing; **Border/Edge:** Maroon; **Quantity:** 21,000.
$ Value, References: $8-$20 (3,6,x)
$ Value, Internet Auctions: —; **# Sales:** —

The Signature Series adds five trays. The third by Jeanne Mack, with an attractive blue background, is titled *Mailboxes*. Pamela Renfroe adds two, *The Gathering Place* and *Jacob's Pharmacy* (the building where Coca-Cola was first served). New to the series, artist Jim Harrison begins his covered bridge series with *Summer Bridge* and John Sandridge has *Birthday Smiles*, the second in his *Just Smiles* series.

Name: Mailboxes; **Issued:** 1995-1997
Comments: Original painting, eight mailboxes, one mailbox with Coke inside, by Jeanne Mack. Reference information indicates initials and names in image are of friends and family, # three from artist; **Shape:** Large Deep Oval; **Size:** 12.5" x 15.5"; **Story:** Yes; **Country:** US; **Mfr/Dist:** Ohio Art Company, distributed by Trademark Marketing; **Border/Edge:** Royal Blue; **Quantity:** 11,500.
$ Value, References: $8-$15 (3,6,x)
$ Value, Internet Auctions: —; **# Sales:** —

Name: 1905 Summer Bridge; **Issued:** 1995-1997
Comments: Original painting, covered bridge with Coke sign, by Jim Harrison, # one from artist; **Shape:** Large Rectangle; **Size:** 13.5" x 18.5"; **Story:** Yes; **Country:** US; **Mfr/Dist:** Ohio Art Company, distributed by Trademark Marketing; **Border/Edge:** Dark Blue; **Quantity:** 48,000.
$ Value, References: $10-$25 (6,7,x)
$ Value, Internet Auctions: $8; **# Sales:** 5

Name: The Gathering Place; **Issued:** 1995-1998, ©1992
Comments: Original painting, country store and old cars, by Pamela C. Renfroe, # three from artist; **Shape:** Large Rectangle; **Size:** 13.5" x 18.5"; **Story:** Yes; **Country:** US; **Mfr/Dist:** Ohio Art Company, distributed by Trademark Marketing; **Border/Edge:** Dark Blue; **Quantity:** 45,000.
$ Value, References: $8-$15 (3,6,x)
$ Value, Internet Auctions: $20 (for info only); **# Sales:** 2

Name: Birthday Smiles; **Issued:** 1995-1998
Comments: Original painting, two children at birthday party, by John Sandridge, *Just Smiles Series*, # two from artist; **Shape:** Std Rectangle; **Size:** 10.5" x 13.25"; **Story:** Yes; **Country:** US; **Mfr/Dist:** Ohio Art Company, distributed by Trademark Marketing; **Mfr/Dist: Border/Edge:** Black, gold edge; **Quantity:** 10,500.
$ Value, References: $8-$15 (3,6,x)
$ Value, Internet Auctions: $15; **# Sales:** 3

1996

Eleven trays from 1996, all pictured, include eight of *The Signature Series* trays, the most issued in one year (at least in the 1990s).

Pamela Renfroe has two *trays, A Winning Combination* and *Fillin' Up on Memories*. These two are the first to be cross-licensed and feature other products in addition to Coke—Dairy Queen and John Deere Tractors. The fourth from Jeanne Mack features an Atlanta landmark from Coke's history, *Fleeman's Pharmacy*. Mack also has *Varsity Drive-In*, another Atlanta landmark, and *Bottles on a Sill*. Jim Harrison's covered bridge series gets through the second season with *Winter Bridge*. An additional John Sandridge *Just Smiles* painting is *Last Drip*. One last tray is a second Sandra K. Porter collage, *Through All the Years II*. This time the tray has over fifty items of Coke Memorabilia pictured.

A simple round tray with a Coke logo, from Germany, has a surface that is slightly sticky to the touch but prevents items on the tray from slipping. The polar bears, on a small tray, and another reproduction of the 1951 Santa ad *Good Boys and Girls* complete the 1996 group.

Name: Fleeman's Pharmacy – Atlanta GA; **Issued:** 1996-current
Comments: Original painting, Atlanta pharmacy used 1914-1995, Coke sign on side of building, by Jeanne Mack, # four from artist; **Shape:** Large Rectangle; **Size:** 13.5" x 18.5"; **Story:** Yes; **Country:** US; **Mfr/Dist:** Ohio Art Company, distributed by Trademark Marketing; **Border/Edge:** Green; **Quantity:** 21,000.
$ Value, References: $8-$20 (3,6,x)
$ Value, Internet Auctions: $5; **# Sales:** 6

Name: A Winning Combination; **Issued:** 1996-1998
Comments: Original painting, 1963 scene at Dairy Queen, cross-licensed, by Pamela C. Renfroe, # five from artist; **Shape:** Std Rectangle; **Size:** 10.5" x 13.25"; **Story:** Yes; **Country:** US; **Mfr/Dist:** Ohio Art Company, distributed by Trademark Marketing; **Border/Edge:** Dark Blue; **Quantity:** 35,000.
$ Value, References: est $8-$15 (6,x)
$ Value, Internet Auctions: $9; **# Sales:** 8

Name: The Varsity, Atlanta, GA; **Issued:** 1996-1998
Comments: Original painting, landmark Atlanta drive-in established 1928, by Jeanne Mack, # five from artist; **Shape:** Large Rectangle; **Size:** 13.5" x 18.5"; **Story:** Yes; **Country:** US; **Mfr/Dist:** Ohio Art Company, distributed by Trademark Marketing; **Border/Edge:** Black; **Quantity:** 11,000.
$ Value, References: $8-$20 (3,6,x)
$ Value, Internet Auctions: $12.50 (for info only); **# Sales:** 1

Name: Fillin' Up On Memories; **Issued:** 1996-1998
Comments: Original painting, John Deere Tractors and gasoline station, cross-licensed with John Deere Tractors, by Pamela C. Renfroe; # six from artist; **Shape:** Std Rectangle; **Size:** 10.5" x 13.25"; **Story:** Yes; **Country:** US; **Mfr/Dist:** Ohio Art Company, distributed by Trademark Marketing; **Border/Edge:** Green; **Quantity:** 28,500.
$ Value, References: est $8-$15 (6,x)
$ Value, Internet Auctions: $10; **# Sales:** 7

Name: Bottles on a Sill; **Issued:** 1996-current
Comments: Original painting, nine bottles including two Coke bottles, by Jeanne Mack, # six from artist; **Shape:** Long Rectangle; **Size:** 8.5" x 19.0"; **Story:** Yes; **Country:** US; **Mfr/Dist:** Ohio Art Company, distributed by Trademark Marketing; **Border/Edge:** Blue with flowers; **Quantity:** 10,000+.
$ Value, References: est $8-$15 (6,x)
$ Value, Internet Auctions: $11; **# Sales:** 3

Name: Winter Bridge; **Issued:** 1996-1998
Comments: Original painting, covered bridge with Coke sign, by Jim Harrison, # two from artist; **Shape:** Large Rectangle; **Size:** 13.5" x 18.5"; **Story:** Yes; **Country:** US; **Mfr/Dist:** Ohio Art Company, distributed by Trademark Marketing; **Border/Edge:** Maroon; **Quantity:** 17,000.
$ Value, References: est $8-$18 (6,x)
$ Value, Internet Auctions: $16 (for info only); **# Sales:** 1

Name: Coke Bottle; **Issued:** 1996
Comments: Logo tray, face of tray is treated with sticky substance that promises a non-slip surface; **Shape:** Deep Round; **Size:** 13.5"; **Story:** Yes; **Country:** Germany; **Mfr/Dist:** —; **Border/Edge:** Red; **Quantity:** —; *Courtesy of Ann Poppenheimer Sherrod and Dave Sherrod, Pop's Mail Order Collectible.*
$ Value, References: est $18-$30 (6,x)
$ Value, Internet Auctions: —; **# Sales:** —

Name: Last Drip;
Issued: 1996-current, ©1989
Comments: Original painting, child drinking *all* his Coke, by John Sandridge, *Just Smiles Series*, # three from artist; **Shape:** Std Rectangle; **Size:** 10.5" x 13.25"; **Story:** Yes; **Country:** US; **Mfr/Dist:** Ohio Art Company, distributed by Trademark Marketing; **Border/Edge:** Black, gold edge; **Quantity:** 15,500+.
$ Value, References: $8-$15 (3,6,x)
$ Value, Internet Auctions: $10; **# Sales:** 9

Name: Polar Bear Push; **Issued:** 1996-1998
Comments: Reproduction of 1995 TV ad, polar bear mother and polar bear babies in frozen Polar Bear Land with *unfrozen* bottles of Coke; **Shape:** Small Oval; **Size:** 8.5" x 11.0"; **Story:** Yes; **Country:** US; **Mfr/Dist:** Ohio Art Company, distributed by Trademark Marketing; **Border/Edge:** White, red stripe; **Quantity:** 41,000.
$ Value, References: est $7-$15 (6,x)
$ Value, Internet Auctions: $10; **# Sales:** 3

Name: Through All The Years II; **Issued:** 1996-1998, ©1994
Comments: Collage, more than fifty Coke Memorabilia items, by Sandra K. Porter, # two from artist; **Shape:** Std Rectangle; **Size:** 10.5" x 13.25"; **Story:** Yes; **Country:** US; **Mfr/Dist:** Ohio Art Company, distributed by Trademark Marketing; **Border/Edge:** Black; **Quantity:** 20,000.
$ Value, References: est $8-$20 (x)
$ Value, Internet Auctions: $7 (for info only); **# Sales:** 2

Name: Good Boys and Girls; **Issued:** 1996-current
Comments: Reproduction of 1951 ad, Santa and the list, by Haddon Sundblom; **Shape:** Std Rectangle; **Size:** 10.5" x 13.25"; **Story:** Yes; **Country:** US; **Mfr/Dist:** Ohio Art Company, distributed by Trademark Marketing; **Border/Edge:** Red, green trim; **Quantity:** 14,000+.
$ Value, References: est $8-$15 (6,x)
$ Value, Internet Auctions: $5 (for info only); **# Sales:** 2

1997

This year marks the 100th anniversary of the year that a single tray, *Victorian Girl*, became the first identified Coca-Cola tray. Thirteen trays are identified and pictured for this year, with eleven licensed for retail distribution.

The Signature Series adds five trays in 1997. Jeanne Mack has two, Jim Harrison does the third season in his *Autumn Bridge*, Pamela Renfroe and John Sandridge each complete one. Details on all these trays can be found in the captions under each picture.

Name: Autumn Bridge; **Issued:** 1997-current
Comments: Original painting, covered bridge with Coke sign, by Jim Harrison, # three from artist; **Shape:** Large Rectangle; **Size:** 13.5" x 18.5"; **Story:** Yes; **Country:** US; **Mfr/Dist:** Ohio Art Company, distributed by Trademark Marketing; **Border/Edge:** Black; **Quantity:** 17,000+.
$ Value, References: est $7-$15 (6,x)
$ Value, Internet Auctions: $7; **# Sales:** 5

Name: Gen. Mdse.; **Issued:** 1997-current
Comments: Original painting, general merchandise store, Coke sign, by Jeanne Mack, # seven from artist; **Shape:** Large Rectangle; **Size:** 13.5" x 18.5"; **Story:** Yes; **Country:** US; **Mfr/Dist:** Ohio Art Company, distributed by Trademark Marketing; **Border/Edge:** Black; **Quantity:** 13,000+.
$ Value, References: est $8-$15 (6,x)
$ Value, Internet Auctions: $10; **# Sales:** 5

Name: All Aboard;
Issued: 1997-current
Comments: Original painting, delivery truck and #290 4-6-2 steam locomotive, by Pamela C. Renfroe, # seven from artist; **Shape:** Std Rectangle; **Size:** 10.5" x 13.25"; **Story:** Yes; **Country:** US; **Mfr/Dist:** Ohio Art Company, distributed by Trademark Marketing; **Border/Edge:** Red; **Quantity:** 16,500+.
$ Value, References: est $8-$15 (6,x)
$ Value, Internet Auctions: —; **# Sales:** —

Name: Birdhouses; **Issued:** 1997-1998
Comments: Original painting, three birdhouses with one old small gasoline station for birds, Coke signs, by Jeanne Mack, # eight from artist; **Shape:** Std Rectangle; **Size:** 10.5" x 13.25"; **Story:** Yes; **Country:** US; **Mfr/Dist:** Ohio Art Company, distributed by Trademark Marketing; **Border/Edge:** Black; **Quantity:** 10,500.
$ Value, References: est $8-$15 (6,x)
$ Value, Internet Auctions: $12; **# Sales:** 5

Name: Clean Smile; **Issued:** 1997-current
Comments: Original painting, child shaving man's head, by John Sandridge, *Just Smiles Series*, # four from artist; **Shape:** Std Rectangle; **Size:** 10.5" x 13.25"; **Story:** Yes; **Country:** US; **Mfr/Dist:** Ohio Art Company, distributed by Trademark Marketing; **Border/Edge:** Black, gold edge; **Quantity:** 9,500+.
$ Value, References: est $8-$15 (6,x)
$ Value, Internet Auctions: $11; **# Sales:** 5

Two Coke Collectors commemorative trays include *Work Refreshed*, a 1993 reproduction that now has a sticker affixed to the back of the tray to note the *Badger Spring Pause*. The other commemorative is the popular *Smokey Bear* from the 23rd annual Coca-Cola Collectors convention. Part of the popularity and value of this tray is due to crossover interest from collectors of Smokey Bear memorabilia.

Two ad reproductions and a collage are licensed trays. The reproductions are a Santa tray from a 1952 ad and a striking, light green color tray picturing a beautiful woman who appeared in a 1950 U.S. ad, the 1951 Mexican calendar, and on a 1951 Mexican tray. The tray is called *Reanimese!* or *Refresh!* The collage is not a picture of Coke Memorabilia, but is more similar to the 1983 tray *Memphis, A Good Place to Be*. Wayland Moore created this image of twelve city scenes called *Atlanta – Our Town*.

Name: Gift for Thirst; **Issued:** 1997-current
Comments: Reproduction of 1952 ad, *. . . and now the gift for thirst . . .*, Christmas morning, by Haddon Sundblom; **Shape:** Long Rectangle; **Size:** 8.5" x 19.0"; **Story:** Yes; **Country:** US; **Mfr/Dist:** Ohio Art Company, distributed by Trademark Marketing; **Border/Edge:** Red; **Quantity:** 8,500+.
$ Value, References: est $7-$18 (6,x)
$ Value, Internet Auctions: $7 (for info only); **# Sales:** 1

Name: Work Refreshed, *Badger Spring Pause*; **Issued:** 1997
Comments: Back of tray pictured. Reproduction of 1941 ad, by Charles E. Heizerling, first reproduced as tray in 1993. This reissue adds sticker on the back to commemorate a Coca-Cola Collectors event, *Badger Spring Pause, 1987-1997, 10 Years on the Job*; **Shape:** Flat Rectangle; **Size:** 11.0" x 15.0"; **Story:** Yes; **Country:** US; **Mfr/Dist:** Ohio Art Company; **Border/Edge:** Red; **Quantity:** est 2,000; *Courtesy of John E. Peterson.*
$ Value, References: est $10-$18 (x)
$ Value, Internet Auctions: —; **# Sales:** —

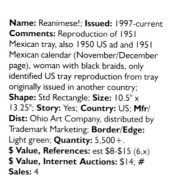

Name: Reanimese!; **Issued:** 1997-current
Comments: Reproduction of 1951 Mexican tray, also 1950 US ad and 1951 Mexican calendar (November/December page), woman with black braids, only identified US tray reproduction from tray originally issued in another country; **Shape:** Std Rectangle; **Size:** 10.5" x 13.25"; **Story:** Yes; **Country:** US; **Mfr/Dist:** Ohio Art Company, distributed by Trademark Marketing; **Border/Edge:** Light green; **Quantity:** 5,500+.
$ Value, References: est $8-$15 (6,x)
$ Value, Internet Auctions: $14; **# Sales:** 4

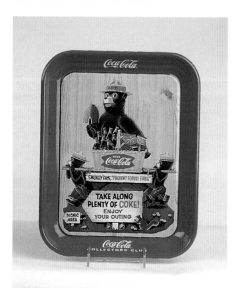

Name: Smokey Bear; **Issued:** 1997
Comments: Commemorative of 23rd National Convention, Coca-Cola Collectors, Colorado Springs, Colorado. Tray value increased by crossover of Smokey Bear collectors; **Shape:** Std Rectangle; **Size:** 10.5" x 13.25"; **Story:** Yes; **Country:** US; **Mfr/Dist:** —; **Border/Edge:** Red; **Quantity:** 2,000; *Courtesy of John E. Peterson.*
$ Value, References: est $45-$90 (x)
$ Value, Internet Auctions: $36; **# Sales:** 9

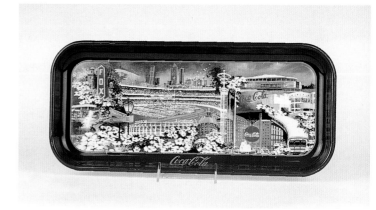

Name: Atlanta-Our Town; **Issued:** 1997-current
Comments: Collage of twelve city sights, by Wayland Moore; **Shape:** Long Rectangle; **Size:** 8.5" x 19.0"; **Story:** Yes; **Country:** US; **Mfr/Dist:** Ohio Art Company, distributed by Trademark Marketing; **Border/Edge:** Green; **Quantity:** 18,500+.
$ Value, References: est $8-$15 (6,x)
$ Value, Internet Auctions: $5 (for info only); **# Sales:** 2

Three additional *snack trays*, first listed in 1993, are copyrighted this year. The cropped images on the tray appear to be from paintings by Pamela C. Renfroe.

This year has seventeen identified trays, all pictured. Fifteen are licensed for retail distribution.

Five collage trays have already been listed in the 1990s. Three picture Coca-Cola memorabilia and contain over *ninety* items: *Through The Years*, the 1990 reissue, has at least thirty items; *Sign Art*, 1995, adds eleven; and *Through All the Years II*, 1996, contains at least fifty. All three were best selling trays. In 1998 four additional collage trays are added, with pictures of another *seventy* items. Twelve are on *1950s Six Pack Carton*, fourteen are on *Decades of Collectibles 1940s*, *Decades of Collectibles 1950s* adds sixteen, and *Tray of Trays* has twenty-six trays and coasters. These seven trays contain over *one hundred-sixty* Coke Memorabilia items. How many of them do YOU have?

Name: Snack Tray, Blue; **Issued:** c.1997
Comments: Tray reproduces part of image from *The Pause that Refreshes*, first tray by Pamela C. Renfroe; **Shape:** Snack Tray, Round; **Size:** 10.5" dia. x 2.5" depth, sloping sides; **Story:** —; **Country:** US; **Mfr/Dist:** The Tin Box Company; **Border/Edge:** Blue, four insets of image from different views, white trim; **Quantity:** —.
$ Value, References: est $5-$12 (x)
$ Value, Internet Auctions: $9 (for info only); **# Sales:** 2

Name: Snack Tray, Green; **Issued:** c.1997
Comments: Tray reproduces part of a painting from Pamela C. Renfroe, ©1993, that was later issued as a 1999 tray, *Looking Back*; **Shape:** Snack Tray, Round; **Size:** 10.5" dia. x 2.5" depth, sloping sides; **Story:** —; **Country:** US; **Mfr/Dist:** The Tin Box Company; **Border/Edge:** Green, four insets of image from different views, white trim; **Quantity:** —.
$ Value, References: est $5-$12 (x)
$ Value, Internet Auctions: $9 (for info only); **# Sales:** 2

Name: 1950s 6 Pack Carton; **Issued:** 1998-current
Comments: Collage, twelve signs and ads, 1902-1960; **Shape:** Deep Round; **Size:** 12.0"; **Story:** Yes; **Country:** US; **Mfr/Dist:** Ohio Art Company, distributed by Trademark Marketing; **Border/Edge:** Red; **Quantity:** 17,000+.
$ Value, References: est $8-$16 (x)
$ Value, Internet Auctions: $12.50; **# Sales:** 8

Name: Snack Tray, Red; **Issued:** c.1997
Comments: Tray has part of image resembling a Renfroe painting, but not identified with any painting in her series; **Shape:** Snack Tray, Round; **Size:** 10.5" dia. x 2.5" depth, sloping sides; **Story:** —; **Country:** US; **Mfr/Dist:** The Tin Box Company; **Border/Edge:** Red, four insets of image from different views, white trim; **Quantity:** —.
$ Value, References: est $5-$12 (x)
$ Value, Internet Auctions: $9 (for info only); **# Sales:** 2

Name: Decades of Collectibles, 1940s; **Issued:** 1998-current
Comments: Collage, fourteen items of Coca-Cola memorabilia, key on back of tray; **Shape:** Large Rectangle; **Size:** 13.5" x 18.5"; **Story:** Yes; **Country:** US; **Mfr/Dist:** Ohio Art Company, distributed by Trademark Marketing; **Border/Edge:** Green; **Quantity:** 10,000+.
$ Value, References: est $8-$15 (6,x)
$ Value, Internet Auctions: $9; **# Sales:** 4

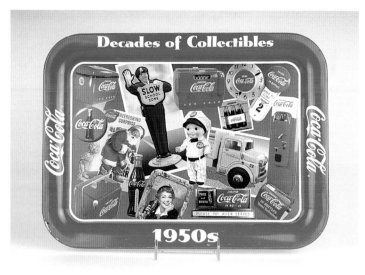

Name: Decades of Collectibles, 1950s; **Issued:** 1998-current
Comments: Collage, sixteen items of Coca-Cola memorabilia, key on back of tray;
Shape: Large Rectangle; **Size:** 13.5" x 18.5"; **Story:** Yes; **Country:** US; **Mfr/Dist:** Ohio Art Company, distributed by Trademark Marketing;
Border/Edge: Red; **Quantity:** 8,000+.
$ Value, References: est $8-$15 (6,x)
$ Value, Internet Auctions: $10; **# Sales:** 6

Eight 1998 *Signature Series* trays include four from Pamela Renfroe. Two are the second group of cross-licensed trays with Dairy Queen and John Deere. Jim Harrison, with his fourth tray, makes it through all the seasons with *Springtime Covered Bridge*. Two trays from Jeanne Mack paintings include the first of her popular lighthouses, another crossover collector item. *Sweet Memories*, by John Sandridge, is the first tray that is not one of the *Just Smiles* series.

Name: Refreshing Times; **Issued:** 1998-current
Comments: Original painting, 1955 scene at Dairy Queen, second DQ product tray cross-licensed, by Pamela C. Renfroe, # eight from artist;
Shape: Std Rectangle; **Size:** 10.5 x 13.25"; **Story:** Yes; **Country:** US;
Mfr/Dist: Ohio Art Company, distributed by Trademark Marketing;
Border/Edge: Green; **Quantity:** 10,000+.
$ Value, References: est $8-$15 (6,x)
$ Value, Internet Auctions: $10; **# Sales:** 9

Name: Tray of Trays; **Issued:** 1998-current
Comments: Collage, twenty-six items of Coca-Cola memorabilia (seventeen trays, six tip trays and three coasters), key on back of tray; **Shape:** Large Rectangle; **Size:** 13.5" x 18.5"; **Story:** Yes; **Country:** US; **Mfr/Dist:** Ohio Art Company, distributed by Trademark Marketing; **Border/Edge:** Red; **Quantity:** 4,000+.
$ Value, References: est $8-$15 (6,x)
$ Value, Internet Auctions: $14; **# Sales:** 5

Name: Virgil's Shop; **Issued:** 1998-current
Comments: Original painting, garage, John Deere Locke Mowers, second Deere tray cross-licensed, Pamela C. Renfroe, # nine from artist; **Shape:** Large Rectangle; **Size:** 13.5" x 18.5"; **Story:** Yes; **Country:** US; **Mfr/Dist:** Ohio Art Company, distributed by Trademark Marketing; **Border/Edge:** Picture extends into border; **Quantity:** 11,000+.
$ Value, References: est $8-$17 (6,x)
$ Value, Internet Auctions: $11; **# Sales:** 4

Name: Coca-Cola Goes Along; **Issued:** 1998-current
Comments: Original painting, 1930s airport and Waco F-5 airplane, by Pamela C. Renfroe, # ten from artist; **Shape:** Large Rectangle; **Size:** 13.5" x 18.5";
Story: Yes; **Country:** US; **Mfr/Dist:** Ohio Art Company, distributed by Trademark Marketing; **Border/Edge:** Red; **Quantity:** 10,000+.
$ Value, References: est $8-$18 (6,x)
$ Value, Internet Auctions: $11; **# Sales:** 15

Name: Coke by the Sea; **Issued:** 1998-current
Comments: Original painting, Cape Hatteras Lighthouse in Hatteras, North Carolina, by Jeanne Mack, # nine from artist, crossover interest with lighthouse collectors; **Shape:** Large Rectangle; **Size:** 13.5" x 18.5"; **Story:** Yes; **Country:** US; **Mfr/Dist:** Ohio Art Company, distributed by Trademark Marketing; **Border/Edge:** Black; **Quantity:** 13,500+.
$ Value, References: est $8-$15 (6,x)
$ Value, Internet Auctions: $11; **# Sales:** 25

Name: REA Brings a Nicer Day;
Issued: 1998-current
Comments: Original painting, electric lights arrive, also with John Deere products, by Pamela C. Renfroe, # eleven from artist; **Shape:** Large Rectangle; **Size:** 13.5" x 18.5"; **Story:** Yes; **Country:** US; **Mfr/Dist:** Ohio Art Company, distributed by Trademark Marketing; **Border/Edge:** Maroon; **Quantity:** 10,500+.
$ Value, References: est $8-$15 (6,x)
$ Value, Internet Auctions: $10;
 # Sales: 9

Name: The Old Sautee Store; **Issued:** 1998-current
Comments: Original painting, store in North Georgia, Coke sign, by Jeanne Mack, # ten from artist; **Shape:** Large Rectangle; **Size:** 13.5" x 18.5"; **Story:** Yes; **Country:** US; **Mfr/Dist:** Ohio Art Company, distributed by Trademark Marketing; **Border/Edge:** Image extends into border; **Quantity:** 17,500+.
$ Value, References: est $8-$17 (6,x)
$ Value, Internet Auctions: $9; **# Sales:** 7

Name: Springtime Covered Bridge; **Issued:** 1998-current
Comments: Original painting, covered bridge with Coke sign, by Jim Harrison, # four from artist (all the seasons now covered); **Shape:** Large Standard; **Size:** 13.5" x 18.5"; **Story:** Yes; **Country:** US; **Mfr/Dist:** Ohio Art Company, distributed by Trademark Marketing; **Border/Edge:** Green; **Quantity:** 5,000+.
$ Value, References: est $8-$15 (6,x)
$ Value, Internet Auctions: $10; **# Sales:** 7

Name: Sweet Memories; **Issued:** 1998-current
Comments: Original painting, Teddy bears and Coke bottles, by John Sandridge, # five from artist, *not* part of *Just Smiles Series*; **Shape:** Large Rectangle; **Size:** 13.5" x 18.5"; **Story:** Yes; **Country:** US; **Mfr/Dist:** Ohio Art Company, distributed by Trademark Marketing; **Border/Edge:** Blue; **Quantity:** 6,500+.
$ Value, References: est $8-$15 (6,x)
$ Value, Internet Auctions: $9; **# Sales:** 5

Name: Prom Night; **Issued:** 1998-current **Comments:** Reproduction of 1948 ad, teenagers around Coke cooler, by Haddon Sundblom; **Shape:** Large Rectangle; **Size:** 11.0" x 15.0"; **Story:** Yes; **Country:** US; **Mfr/Dist:** Ohio Art Company, distributed by Trademark Marketing; **Border/Edge:** Red; **Quantity:** 4,000+.
$ Value, References: est $8-$15 (6,x)
$ Value, Internet Auctions: $12; **# Sales:** 5

The year has five trays reproduced from ads. One is a 1923 Christmas ad *not* from a Santa image. *Prom Night*, reproduced from a 1948 ad, is another colorful image that so beautifully depicted life in America. As with so many of these images, the artist is Haddon Sundblom. A small tray of basketball and baseball playing polar bears is titled *Always*. Two ads are on Coke Collectors commemorative trays. One is a 1958 Santa ad on *Springtime in Atlanta*, celebrating the 20th Anniversary of this event. Two other trays for this event were dated 1981 and 1993. The 24th Annual Coke Collectors Convention is commemorated with a tray that reproduces a 1936 ad.

Name: Always Coca-Cola; **Issued:** c.1997-1998
Comments: Athletic bears playing basketball *and* baseball; **Shape:** Small Oval; **Size:** 8.5" x 11.0"; **Story:** —; **Country:** US; **Mfr/Dist:** Golden Harvest Products; **Border/Edge:** White; **Quantity:** —.
$ Value, References: est $5-$10 (x)
$ Value, Internet Auctions: $5; **# Sales:** 13

Name: Thirst Knows no Season; **Issued:** 1998-current
Comments: Reproduction of 1923 ad, Christmas holiday theme; **Shape:** Deep Round; **Size:** 13.5"; **Story:** Yes; **Country:** US; **Mfr/Dist:** Ohio Art Company, distributed by Trademark Marketing; **Border/Edge:** Gold; **Quantity:** 10,000, individually numbered.
$ Value, References: est $8-$15 (6,x)
$ Value, Internet Auctions: $12 (for info only); **# Sales:** 2

Name: Celebration of Santa; **Issued:** 1998-current **Comments:** Reproduction of 1958 ad, *The Pause that Refreshes*, by Haddon Sundblom, Commemorative of Coca-Cola Collectors Event, Springtime in Atlanta; **Shape:** Std Rectangle; **Size:** 10.5" x 13.25"; **Story:** Yes; **Country:** US; **Mfr/Dist:** Ohio Art Company, distributed by Trademark Marketing; **Border/Edge:** Dark Green, red stripe; **Quantity:** 2,000.
$ Value, References: est $15-$30 (6,x)
$ Value, Internet Auctions: $6; **# Sales:** 6

Name: Woman at Wheel of Boat; **Issued:** 1998
Comments: Reproduction of 1936 ad, commemorative of 24ᵗʰ National Convention, Coca-Cola Collectors, Minneapolis, Minnesota; **Shape:** Std Rectangle; **Size:** 10.5" x 13.25"; **Story:** Yes; **Country:** US; **Mfr/Dist:** —; **Border/Edge:** Gray; **Quantity:** 2,000.
$ Value, References: est $15-$30 (6,x)
$ Value, Internet Auctions: $14; **# Sales:** 4

Name: The Delivery; **Issued:** 1999-current
Comments: Collage, eight pictures, Coca-Cola delivery trucks dating from 1915;
Shape: Flat Rectangle; **Size:** 11.0" x 15.0"; **Story:** Yes; **Country:** US; **Mfr/Dist:** Distributed by Trademark Marketing; **Border/Edge:** Red; **Quantity:** —.
$ Value, References: est $8-$15 (x)
$ Value, Internet Auctions: $10; **# Sales:** 7

1999

The last year of the decade contains twenty-two trays, the most of any year of the 1990s. Twenty-one are shown in this section.

Two licensed trays, *Evolution* and *Delivery*, both picture change over time.

Collage trays issued in 1999 are different. These trays blend images from multiple ads rather than picturing a group of Coke Memorabilia or other items. One 1999 example, *Thank you, have a Coke*, reproduces models from ads of 1944, 1947, and 1948 and attempts to blend the three into the appearance of one image. Four 1999 Santa trays include three of these blended image collages. The best example is the deep round tray titled *Happy Holidays*. The caption detail lists six pieces of ads that were reproduced to create this tray. Why?

Name: Thank You, Have a Coke;
Issued: 1999-current, ©1999
Comments: Collage, reproductions from three 1940s ads, *left model 1947, center model 1948, right model 1944*, litho by J. V. Reed and Company; **Shape:** Flat Rectangle;
Size: 10.75" x 14.75"; **Story:** —;
Country: US;
Mfr/Dist: Sheadle Company;
Border/Edge: Black; **Quantity:** —.
$ Value, References: est $5-$12 (x)
$ Value, Internet Auctions: $6 (for info only); **# Sales:** 1

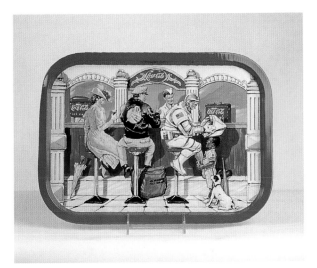

Name: Evolution; **Issued:** 1999, ©1998
Comments: Collage, people over time at soda fountain, 1890s *Gay '90s*, 1940s *The Fabulous Forties*, c.1990s *Astronauts*, plus young boy in baseball uniform, soda jerk, and dog. Note 1938 ad *Girl in White Bathing Suit* on leather jacket;
Shape: Large Flat Rectangle; **Size:** 11.5" x 15.75"; **Story:** Yes; **Country:** US;
Mfr/Dist: —; **Border/Edge:** Red; **Quantity:** —; *Courtesy of John E. Peterson.*
$ Value, References: est $18-$35 (x)
$ Value, Internet Auctions: $16 (for info only); **# Sales:** 1

Name: Happy Holidays; **Issued:** c.1998-1999-current
Comments: Reproduction of 1936 ad, *Old Santa says, Me Too*, Santa under tree with toys, by Haddon Sundblom. Back of tray: *Time to Pause*; **Shape:** Std Rectangle;
Size: 10.5" x 13.25"; **Story:** Yes; **Country:** US; **Mfr/Dist:** Distributed by Trademark Marketing; **Border/Edge:** Silver; **Quantity:** 2,000+.
$ Value, References: est $7-$12 (x)
$ Value, Internet Auctions: $11; **# Sales:** 5

Name: 1999 Season's Greeting; **Issued:** 1999-current
Comments: Collage, reproduction from two Santa ads: Santa with bag from *Wherever I Go*, c.1943; and the reindeer from 1949's *Travel Refreshed*, all original ads by Haddon Sundblom; **Shape:** Large Rectangle; **Size:** 13.5" x 18.5"; **Story:** Yes; **Country:** US; **Mfr/Dist:** Distributed by Trademark Marketing; **Border/Edge:** Gold; **Quantity:** 10,000.
$ Value, References: est $10-$18 (x)
$ Value, Internet Auctions: $9; **# Sales:** 5

Name: Santa, Happy Holidays; **Issued:** 1999
Comments: Collage, reproductions from multiple Santa ads: young girl on left and Santa's belt buckle, 1964; young girl on right, 1938; Santa's face and hand, 1960. On tray back: Santa's hat, face, and body, 1950; Santa's arm, 1949; Santa's hand with bottle 1951, all original ads by Haddon Sundblom, litho by J. V. Reed and Company; **Shape:** Deep Round; **Size:** 13.0" dia. x 1.75" depth; **Story:** —; **Country:** US; **Mfr/Dist:** Sheadle Company; **Border/Edge:** Green; **Quantity:** —.
$ Value, References: est $8-$15 (x)
$ Value, Internet Auctions: $9 (for info only); **# Sales:** 2

Name: Santa, Happy Holidays; **Issued:** 1999
Comments: Collage, reproductions from multiple Santa ads: Santa's face and hand, c.1943 (ad without a name); right arm, belt, and child, 1953; and the dog from 1961, all original ads by Haddon Sundblom. Back of tray treated to provide non-skid surface, litho by J. V. Reed and Company; **Shape:** Large Rectangle; **Size:** 10.75" x 14.75"; **Story:** —; **Country:** US; **Mfr/Dist:** Sheadle Company; **Border/Edge:** Green; **Quantity:** —.
$ Value, References: est $7-$15 (x)
$ Value, Internet Auctions: $6; **# Sales:** 3

Name: Santa, Happy Holidays; **Issued:** 1999
Comments: Back of round *Happy Holidays* tray.

Name: Santa, Happy Holidays; **Issued:** 1999
Comments: Back of tray, metal has been treated so that it is a non-skid surface.

Six *Signature Series* trays include two from Pamela Renfroe, bringing her total to thirteen, plus one each from Jeanne Mack, Jim Harrison, and John Sandridge. Those latter artists now total twenty-two trays, with Mack having eleven, Harrison five, and Sandridge six. The sixth *Signature Series* tray pictures the first painting from Steve Johnson. Add in the two *Signature Series* trays from Sandra Porter and the total of 1990s trays from these six artists totals thirty-eight over seven years.

Name: Looking Back; **Issued:** 1999-current, ©1993
Comments: Original painting, 1930s summer scene of general store and cars, by Pamela C. Renfroe, # twelve from artist; **Shape:** Large Rectangle; **Size:** 13.5" x 18.5"; **Story:** Yes; **Country:** US; **Mfr/Dist:** Ohio Art Company, distributed by Trademark Marketing; **Border/Edge:** Red; **Quantity:** —.
$ Value, References: est $8-$15 (x)
$ Value, Internet Auctions: $11; **# Sales:** 6

Name: Crossing-Creek Bridge; **Issued:** 1999-current
Comments: Original painting, covered bridge in green leafy setting, by Jim Harrison, # five from artist (is it *Spring* or *Summer* again?); **Shape:** Std Rectangle; **Size:** 10.5" x 13.25"; **Story:** Yes; **Country:** US; **Mfr/Dist:** Ohio Art Company, distributed by Trademark Marketing; **Border/Edge:** Image extends into border; **Quantity:** —.
$ Value, References: est $8-$15 (x)
$ Value, Internet Auctions: $10; **# Sales:** 7

Name: Summer Smiles;
Issued: 1999-current
Comments: Original painting, child on roller skates with band aids, by John Sandridge, # six from artist, # five in *Just Smiles Series*; **Shape:** Std Rectangle; **Size:** 10.5" x 13.25"; **Story:** Yes; **Country:** US; **Mfr/Dist:** Ohio Art Company, distributed by Trademark Marketing; **Border/Edge:** Black, gold edge; **Quantity:** 1,000+ (partial year only).
$ Value, References: est $8-$15 (x)
$ Value, Internet Auctions: $10; **# Sales:** 7

Name: Yuletide Delivery; **Issued:** 1999-current
Comments: Original painting, snow scene with Coca-Cola truck delivering to a store, by Pamela C. Renfroe, # thirteen from artist; **Shape:** Large Rectangle; **Size:** 13.5" x 18.5"; **Story:** Yes; **Country:** US; **Mfr/Dist:** Ohio Art Company, distributed by Trademark Marketing; **Border/Edge:** Red; **Quantity:** —.
$ Value, References: est $8-$15 (x)
$ Value, Internet Auctions: $11; **# Sales:** 3

Name: Boston Lighthouse;
Issued: 1999-current
Comments: Original painting, Boston Harbor Lighthouse, by Jeanne Mack, # eleven from artist, second lighthouse tray; **Shape:** Large Rectangle; **Size:** 13.5" x 18.5"; **Story:** Yes; **Country:** US; **Mfr/Dist:** Ohio Art Company, distributed by Trademark Marketing; **Border/Edge:** Yellow; **Quantity:** —.
$ Value, References: est $8-$15 (x)
$ Value, Internet Auctions: $12; **# Sales:** 14

Name: A Boy and His Dog; **Issued:** 1999-current
Comments: Original painting, boy and dog in front of brick wall with Coke ad, by Steve Johnson, # one from artist; **Shape:** Large Rectangle; **Size:** 13.5" x 18.5"; **Story:** Yes; **Country:** US; **Mfr/Dist:** Ohio Art Company, distributed by Trademark Marketing; **Border/Edge:** Image extends into Border; **Quantity:** 3,000+ (partial year only).
$ Value, References: est $8-$15 (x)
$ Value, Internet Auctions: $11; **# Sales:** 6

Relax Refreshed reproduces a beautiful c.1952-1954 ad by the artist Gil Elvgren. Two additional ad reproductions and an eclectic group of six miscellaneous trays, five pictured, complete the 1999 group.

Name: Travel Tray; **Issued:** 1999
Comments: Reproduction of 1907 glass change tray, same design on back of tray, litho by J. V. Reed and Company; **Shape:** Deep Round; **Size:** 13.0"; **Story:** —; **Country:** US; **Mfr/Dist:** Sheadle Company; **Border/Edge:** Black; **Quantity:** —.
$ Value, References: est $7-$12 (x)
$ Value, Internet Auctions: —; **# Sales:** —

Name: Relax Refreshed; **Issued:** 1999-current
Comments: Reproduction of c.1952-1954 ad, *Girl with Dog*, by Gil Elvgren. A young girl on sailboat, considered by many to be one of the most beautiful ads ever released by The Coca-Cola Company. **Shape:** Std Rectangle; **Size:** 10.5" x 13.25"; **Story:** Yes; **Country:** US; **Mfr/Dist:** Ohio Art Company, distributed by Trademark Marketing **Border/Edge:** Red; **Quantity:** 5,000 (partial year only).
$ Value, References: est $7-$15 (x)
$ Value, Internet Auctions: $12; **# Sales:** 8

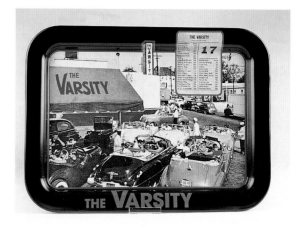

Name: The Varsity; **Issued:** 1999
Comments: Pictures c.1950s Atlanta landmark drive-in, established 1928, plus menu, Coke on menu for 5¢. *Not* a Coca-Cola Licensed tray; **Shape:** Std Rectangle; **Size:** 10.5" x 13.25"; **Story:** Yes; **Country:** US; **Mfr/Dist:** Distributed by Trademark Marketing for *The Varsity*;
Border/Edge: Black; **Quantity:** —.
$ Value, References: est $5-$10 (x)
$ Value, Internet Auctions: $12; **# Sales:** 11

Name: Ice Cold Coke Sold Here; **Issued:** 1999
Comments: Reproduction of 1934 ad, tin sign, litho by J. V. Reed and Company; **Shape:** Flat Rectangle; **Size:** 10.75" x 14.75"; **Story:** —; **Country:** US; **Mfr/Dist:** Sheadle Company; **Border/Edge:** Black; **Quantity:** —.
$ Value, References: est $7-$15 (x)
$ Value, Internet Auctions: $6; **# Sales:** 4

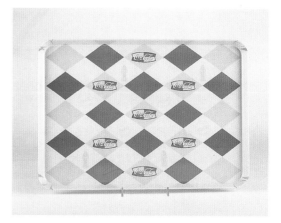

Name: Checkerboard *or* The Cafeteria Tray; **Issued:** 1999-current
Comments: Logo tray, fishtail logo c.1958-1964, heavy plastic; **Shape:** Large Rectangle; **Size:** 12.25" x 17.75"; **Story:** —; **Country:** US; **Mfr/Dist:** Mfr Italy, distributed by Trademark Marketing; **Border/Edge:** Light green; **Quantity:** —.
$ Value, References: est $15-$25 (x)
$ Value, Internet Auctions: $13 (for info only); **# Sales:** 1

Name: Polar Bears with Ice; **Issued:** 1999
Comments: Two bears sliding on ice, an adult bear and friendly seal look
on; **Shape:** Oval (wavy sides); **Size:** 12.0" x 16.0"; **Story:** —; **Country:**
US; **Mfr/Dist:** Giffoo, Inc.; **Border/Edge:** Red; **Quantity:** —.
$ Value, References: est $12-$25 (x)
$ Value, Internet Auctions: $9; **# Sales:** 6

Name: Enjoy Coca-Cola; **Issued:** c.1999
Comments: Tray face is metal with small center image,
c.1940s woman getting bottle of Coke from cooler; **Shape:**
Large Rectangle; **Size:** 12.5" x 16.5"; **Story:** —; **Country:**
— (Belgium?); **Mfr/Dist:** —; **Border/Edge:** Silver;
Quantity: —; *Courtesy of John E. Peterson.*
$ Value, References: est $8-$15 (x)
$ Value, Internet Auctions: —; **# Sales:** —

Name: Stars and Buttons; **Issued:** c.1999
Comments: Platter, with Stars and Buttons design, plastic; **Shape:**
Large Deep Oval; **Size:** 14.5" x 17.0" x 2.75"; **Story:** —; **Country:**
US; **Mfr/Dist:** Ullman Co.; **Border/Edge:** Dark blue; **Quantity:** —.
$ Value, References: est $5-$20 (x)
$ Value, Internet Auctions: —; **# Sales:** —

2000 and Beyond

This book identifies two trays from the year 2000. But, we can all
be sure more are out there . . . or will be soon. We can also be sure that
other trays from earlier years have not been identified in this effort. The
Internet, especially for items such as Coca-Cola memorabilia, really is
an international yard sale. Hardly a day of reviewing auctions passes
without identifying a previously unidentified tray.

One tray (not pictured) has the logo and characters from the Sydney
2000 Olympic Games. This tray can be categorized as a commemorative, although it certainly differs from all previous trays of this type as it
does not feature players, records, or posters. The last tray pictured is
titled *Pop's General Store*, and is licensed and distributed by Trademark
Marketing, International. It is not by any identified artist and not listed as
a *Signature Series* tray. New directions?

Name: Pop's General Store; **Issued:** 2000
Comments: New image of an older scene, story on back, artist not identified;
Shape: Std Rectangle; **Size:** 10.5" x 13.25"; **Story:** Yes (partial); **Country:** US; **Mfr/
Dist:** Mfr. China, distributed by Trademark Marketing; **Border/Edge:** Maroon,
Coca-Cola script logo in bottom border is centered in right half of tray;
Quantity: —.
$ Value, References: est $8-$12 (x)
$ Value, Internet Auctions: $10; **# Sales:** 3

Hopefully, readers will communicate if they know of additional trays,
are able to supply missing information, can complete incomplete data,
and/or correct incorrect items. If what has been presented in these
pages generates enough interest, a second edition would have the ability to update dollar values and present new and/or corrected information.

## Chapter Seven

Another Look: Tray Groups and Series

Chapters One through Six presented pictures and details on trays in chronological order. This chapter will sort many of the same trays into various groups and series, regardless of their year of issue. Some details are listed on each tray in a group, and the year issued or other references will guide the reader to the location of the picture in an earlier chapter.

The purpose of this chapter is to help avoid confusion, since many images are found on more than one tray, as well as to facilitate collectors who may want to concentrate on a specific area of interest. The tray groups featured in this chapter are listed below, followed by the detailed list on each. Note that a tray can be included in more than one group.

I. Reproduction Trays of Earlier Tray Images
II. Reproduction Trays of Earlier Advertising Images (Except Santa Claus)
III. Reproduction Trays of Earlier Santa Claus Advertising Images
IV. Commemorative Trays
V. Tray Groups or Series

For easy reference, the years covered in each previous Chapter and the page numbers are:

I. Reproduction Trays of Earlier Tray Images

Reproduction trays have images that first appeared on *classic* trays dating from 1897 through the 1960s. Beginning in 1968, twenty-four earlier trays have been reproduced at least once, some more than once. Eighty-four tray reproductions are listed below. All of the twenty-four original trays have pictures in Chapters One, Two, or Three. And, seventy-four of the reproductions have pictures in Chapters Three through Six. Details on the trays *without* pictures will be found in the Appendix.

The reproductions include fifty-six U.S. trays, seventeen Canadian, ten Italian, and one German. Eight of the twenty-four original trays have one identified reproduction; eight more have been reproduced twice. The remaining eight trays with three or more reproductions are listed below:

Summer Girl, 1921, and *Girl at Shade*, 1938, each have three identified reproduction trays.

Bottle 5¢, 1903, is found on four reproductions, all Coca-Cola bottler anniversary trays.

Lillian Nordica with Bottle, 1905, was the *first* original tray to be reproduced. This tray is found on seven reproductions.

The Coca-Cola Girl, 1910; *Elaine*, 1916; and *Flapper Girl*, 1923, are tied for second place with eight reproductions each. *Elaine* was reproduced in four shapes, all dated in the 1970s. *The Coca-Cola Girl* was reproduced in five shapes on trays of the 1970s and 1980s. The diversity champ of reproduction trays is *Flapper Girl*. Reproductions of this tray are found in five shapes, come from four countries, and are dated in three decades.

Hilda with Glass and Note, 1900, is found on *nineteen* reproductions, the most of any tray. All were round in shape and issued in the late 1970s.

Chapter One (1897-1919) has *eleven* of the twenty-four original trays found on a total of *fifty-six* reproductions.

Chapter Two (1920-1949) contains *ten* trays reproduced on *twenty-five* later trays.

Chapter Three (1950-1969) has the remaining *three* trays that were reproduced *three* times.

The reproduction trays first appear in Chapter Three, with two identified in 1968. They are concentrated in Chapter Four (1970-1979), when fifty-six trays were issued. Chapter Five (1980-1989) has twenty and Chapter Six (1990-1999) has six. In the following table, the first line of headings after each number provides the original tray name, year issued, shape, color, and country. The second line provides the total number of reproductions of that tray, the year issued, shape, color, country, and whether the reproduction was a commemorative tray (with the number of commemoratives if more than one tray).

Name of Original	Year Issued	Shape	Color/ Border	Country
(# of Repros)	Yr of Repro	Shape	Color/ Border	Country, Commemorative
1. Victorian Girl	**1897**	**Round**	**Red**	**US**
(1 repro)	1970s	Deep Round	Red	US
2. Hilda with Pen	**1899**	**Round**	**Black**	**US**
(1 repro)	1987	Flat Round	Black	US
3. Hilda with Glass	**1900**	**Round**	**Red**	**US**
(19 repros)	1976	Flat Round	Red	US
	1976	Flat Round	Red	US, Commem (8)
	1977	Flat Round	Red	US, Commem (10)*
4. Hilda with Roses	**1901**	**Round**	**Black**	**US**
(2 repros)	1975	Std Rect	Red	US, Commem
	1985	Lge Rect	Black	US
5. Bottle 5¢	**1903**	**Round**	**Yellow**	**US**
(4 repros)	1978	Round	Yellow	US, Commem (3)**
	1980	Round	Yellow	US, Commem
6. L. Nordica w/Bottle	**1905**	**Oval**	**Green**	**US**
(7 repros)	1968	Flat Rect	Green	English Can.*
	1968	Flat Rect	Green	French Can.
	1975	Std Rect	Green	US, Commem
	1977	Std Rect	Green	US, Commem (3)
	1977	Std Rect	Green	Italy, Commem*
7. Relieves Fatigue	**1907**	**Oval**	**Gold**	**US**
(2 repros)	1981	Lge Dp Oval	Brown	US, Commem
	1982	Std Rect	Maroon	US, Commem
8. Coca-Cola Girl	**1910**	**Std Rect**	**Red**	**US**
(8 repros)	1971	Flat Rect	Red	English Can.*
	1971	Flat Rect	Red	French Can.
	1972	Flat Rect	Red	US
	1972	Std Rect	Gold	US
	1980s	Std Rect	Yellow	US
	1980s	Lge Rect	Yellow/Red	US

Name of Original	Year Issued	Shape	Color/ Border	Country
(# of Repros)	Yr of Repro	Shape	Color/ Border	Country, Commemorative
8. Coca-Cola Girl	1980s	Lge Rect	Red/Glass	US*
(cont'd)	1982	Round	Red	Italy
9. Hamilton King Girl	**1913**	**Std Rect**	**Black**	**US**
(2 repros)	1973	Std Rect	Green	US
	1988	Deep Round	Red	Italy
10. Betty Girl	**1914**	**Std Rect**	**Black**	**US**
(2 repros)	1973	Lge Dp Oval	Black	US
	1980s	Deep Round	Dark Blue	US
11. Elaine	**1916**	**Long Rect**	**Gold**	**US**
(8 repros)	1970s	Long Rect	Gold	US
	1973	Long Rect	Gold	US
	1976	Flat Oval	Yellow	English Can.
	1976	Flat Oval	Yellow	French Can.
	1976	Lge Flt Oval	Yellow	English Can.
	1976	Lge Flt Oval	Yellow	French Can.
	1976	Flat Oval	Yellow	Can., Commem
	1979	Std Rect	Orange	Italy, Commem
12. Golfer Girl	**1920**	**Std Rect**	**Red**	**US**
(1 repro)	1980	Std Rect	Green	Can., Commem
13. Summer Girl	**1921**	**Std Rect**	**Black/Gold**	**US**
(3 repros)	1984	Std Rect	Beige	Italy, Commem*
	1991	Sm Rect	Blue	US
	1991	Sm Rect	Blue	US, Commem
14. Autumn Girl	**1922**	**Std Rect**	**Black**	**US**
(2 repros)	1974	Long Rect	Gold	US
	1983	Long Rect	Green	US
15. Flapper Girl	**1923**	**Std Rect**	**Black**	**US**
(8 repros)	1974	Lge Dp Oval	Brown	US
	1974	Round	Dk Green	German*
	1979	Std Rect	Brown	English Can.
	1980	Std Rect	Brown	Can., Commem
	1983	Lge Dp Oval	Brown	US
	1986	Std Rect	Maroon	Italy, Commem
	1987	Deep Round	Green	Italy
	1995	Sm Dp Rect	Green	Italy
16. Party Girl	**1925**	**Std Rect**	**Black**	**US**
(2 repros)	1974	Std Rect	Brown	US
	1982	Std Rect	Green	Italy, Commem
17. Golfers	**1926**	**Std Rect**	**Red**	**US**
(2 repros)	1976	Flat Rect	Red	English Can.
	1976	Flat Rect	Red	French Can.
18. Barefoot Boy	**1931**	**Std Rect**	**Red**	**US**
(2 repros)	1991	Sm Flat Rect	Red	US
	1990s	Std Rect	Yellow	Italian*
19. Tarzan	**1934**	**Std Rect**	**Red**	**US**
(1 repro)	1970s	Std Rect	Red	US
20. Running Girl	**1937**	**Std Rect**	**Red**	**US**
(1 repro)	1970s	Std Rect	Red	US
21. Girl at Shade	**1938**	**Std Rect**	**Red**	**US**
(3 repros)	1977	Flat Oval	Brown	English Can.
	1977	Lge Flt Oval	Brown	English Can.
	1977	Lge Flt Oval	Brown	French Can.
22. Girl w/Wind ...	**1950**	**Std Rect**	**Red**	**US**
(1 repro)	1980s	Std Rect	Red	US
23. Woman w/Braids	**1951**	**Std Rect**	**Yellow/Red**	**Mex.**
(1 repro)	1997	Std Rect	Teal	US
24. Candlelight	**1962**	**TV**	**Brown**	**US**
(1 repro)	1972	TV	Brown	US*

Indicates a tray(s) not pictured in the chronological Chapters

Name: Victorian Girl; **Issued:** 1897
Comments: The first identified tray; **Shape:** Round; **Size:** 9.375";
Country: US; **Border/Edge:** Red, with Cola Beans; **Found In:** Chapter One.

Name: Victorian Girl;
Issued: 1970s
Comments: Reproduction of the first tray;
Shape: Deep Round;
Size: 12.25" dia. x 1.75" depth; **Country:** US;
Border/Edge: Red;
Found In: Chapter Four.

II. Reproduction Trays of Earlier Advertising Images (Except Santa Claus)

This section lists trays with images reproduced from earlier advertising materials dating from around the beginning of the twentieth century through television ads of the early 1990s. Note that the eighty-four trays reproduced from earlier *tray* images are not listed in this section (they are found in the section above), although many of those images were also found on advertising items of the same time period. Similarly, the forty-six *Santa* trays reproduced from ads are not shown here (but will be found in the section following this one).

One hundred eleven trays have been reproduced from eighty earlier ads. Sixteen advertising images are found on more than one tray and total forty-seven of the reproductions. The 1904 calendar of *Lillian Nordica with Sign* is found on *seven* trays, the most of any advertising image. *Four Seasons*, 1922, is on five trays. While hundreds of ads were reviewed to confirm the listed tray reproductions, some have probably been missed. Reference materials on international advertising images are not as well documented as U.S. ads. Eighty of the reproduction trays are U.S, Italy has sixteen, Canada and Mexico have five each, and three other countries have a total of five trays.

Ads that have been reproduced are concentrated in the classic collectible period. By decades the totals are: 1800s through 1909 (11), 1910-1919 (10), 1920-1929 (10), 1930-1939 (17), 1940-1949 (18), 1950-1959 (11), 1980-1989 (1), and 1990-1999 (2).

Trays from ad reproductions are spread over the same four "recent" decades as reproductions from earlier trays. One hundred-five of the 111 listed trays are pictured. Chapter Three has three (in the 1960s), Chapter Four (1970-1979) contains ten, Chapter Five (1980-1989) has thirty-nine and Chapter Six (1990-1999) lists the highest number, fifty-nine—over fifty percent of the total trays from ad reproductions.

A name or description of the ad is generally used in the list rather than attempting to name or describe one or more types of ad materials, since images usually appeared on multiple items. The list is in order by date of ad and trays are listed with the ads they reproduce. Shape, color, and country are included to help differentiate similar trays.

# Name of Ad	Year of Ad	Year of Repro	Shape	Color/ Border	Country
1. Girl w/ Tennis Racquet	1891	c.1992-95	Sm Dp Rect	Teal	Italy
2. Hilda with The Glass	1900	c.1992-95	Sm Dp Rect	Silver	Italy
3. Ask at the Soda Fountain	c.1900	1992	Sm Rect	Green	US
4. Girl with Pansies	1901	c.1992-95	Sm Dp Rect	Maroon	Italy
5. Drink Coca-Cola 5¢	1901	c.1992-95	Sm Dp Rect	Red	Italy*
6. Lillian Nordica w/Sign	1904	1969	Flt Rect	Yellow	Eng Can.
		1969	Flt Rect	Yellow	Frn Can.
		1978	Std Rect	Yellow	US, C (3)
		1979	Std Rect	Yellow	US, C
		1990s	Sm Rect	Yellow	Italy
7. Baseball (Massengale Ad)	1907	1989	Std Rect	Red	US
8. Keep Cool (Uncle Sam)	1907	1994	Flt Rect	Red	US
9. Drink Coca-Cola 5¢	1907	1999	Dp Round	Blk/Yel	US
10. Soda Fountain	c.1908	1980s	Round	Brown	US
		1989	Lg Rect	Blue	US
11. Lady in Red	1908	1987	Lg Dp Oval	Black	US
12. Gibson Girl	1910	1980s	Dp Round	Brown	US
13. Duster Girl	1911	1972	Flt Rect	Red	Eng Can.
		1972	Flt Rect	Red	Frn Can.
		1980s	Std Rect	Red/Org	US
		1980s	Std Rect	Red	US
14. Duster Girls	1912	c.1985	Lg Dp Oval	Black	US
		1988	Lg Dp Oval	Black	US, C*
15. 1912 Calendar Girl	1912	1991	Lg Dp Oval	Dk Blue	US
16. Syrup Label	c.1914	c.1981	Flt Round	Red	US
17. Supremely Satisfying	1914	1992	Sm Rect	Black	US
18. Constance	1917	1987	Dp Round	Red	Mex.
		c.1993	Rnd, Snack	Blue	US
19. Atlantic City Girl	1918	c.1985	Long Rect	Black	US
		c.1993	Rnd, Snack	Green	US
20. Girls at the Seashore	1918	1987	Dp Round	Red	Mex.
		c.1993	Rnd, Snack	Red	US
		c.1993	Rnd, Snack	Red	US
21. Girl with Glass	1919	1980s	Lg Rect	Red	US
		1980s	Round	Red	US
		1980s	Oval, Tip	Red	US
22. Circus Has Come ...	1920	1991	Std Rect	Red	US
23. Court Day	1921	1990	Std Rect	Red	US
24. Four Seasons	1922	1981	Lg Dp Oval	Blk/Yel	US
		1981	Lg Dp Oval	Blk/Yel	US, C*
		1984	Lg Dp Oval	Blk/Yel	US, C*
		1980s	Lg Rect	Red	US
		1990	Sm Rect	Black	US
25. Thirst Knows no Seas.	1923	1998	Dp Round	Gold	US
26. Lady with Mums	c.1923	1987	Flt Rect	Black	US
		1987	Flt Rect	Black	US
27. Swimsuit Girls	1924	1991	Lg Rect	Blue	France
28. Touring Car	1924	1987	Lg Rect	Red	US
		1987	Lg Rect	Red	US (lap)

# Name of Ad	Year of Ad	Year of Repro	Shape	Color/ Border	Country
28. Touring Car (cont'd)		1989	Lg Rect	Red	US, C
		1990	Lg Rect	Red	US, C
29. What's Really Good ...	1926	1992	Sm Flt Rect	Black	US
30. 1927 Calendar Girl	1927	1974	Flt Rect	Maroon	Can.
		1979	Lg Rect	Black	Mex.
		1981	Std Rect	Blue	Italy, C*
31. Women with bottles ...	1929	1976	Dp Round	Black	Mex.
32. The Old Oaken Bucket	1932	1981	Std Rect	Black	US
33. The Village Blacksmith	1933	1982	Lg Flt Oval	Blk/Red	US
		1987	Std Rect	Red	US
34. Old Kentucky Home	1934	1981	Std Rect	Blk/Gld	US
35. Ice Cold Coke (Sign)	1934	1999	Lg Rect	Black	US
36. Out Fishin'	1935	1981	Std Rect	Black	US
		c.1992-95	Sm Dp Rect	Green	Italy
37. Boys on the Curb	1935	1993	Sm Flt Rect	Red	US
38. Sea Captain	1936	1987	Sm Flt Rect	Yellow	US
39. Circus Scene	1936	1990s	Dp Round	Red	Arg.
40. Woman at Helm of Boat	1936	1998	Std Rect	Grey	US, C
41. Boy and Dog	1937	1988	Std Rect	Green	Italy, C
42. Blue Lady (Magazine)	1937	1992	Flt Round	Blue	US
43. Mother and Daughter...	1937	1990s	Dp Round	Red	Arg.
44. Girl in Wht Bathing Suit	1938	c.1992-95	Sm Dp Rect	White	Italy
45. 7 Million a Day	c.1930	1990	Lg Rect	Red	US
46. Whatddya, Know?	c.1930s	1993	Std Rect	Black	US
47. Lady with Pansies	c.1930s	1987	Long Rect	Black	US
48. Thirst asks nothing ...	c.1930s	1992	Sm Flt Rect	Orange	US*
49. Sprite Boy w/ Bottle	1941	1960	Lg Rect	Red	Mex.
		c.1992-95	Sm Dp Rect	Red	Italy
50. Work Refreshed	1941	1993	Flt Rect	Red	US
		1997	Flt Rect	Red	US, C
51. Female Aviator	1941	c.1992-95	Sm Dp Rect	Red	Italy
52. Couple with Snowman	1942	c.1992-95	Sm Dp Rect	Gold	Italy
53. Howdy Friend	1942	1992	Flt Rect	Red	US
54. Welcome	1943	1991	Long Rect	Red	US
55. After the Tattoo Artist	1944	1977	Lg Irreg Oval	Green	UK
56. He's Coming Home ...	1944	1991	Sm Flt Rect	Green	US
57. The Family	1945	1991	Flt Round	Maroon	US
58. Why Grow Thirsty?	1945	1993	Std Rect	White	US, C
59. Sprite Boy w/ Carton	1946	c.1992-95	Sm Dp Rect	Red	Italy
60. Winter Girl	1948	c.1992-95	Sm Dp Rect	Green	Italy
61. Have a Coke (Couple)	1948	1991	Lg Rect	Red	US
62. Pause for Coke (Baseball)	1948	1992	Sm Flt Rect	Red	US
63. Shop Refreshed	1948	1995	Long Rect	Yellow	US
64. Prom Night	1948	1998	Flt Rect	Red	US
65. Hospitality (Couples)	1940s	1990s	Dp Round	Red	Arg.
66. Refreshing (Hat & Veil)	c.1940s	1980s	Dp Round	Brown	Italy
67. Drive Refreshed	1950	1990	Long Rect	Red	US
68. Travel Refreshed	1950	1991 (2)	Long Rect	Red	US
69. Play Refreshed	1950	1992	Long Rect	Red	US
70. Reflections in the Mirror	1950	1993	Std Rect	Green	US
71. Sprite Boy	1951	1982	Std Rect	Red	US, C
72. To Play Refreshed	1951	1990	Long Rect	Red	US
73. Girl's Softball Team	1952	1994	Flt Round	Blue	US
74. Relax Refreshed	c.1952	1999	Std Rect	Red	US
75. Hand with Bottle	1956	1987	Sm Dp Rect	Blue	Italy, C
76. Be Really Refreshed	1958	1992	Sm Flt Rect	Red	US
77. Family Drive-In	1958	1995	Std Rect	Black	US
78. Refreshment Time	c.1980s	1980s	Oval	White	US, C
79. Always Cool (TV Ad)	c.1992	1993	Std Rect	Red	US
80. Polar Bear Push (TV Ad)	1995	1996	Sm Oval	White	US

C= commemorative

*Indicates a tray that is not pictured in the chronological Chapters

III. Reproduction Trays of Earlier Santa Claus Advertising Images

The Santa Claus created by Haddon Sundblom is considered by many to define the look of Santa in the twentieth century. Several reference books in the Bibliography have sections on Santa ads and other advertising items that have appeared since the 1930s. Two of the most comprehensive are *The Illustrated Guide to the Collectibles of Coca-Cola* by Cecil Munsey and *Dream of Santa, Haddon Sundblom's Advertising Paintings for Christmas, 1931-1964* by Barbara Fahs Charles and J. R. Taylor.

Coca-Cola in the refrigerator, Coke instead of milk under the tree or on the fireplace mantle for Santa, Coke as a reward for Santa's work, and Santa's list of Good Boys and Girls are some of the familiar images created in these ads (and trays).

Name: Santa Dolls; **Issued:** Black boots: 1950s, white boots: 1970s
Comments: Two Santa dolls by Rushton Mfg., examples of the many other types of Coke advertising items created using the image of Sundblom's Santas; **Size:** 15.0"-16.0"; *Courtesy of Michele LaMarca.*

In addition to his Santa images, Sundblom created other paintings that appeared in Coca-Cola advertising items and on trays. *Skater Girl*, 1941, and *Girl with Wind in Hair*, 1950, are two examples. The artist also created *Sprite Boy*, reproduced on several trays.

The Santa trays provide an interesting specialty for a collector. The trays are colorful, not impossible to find, not too expensive to acquire, and fun!

Forty-six trays are listed. They reproduce over twenty Santa ads that originally appeared in the 1930s, 1940s, 1950s, and 1960s. Twenty-nine trays are dated in the 1990s, fourteen from the 1980s, and three from the 1970s. No *original* tray has been found with a Santa image (i.e., a tray dated within a year or two of the first appearance of the original ad).

Pictures of original magazine advertisements have been used in this section to show the relationship between the original ad and the reproduction trays (as pictured in Chapters Four through Six).

Santa Ads From the 1930s

Three 1930s ads were reproduced on a total of six trays.

The 1935 ad *It Will Refresh You Too* appears on two very different looking reproductions. The first tray commemorates the anniversary of an Ohio supermarket chain while the other is a 1990s Italian promotional tray.

In 1936 the ad *Old Santa says: "Me too"* shows Santa under a Christmas tree, surrounded by toys. It has been reproduced twice. In the 1999 reproduction, note that Santa has a bag of toys as well as a few other changes not in the original ad. But Sundblom also created variations of many of his ads and reused certain items in subsequent years. This 1936 ad was redone in 1962, with an updated Santa and more modern toys.

When *Thanks for the Pause that Refreshes* was created in a 1938 ad, the slogan had been in use for ten years. This ad has also been reproduced twice.

Name: It will Refresh You; **Issued:** 1935
Comments: December, 1935 ad, *National Geographic Magazine*.

#1-Reproduction Name: Big Bear Supermarket; **Issued:** 1984
Comments: Commemorative of 50th Anniversary of Customer. Reproduction of 1935 ad; **Shape:** Large Rectangle; **Size:** 13.5" x 18.5"; **Country:** US; **Border/Edge:** Gold; **Found In:** Chapter Five.

#2-Reproduction Name: Santa, Refreshing Times; **Issued:** c.1992-1995
Comments: Reproduction of the top part of 1935 ad. On this tray the wreath is added for the reproduction; **Shape:** Small Rectangle; **Size:** 8.0" x 11.0" x 1.0"; **Country:** Italy; **Border/Edge:** Red; **Found In:** Chapter Six.

Name: Old Santa says, "Me too"; **Issued:** 1936
Comments: December, 1936 ad, *National Geographic Magazine.*

#1-Reproduction Name: Can't Beat the Feeling; **Issued:** 1989
Comments: Reproduction of 1936 ad, *Old Santa says, "Me too"*; **Shape:** Small Flat Rectangle; **Size:** 10.5" x 14.0"; **Country:** US; **Border/Edge:** Red; **Found In:** Chapter Five.

#2-Reproduction Name: Happy Holidays; **Issued:** 1999-current
Comments: Reproductions of 1936 ad, *Old Santa says, "Me too,"* back of tray words: *Time to Pause*; **Shape:** Std Rectangle; **Size:** 10.5" x 13.25"; **Country:** US; **Border/Edge:** Silver; **Found In:** Chapter Six.

Santa Ads From the 1940s

Ad materials from this decade are used on ten reproduction trays. Three ads are pictured below that account for four reproduction trays. Three ads are not pictured, although one in 1948 is a variation of the ad pictured for 1947. Not all of the Sundblom Santa ads and their variations appeared as magazine ads. Some images were only found on cardboard cutout signs, billboards, or other types of ad items.

The first full-length image of Santa is in the 1942 ad *That Extra Something! . . .* The green banner was used in other ads supporting the country during World War II. The 1992 reproduction tray has again added a bag of toys.

Wherever I Go, a 1943 ad with a World War II theme, is reproduced on three trays. Two show Santa with war bonds in his bag. This image was originally a cardboard sign and no magazine ad has been identified. Note that in the c.1992 Italian reproduction, additional *toys* replace the bonds. *They knew what I wanted,* from 1945, was used on billboards; a magazine ad of the image has not been found. The 1992 reproduction is one of the two long rectangle shapes found in Santa trays.

Several ad variations in 1947 and 1948 were titled *Busy Man's Pause* or *Hospitality.* The theme was Santa working on toys, sometimes in front of a refrigerator. A 1947 ad is shown here. Three trays reproduce 1947 and 1948 versions of this theme.

Only one ad had Santa actually drinking a bottle of Coca-Cola. That 1949 ad, with Sprite Boy and reindeer, is called *Travel Refreshed.* It has been reproduced twice.

Name: Thanks for the Pause; **Issued:** 1938
Comments: December, 1938 ad, *National Geographic Magazine.*

#1-Reproduction Name: Thanks for the Pause; **Issued:** 1983
Comments: Reproduction of 1938 ad; **Shape:** Std Rectangle; **Size:** 10.5" x 13.25"; **Country:** US; **Border/Edge:** Green with trim; **Found In:** Chapter Five

#2-Reproduction Name: Thanks for the Pause that Refreshes; **Issued:** 1995-1996
Comments: Reproduction of 1938 ad; **Shape:** Small Deep Oval; **Size:** 8.5" x 11.0"; **Country:** US; **Border/Edge:** Red; **Found In:** Chapter Six

Name: That Extra Something! They Remembered Me; **Issued:** 1942
Comments: December, 1942 ad, *National Geographic Magazine.*

#1-Reproduction Name: Season's Greetings; **Issued:** 1992-1998
Comments: Reproduction of 1942 ad; **Shape:** Std Rectangle; **Size:** 10.5" x 13.25"; **Country:** US; **Border/Edge:** Red; **Found In:** Chapter Six.

Name: Wherever I Go (1943 ad, no picture):

#1-Reproduction Name: Wherever I Go; **Issued:** 1991-1996
Comments: Reproduction of c.1943 ad, war bonds in Santa's bag; **Shape:** Small Flat Rectangle; **Size:** 10.5" x 14.0"; **Country:** US; **Border/Edge:** Red; **Found In:** Chapter Six.

#2-Reproduction Name: Santa Around the World; **Issued:** 1991-1996
Comments: Reproduction (with variation) of c.1943 ad, *Wherever I Go*; **Shape:** Round; **Size:** 12.0"; **Country:** US; **Border/Edge:** White; **Found In:** Chapter Six.

#3-Reproduction Name: Wherever I Go; **Issued:** c.1992-1995
Comments: Reproduction (with variation) of c.1943 ad, Santa's bag has all toys and no war bonds; **Shape:** Small Rectangle; **Size:** 8.0" x 11.0" x 1.0"; **Country:** Italy; **Border/Edge:** Gold; **Found In:** Chapter Six.

Name: They knew what I wanted (1945 ad, no picture):

#1-Reproduction Name: They Knew What I Wanted; **Issued:** 1992-1999
Comments: Reproduction of 1945 ad, end of WWII, the theme is *return*; **Shape:** Long Rectangle; **Size:** 8.5" x 19.0"; **Country:** US; **Border/Edge:** Red; **Found In:** Chapter Six.

Name: Travel Refreshed; **Issued:** 1949
Comments: December, 1949 ad, *National Geographic Magazine*.

#1-Reproduction Name: Santa; **Issued:** 1992-1997
Comments: Reproduction of 1949 ad, *Travel Refreshed*; **Shape:** Round; **Size:** 12.5"; **Country:** US; **Border/Edge:** Green, gold edge; **Found In:** Chapter Six.

#2-Reproduction Name: Travel Refreshed; **Issued:** c.1992-1995
Comments: Reproduction of 1949 ad; **Shape:** Small Rectangle; **Size:** 8.0" x 11.0" x 1.0"; **Country:** Italy; **Border/Edge:** Green; **Found In:** Chapter Six.

Santa Ads From the 1950s

Fourteen trays reproduce ads from the 1950s. The ads from this decade have been responsible for the highest number of reproduction trays.

Good Boys and Girls, a 1951 ad, has been reproduced *five* times in *four* different tray shapes. The image is an updated version of Santa working at his North Pole desk on the important list showing who is naughty versus who is nice. Note that in Sundblom's and Coke's version the list contains only the *nice* (or *good*) girls and boys. Two reproductions, from 1983 and 1989, initially look identical in the pictures but the trays are in two sizes and the picture is cut or cropped differently on each tray.

Santa ads were sometimes created in horizontal *and* vertical versions. The 1952 ad, *. . . and now the gift for thirst . . .* is shown here in a vertical version. A 1993 tray was reproduced from that version and a 1997 tray uses the horizontal version of the ad (not pictured).

Some years, such as 1952, have one ad in multiple versions; other years have more than one ad image for that year's advertising materials. An example of the latter instance is the year 1953. *The Pause that refreshes . . .* is found on two trays (ad not pictured) and *For Sparkling Holidays*, a view of Santa's North Pole Workshop, is found on one tray.

Several ads show Santa resting and relaxing with a fawn nearby. One such ad in 1958 titled *The Pause That Refreshes*, was reproduced on two trays. One tray commemorates a 1998 Coke Collectors meeting.

The 1959 ad *Refreshing Surprise* is reproduced on two 1990s Italian trays that differ only in the border color.

Name: Hospitality in Your Refrigerator; **Issued:** 1947
Comments: December, 1947 ad, *National Geographic Magazine*. (Note that #2 and #3 below are reproductions from a 1948 variation of this ad.)

#1-Reproduction Name: Busy Man's Pause; **Issued:** 1990-1991
Comments: Reproduction of 1947 ad, *Hospitality*; **Shape:** Large Rectangle; **Size:** 13.5" x 18.5"; **Country:** US; **Border/Edge:** Green, red ribbon trim; **Found In:** Chapter Six.

#2-Reproduction Name: Hospitality; **Issued:** 1987-1991
Comments: Reproduction of 1948 ad; **Shape:** Large Deep Oval; **Size:** 12.5" x 15.5"; **Country:** US; **Border/Edge:** Red; **Found In:** Chapter Five.

#3-Reproduction Name: Hospitality; **Issued:** c.1992-1995
Comments: Reproduction of 1948 ad; **Shape:** Small Rectangle; **Size:** 8.0" x 11.0" x 1.0"; **Country:** Italy; **Border/Edge:** Green; **Found In:** Chapter Six.

Name: Good Boys and Girls; **Issued:** 1951
Comments: December, 1951 ad, *National Geographic Magazine*. Ad words: *. . . talk about being good!*

#1-Reproduction Name: Good Boys and Girls; **Issued:** 1983
Comments: Reproduction of 1951 ad; **Shape:** Std Rectangle; **Size:** 10.5" x 13.25"; **Country:** US; **Border/Edge:** Green with trim; **Found In:** Chapter Five.

#2-Reproduction Name: Good Boys and Girls; **Issued:** 1989
Comments: Reproduction of 1951 ad; **Shape:** Large Rectangle; **Size:** 13.5" x 18.5"; **Country:** US; **Border/Edge:** Green with trim; **Found In:** Chapter Five.

#3-Reproduction Name: Good Boys and Girls; **Issued:** c.1992-1995
Comments: Reproduction of 1951 ad; **Shape:** Small Rectangle; **Size:** 8.0" x 11.0" x 1.0"; **Country:** US; **Border/Edge:** Red; **Found In:** Chapter Six.

#4-Reproduction Name: Good Boys and Girls; **Issued:** c.1994
Comments: Reproduction of 1951 ad; **Shape:** Cookie Tray, Round; **Size:** 13.125"; **Country:** US; **Border/Edge:** Red, Green, Gold, Holiday trim; **Found In:** Chapter Six..

#5-Reproduction Name: Good Boys and Girls; **Issued:** 1997-current
Comments: Reproduction of 1951 ad; **Shape:** Std Rectangle; **Size:** 10.5" x 13.25"; **Country:** US; **Border/Edge:** Red, green trim; **Found In:** Chapter Six.

Name: The Pause That Refreshes (1953 ad, no picture):

#1-Reproduction Name: The Pause That Refreshes; **Issued:** 1981
Comments: Reproduction of 1953 ad, Santa in chair, two children serve him Coke; **Shape:** Std Rectangle; **Size:** 10.5" x 13.25"; **Country:** US; **Border/Edge:** Black, Holiday trim; **Found In:** Chapter Five.

#2-Reproduction Name: The Pause That Refreshes; **Issued:** 1995
Comments: Reproduction of 1953 ad, Santa in chair, two children serve him Coke; **Shape:** Small Deep Oval; **Size:** 8.5" x 11.0"; **Country:** US; **Border/Edge:** Red; **Found In:** Chapter Six.

Name: For Sparkling Holidays; **Issued:** 1953
Comments: December, 1953 ad, *National Geographic Magazine*. Ad words: *The Pause That Refreshes.*

#1-Reproduction Name: For Sparkling Holidays; **Issued:** 1992
Comments: Reproduction of 1953 ad, Santa and elves in the Workshop; **Shape:** Flat Rectangle; **Size:** 11.0" x 15.0"; **Country:** US; **Border/Edge:** Green; **Found In:** Chapter Six.

Name: *. . . and now the gift for thirst . . .* ; **Issued:** 1952
Comments: December, 1952 ad, *National Geographic Magazine*. (Note: vertical version of ad)

#1-Reproduction Name: My Gift for Thirst; **Issued:** 1993
Comments: Reproduction of 1952 ad, Christmas, morning; **Shape:** Large Deep Oval; **Size:** 12.5" x 15.5"; **Country:** US; **Border/Edge:** Red; **Found In:** Chapter Six.

#2-Reproduction Name: Gift for Thirst; **Issued:** 1997-current
Comments: Reproduction of 1952 ad, Christmas, morning, horizontal version; **Shape:** Long Rectangle; **Size:** 8.5" x 19.0"; **Country:** US; **Border/Edge:** Red; **Found In:** Chapter Six.

Name: The Pause That Refreshes; **Issued:** 1958
Comments: December, 1958 ad, *National Geographic Magazine*.

#1-Reproduction Name: Santa with Deer; **Issued:** 1989
Comments: Reproduction of 1958 ad, *The Pause That Refreshes*; **Shape:** Std Rectangle; **Size:** 10.5" x 13.25"; **Country:** US; **Border/Edge:** Green; **Found In:** Chapter Five.

#2-Reproduction Name: Celebration of Santa; **Issued:** 1998-current
Comments: Reproduction of 1958 ad, *The Pause that Refreshes*, commemorative of Coca-Cola Collectors event, Atlanta, Georgia; **Shape:** Std Rectangle; **Size:** 10.5" x 13.25"; **Country:** US; **Border/Edge:** Dark green, red stripe; **Found In:** Chapter Six.

Name: Refreshing Surprise; **Issued:** 1959
Comments: December, 1959 ad, *National Geographic Magazine*.

#1-Reproduction Name: Refreshing Surprise; **Issued:** c.1992-1995
Comments: Reproduction of 1959 ad; **Shape:** Small Rectangle; **Size:** 8.0" x 11.0" x 1.0";
Country: Italy; **Border/Edge:** *Red*; **Found In:** Chapter Six.

#2-Reproduction Name: Refreshing Surprise; **Issued:** c.1992-1995
Comments: Reproduction of 1959 ad; **Shape:** Small Rectangle; **Size:** 8.0" x 11.0" x 1.0";
Country: Italy; **Border/Edge:** *Blue*; **Found In:** Chapter Six.

Santa Ads From the 1960s

Haddon Sundblom's Santa ads ended during the 1960s, the same time period that many collectors have noted as the end of the classic Coca-Cola collectibles period. Five Sundblom ads from 1960-1964 are the last ones found on tray reproductions. Thirteen trays from these images have been identified.

Elves are back in the 1960 ad, helping Santa to rest and relax. This ad had several versions, some with the elves marching and playing musical instruments. The ad is titled *A Merry Christmas Calls for Coke* and is found on three trays.

The 1961 ad *When Friends Drop In* was reproduced in 1988 on the first Santa tray in a round shape.

In 1962 an update of the 1936 ad was created with a different look to Santa and a few new toys. The new version, titled *Season's Greetings*, is fully reproduced once. The face is also used on two c.1992 Italian trays. On these trays it appears that the arm and hand holding a bottle of Coke are not from the ad. The closest match was made from the 1951 *Good Boys and Girls* ad (notice the fingers). The polar bear looks as if it could be from another tray but no specific match was made.

Dear Santa or *Santa at Chimney*, from 1963, was a new image for that year but it reworks and reuses parts of earlier ads. The note on the mantle was used in 1932 and 1945 ads. The name on the book of lists, *Good Boys and Girls*, is first seen in 1951 in an ad of the same name. This 1963 ad was reproduced, and reproduced, and *reproduced*! It was the image on the first Santa tray reproduction in 1973. It was *also* the image on the second tray, the third tray, and the fourth tray reproductions. One of these was the widely distributed promotional tray for the *Long John Silver Seafood Shoppes*. No different Santa ad was reproduced until *1981*. An additional reproduction of *Dear Santa* was issued in 1989. Four of the five reproductions are very similar in appearance.

A 1964 scene of Christmas morning with Santa, children, a dog, and toys, titled *. . . things go better with Coke*, is reproduced on one tray.

Name: A Merry Christmas Calls for Coke; **Issued:** 1960
Comments: December, 1960 ad, *National Geographic Magazine*. Ad words: *The Pause That Refreshes*.

#1-Reproduction Name: A Merry Christmas; **Issued:** c.1982
Comments: Reproduction of 1960 ad, *A Merry Christmas Calls for Coke*, Santa in chair with elves; **Shape:** Std Rectangle; **Size:** 10.5" x 13.25"; **Country:** US; **Border/Edge:** Green, no trim; **Found In:** Chapter Five.

#2-Reproduction Name: A Merry Christmas; **Issued:** c.1982-1983
Comments: Reproduction of 1960 ad, *A Merry Christmas Calls for Coke*, Santa in chair with elves, tray words: *Coke Is It!*; **Shape:** Std Rectangle; **Size:** 10.5" x 13.25"; **Country:** US; **Border/Edge:** Red and yellow, Holiday trim; **Found In:** Chapter Five.

#3-Reproduction Name: A Merry Christmas; **Issued:** 1991-1997
Comments: Reproduction of 1960 ad, *A Merry Christmas Calls for Coke*, Santa in chair with elves; **Shape:** Flat Rectangle; **Size:** 11.0" x 15.0"; **Country:** US; **Border/Edge:** Red; **Found In:** Chapter Six.

Name: When Friends Drop In; **Issued:** 1961
Comments: December, 1961 ad, *National Geographic Magazine*.

#1-Reproduction Name: When Friends Drop In; **Issued:** 1988-1989, 1994-1996
Comments: Reproduction of 1961 ad; **Shape:** Round; **Size:** 12.25"; **Country:** US; **Border/Edge:** Red, green edge; **Found In:** Chapter Five.

Name: Season's Greetings; **Issued:** 1962
Comments: December, 1962 ad, *National Geographic Magazine*.

#1-Reproduction Name: And the Same for You; **Issued:** c.1992-1995
Comments: Reproduction of 1962 ad, *Season's Greetings*, face only; **Shape:** Small Rectangle; **Size:** 8.0" x 11.0" x 1.0"; **Country:** Italy; **Border/Edge:** Red; **Found In:** Chapter Six.

#2-Reproduction Name: Santa and Polar Bear; **Issued:** c.1992-1995
Comments: Reproduction of multiple ads. Santa's face is reproduced from 1962 ad, arm and hand with bottle from 1951. Polar bear is from TV ads, no specific tray has been identified; **Shape:** Small Rectangle; **Size:** 8.0" x 11.0" x 1.0"; **Country:** Italy; **Border/Edge:** Red; **Found In:** Chapter Six.

#3-Reproduction Name: Season's Greeting; **Issued:** 1994
Comments: Reproduction of 1962 ad, Santa under tree playing with toys; **Shape:** Large Rectangle; **Size:** 13.5" x 18.5"; **Country:** US; **Border/Edge:** Green; **Found In:** Chapter Six.

Name: Things go better with Coke; **Issued:** 1964
Comments: December, 1964 ad, *National Geographic Magazine*.

#1-Reproduction Name: Things go better...; **Issued:** 1986
Comments: Reproduction of 1964 ad; **Shape:** Std Rectangle; **Size:** 10.5" x 13.25"; **Country:** US; **Border/Edge:** Red; **Found In:** Chapter Five.

Name: Dear Santa; **Issued:** 1963
Comments: December, 1963 ad, *National Geographic Magazine*.

#1-Reproduction Name: Dear Santa *or* Santa at Chimney; **Issued:** 1973
Comments: Reproduction of 1963 ad, *first Santa tray*, rim words: *Merry Christmas from your Coca-Cola Bottler*; **Shape:** Std Rectangle; **Size:** 10.5" x 13.25"; **Country:** US; **Mfr/Dist:** Ohio Art Company; **Border/Edge:** Green, holiday trim; **Found In:** Chapter Four.

#2-Reproduction Name: Dear Santa *or* Santa at Chimney; **Issued:** 1975
Comments: Reproduction of 1963 ad; **Shape:** Flat Rectangle; **Size:** 10.5" x 14.5"; **Country:** US; **Mfr/Dist:** Ohio Art Company; **Border/Edge:** Green, no trim, no logo; **Found In:** Not pictured (similar to Long John Silver tray except no rim words).

#3-Reproduction Name: Dear Santa *or* Santa at Chimney; **Issued:** 1976
Comments: Reproduction of 1963 ad, for *Long John Silver Seafood Shoppes*; **Shape:** Small Flat Rectangle; **Size:** 10.5" x 14.0"; **Country:** US; **Mfr/Dist:** Donaldson Art Company; **Border/Edge:** Green, holiday trim; **Found In:** Chapter Four.

#4-Reproduction Name: Dear Santa *or* Santa at Chimney; **Issued:** 1980
Comments: Reproduction of 1963 ad, commemorates 25th Anniversary of Santa Village at Bracebridge, Ontario, *"Halfway to the North Pole"*; **Shape:** Std Rectangle; **Size:** 10.5" x 13.25"; **Country:** Canadian (English); **Border/Edge:** Green; **Found In:** Chapter Five.

#5-Reproduction Name: Santa at Chimney; **Issued:** 1989-1990, 1996-1998
Comments: Reproduction of 1963 ad; **Shape:** Std Rectangle; **Size:** 10.5" x 13.25"; **Country:** US; **Mfr/Dist:** Ohio Art Company, distributed by Trademark Marketing; **Border/Edge:** Green with trim; **Found In:** Chapter Five.

Santa Ads, Collage Trays

Three trays, all from 1999, have taken ad variations to a different level by blending pieces of multiple ads from different years to create a single image (or to *try* and create a single image). These ads have an artificial look, as if a committee created them. Since many other original Sundblom Santa ads have *never* been reproduced on a tray, it is questionable (at least visually) as to why this approach has been used.

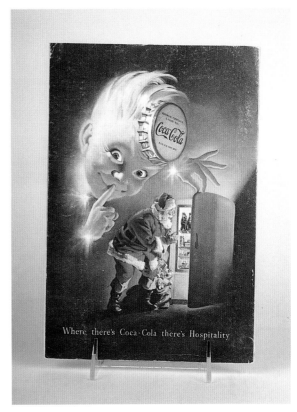

Name: Wherever There's Coca-Cola, There's Hospitality; **Issued:** 1948
Comments: December, 1948 ad, *National Geographic Magazine*. One more Santa ad that could be a future tray reproduction.

Name: For Santa; **Issued:** 1950
Comments: December, 1950 ad, *National Geographic Magazine*. Note: Used in reproduction, 1999, *Santa, Happy Holidays* (Round Shape), on back of tray.

#1-Reproduction Name (Collage): Santa, Happy Holidays; **Issued:** 1999
Comments: Collage, reproductions from multiple Santa ads: young girl on left and Santa's belt buckle, 1964; young girl on right, 1938; Santa's face and hand, 1960. On tray back: Santa's hat, face, and body, 1950; Santa's arm, 1949; Santa's hand with bottle, 1951; litho by J. V. Reed and Company; **Shape:** Deep Round; **Size:** 13.0" dia. x 1.75" depth; **Country:** US; **Border/Edge:** Green; **Found In:** Chapter Six.

#2-Reproduction Name (Collage): Santa, Happy Holidays; **Issued:** 1999
Comments: Collage, reproductions from multiple Santa ads: Santa's face and hand, c.1943 (ad without a name); right arm, belt, and child, 1953; and the dog from 1961; back of tray treated to provide non-skid surface; litho by J. V. Reed and Company; **Shape:** Large Rectangle; **Size:** 10.75" x 14.75"; **Country:** US; **Border/Edge:** Green; **Found In:** Chapter Six.

#3-Reproduction Name (Collage): 1999 Season' Greetings; **Issued:** 1999
Comments: Collage, reproduction from two Santa ads: Santa with Bag from *Wherever I Go*, c.1943; and the reindeer from 1949's *Travel Refreshed*; **Shape:** Large Rectangle; **Size:** 13.5" x 18.5"; **Country:** US; **Border/Edge:** Gold; **Found In:** Chapter Six.

IV. Commemorative Trays

Commemorative trays were first found in the 1960s and today are an endangered species. The 1970s and 1980s contain most of the trays that have been identified. The number of commemorative trays dropped off dramatically in the 1990s, even though the total number of identified trays increased. *WHY?*

Without attempting to unearth *all* the reasons why new commemorative trays have virtually ceased, one big answer is obvious: *ACL*. Technological advances in the ability to print words, colors, and pictures on *bottles* of Coke have made ACL, or *Applied Color Labeling*, the vehicle to create commemorative bottles. Commemorative bottles did exist in the 1970s and 1980s and were issued in addition to trays or in a packaged set along with a commemorative tray.

The bottle, with a lower cost per unit, the increase in ACL graphics ability, easier production of limited volumes, and the local bottler's involvement in distribution have all made the *bottle* today's commemorative item of choice. Collecting bottles is a *hot* area of Coke Memorabilia activity. Commemorative bottles don't take much room, are colorful, easy to display, relatively inexpensive, and not impossible to locate. It is interesting to note that in just one year, 1999, about the same number of commemorative bottles were issued as the *entire* number of commemorative trays issued over the thirty-six years since the first commemorative tray was identified in 1964!

This section identifies 147 commemorative trays issued in the 1960s, 1970s, 1980s, and 1990s. Since *new* commemorative trays are an endangered species, it is logical to assume that commemorative trays issued in past years will become even more collectible and valuable in the future!

The most commonly found commemorative tray is one that celebrates the anniversary of the number of years of operation for a Coca-Cola franchised bottler. Sixty-two trays of this type have been identified. Nine "milestone" years of twenty-five, forty-five, fifty, sixty, seventy-five, eighty, eighty-five, ninety, and one hundred years are commemorated in one or more trays. An additional thirteen trays commemorate some other bottler event.

Of the seventy-five bottler commemorative trays, sixty-five are pictured in Chapters Three through Six.

#	Year	Anniv.	Location	Shape	Volume	Type (Repro, Picture)

Bottler Anniversary Commemoratives

#	Year	Anniv.	Location	Shape	Volume	Type (Repro, Picture)
1.	1964	25th	La Laguna, MX	Deep Round	-	Plant, Artist Rendition
2.	1967	50th	La Victoria, MX	Deep Round	-	Dates and Buildings
3.	1975	75th	Nashville, TN	Std Rectangle	35,000	Repro 1901 Hilda with The Roses
4.	1975	75th	Atlanta, GA	Std Rectangle	100,000	Repro 1905 Lillian Nordica with Bottle
5.	1976	75th	Campbellesville, KY	Flat Round	6,000	Repro 1900 Hilda with Glass
6.	1976	75th	Chicago, IL	Flat Round	4,000	Repro 1900 Hilda with Glass
7.	1976	75th	Cincinnati, OH	Flat Round	80,000	Repro 1900 Hilda with Glass
8.	1976	75th	Columbia, GA	Flat Round	6,000	Repro 1900 Hilda with Glass
9.	1976	75th	Elizabethtown, KY	Flat Round	15,000	Repro 1900 Hilda with Glass
10.	1976	75th	Louisville, KY	Flat Round	71,000	Repro 1900 Hilda with Glass
11.	1976	75th	Norfolk, VA	Flat Round	41,000	Repro 1900 Hilda with Glass
12.	1976	75th	Shelbyville, KY	Flat Round	8,000	Repro 1900 Hilda with Glass
13.	1976	60th	Canada, Hamby's Beverage	Flat Oval	-	Repro 1916 Elaine
14.	1977	75th	Augusta, GA	Flat Round	3,000	Repro 1900 Hilda with Glass
15.	1977	75th	Buffalo, NY	Flat Round	6,000	Repro 1900 Hilda with Glass
16.	1977	75th	Charlotte, NC	Flat Round	42,000	Repro 1900 Hilda with Glass
17.	1977	75th	Coca-Cola Archives (for all bottlers)	Flat Round	2,000	Repro 1900 Hilda with Glass
18.	1977	75th	Columbia, SC	Flat Round	5,000	Repro 1900 Hilda with Glass
19.	1977	75th	Dallas, TX	Flat Round	150,000	Repro 1900 Hilda with Glass
20.	1977	75th	Harrisburg, PA	Flat Round	35,000	Repro 1900 Hilda with Glass
21.	1977	75th	Meridian, MI	Flat Round	-	Repro 1900 Hilda with Glass*
22.	1977	75th	Philadelphia, PA	Flat Round	1,250	Repro 1900 Hilda with Glass
23.	1977	75th	Savannah, GA	Flat Round	2,000	Repro 1900 Hilda with Glass
24.	1977	50th	Italy (#1 of series)	Flat Standard	-	Repro 1905 Lillian Nordica with Bottle*
25.	1977	75th	Louisiana (New Orleans)	Flat Round	43,400	Repro 1905 Lillian Nordica with Bottle
26.	1977	75th	Mid-America (Kansas City)	Std Rectangle	50,000	Repro 1905 Lillian Nordica with Bottle
27.	1977	75th	Womecto Co. (Roanoke, VA)	Std Rectangle	-	Repro 1905 Lillian Nordica with Bottle
28.	1977	75th	Los Angeles, CA	Round	-	Collage of City Scenes
29.	1978	75th	Athens, GA	Std Rectangle	2,000	Repro Ad, 1904 Lillian Nordica with Sign
30.	1978	75th	Rockwood, TN	Std Rectangle	5,000	Repro Ad, 1904 Lillian Nordica with Sign
31.	1978	75th	Selma, AL	Std Rectangle	800	Repro Ad, 1904 Lillian Nordica with Sign
32.	1978	75th	Carolina	Flat Round	-	Repro 1903 Bottle 5¢*
33.	1978	75th	Jackson, MS	Flat Round	-	Repro 1903 Bottle 5¢*
34.	1978	75th	Paducah, KY	Flat Round	8,000	Repro 1903 Bottle 5¢
35.	1979	75th	New York, NY	Sm Rectangle (Plastic)	-	Collage, Bottle & City Scenes
36.	1979	80th	Chattanooga, TN	Std Rectangle	10,000	Repro Ad, 1904 Lillian Nordica with Sign
37.	1979	85th	Biedenharn Candy Co., Vicksburg, MI	Flat Round	-	Plant & Founder, Artist Rendition
38.	1979	50th	Italy (#2 of series)	Std Rectangle	-	Repro, 1916 Elaine
39.	1980	60th	Vancouver (Can)	Std Rectangle	-	Picture of City, c.1920
40.	1980	60th	Vancouver (Can)	Std Rectangle	-	Picture of City and Harbor (in 1980)
41.	1980	60th	Vancouver (Can)	Std Rectangle	-	Repro 1920 Golfer Girl
42.	1980	75th	Houston, TX	Std Rectangle	-	Picture of Plant, Border trim of bottles
43.	1980	75th	Cleveland, OH	Std Rectangle	-	Pictures Euclid Beach, Baseball
44.	1980	75th	Jackson, TN	Flat Round	8,000	Repro 1903 Bottle 5¢
45.	1981	75th	Tullahoma, TN	Lge Deep Oval	10,000	Repro 1907 Relieves Fatigue
46.	1981	50th	Italy (#3 of series)	Std Rectangle	-	Repro Ad, 1927 Calendar Girl*
47.	1982	75th	Corinth, MI	Std Rectangle	10,000	Repro 1907 Relieves Fatigue
48.	1982	75th	Hawaii	Flat Round	-	Collage, Bottle & Scenes
49.	1982	50th	Italy (#4 of series)	Std Rectangle	-	Repro 1925 Party Girl
50.	1984	75th	Zanesville, OH (#1 of series)	Std Rectangle	5,000	Original Art, Leslie Cope
51.	1984	45th	Cape Cod, MA (and new plant)	Deep Oval	-	Repro Ad, 1922 Four Seasons*
52.	1984	50th	Italy (#5 of series)	Std Rectangle	-	Repro 1921 Summer Girl*
53.	1986	75th	Ft. Myers, FL	Std Rectangle	-	City Scene, Artist Rendition
54.	1986	50th	Italy (#6 of series, also Coke 100th Anniv)	Std Rectangle	-	Repro 1923 Flapper Girl
55.	1987	50th	Italy (#7 of series)	Sm Rectangle	-	Repro Ad, 1956 Hand with Bottle (Mondo Bottilliz)
56.	1988	75th	Arkansas (Harrison?)	Lge Deep Oval	-	Repro Ad, 1912 Duster Girls*
57.	1988	50th	Italy (#8 of series)	Std Rectangle	-	Repro Ad, 1937 Fishin' Hole, by N.C. Wyeth
58.	1989	75th	York, PA	Lge Rectangle	-	Repro Ad, 1924 Touring Car
59.	1989	90th	Chattanooga, TN	Std Rectangle	5,000	Picture, Crown Bottling Machine
60.	1989	90th	Chattanooga, TN	Std Rectangle	5,000	Picture, Antique Truck
61.	1993	75th	Coatesville, PA	Std Rectangle	-	Plant and Truck, Artist Rendition
62.	1994	100th	Biedenharn Candy Co., Vicksburg, MI	Sm Flat Rectangle	-	Collage of Memorabilia

Commemoratives for New Plant, Safe Driving, or an Executive

1.	1968	*New Plant*	Pacifico, MX	TV Tray	-		Plant, Artist Rendition*
2.	1970s	*New Plant*	Mante, MX	Sm Rectangle	-		Plant, Artist Rendition
3.	1979	*New Plant*	Calgary (Can)	Sm Rectangle	-		Plant, Artist Rendition
4.	1979	*New Plant*	Goodwill (Can)	Sm Rectangle	-		Plant, Artist Rendition
5.	1980s	*New Plant*	St. John's Newfoundland (Can)	Sm Rectangle	-		Plant, Artist Rendition*
6.	1980s	*Driving*	Safe Driving Award (Can)	Flat Round (Plastic)	-		Graphics of Operations
7.	1981	*50th*	*Executive* (James Carlen), Cooksville, TN	Sm Rectangle	-		Plant and Employee Picture
8.	1981	*New Plant*	Regina Saskatchewan (Can)	Std Rectangle	-		Plant, Artist Rendition
9.	1981	*New Plant*	Lehigh Valley (PA)	Oval	-		Plant, Artist Rendition
10.	1982	*New Plant*	Pembroke Pines, FL	Std Rectangle	750		Picture, Antique Truck
11.	c.1985	*Driving*	Safe Driving Award (Can)	Sm Rectangle	-		Picture, Car & Truck
12.	1986	*Driving*	Driver Safety Achievement (Can)	Std Rectangle	-		Pictures, Seven Trucks
13.	1986	*Driving*	Driver Safety Achievement (Can)	Std Rectangle	-		Picture, Antique Truck

Indicates a tray that is not pictured in the chronological Chapters

Additional commemorative trays have been grouped into seven types. The total number of commemorative trays in these groups is seventy-two. *Customer Commemoratives* are the most frequently found category with sixteen trays. Sixty-six of these have pictures in Chapters Three through Six.

CUSTOMER COMMEMORATIVES

#	Yr Issued	Subject	Shape	Volume	Type (Repro, Picture)
1.	1976	Dear Santa, Long John Silver Seafood	Sm Flat Rectangle	400,000	Repro 1963 Santa Ad
2.	1976	100th Anniv Fred Harvey Shoppes (Coke 90th)	Std Rectangle	10,000	Collage
3.	1978	Happy Joe's Pizza and Ice Cream Parlor	Sm Flat Oval	-	Caricature Drawing
4.	1980s	100th Anniversary, ESSO Oil Company	Oval	-	Repro c.1980s Ad, Girls at Ballet
5.	1980	25th Anniversary, McDonald's & Coke (Can)	Std Rectangle	-	Repro 1923 Flapper Girl
6.	1980	100th Anniversary, Imperial Oil Co. (Can)	Std Rectangle	-	Picture, Antique Car*
7.	1982	McDonald's Convention (US)	Lge Rectangle	-	Collage, San Francisco
8.	1982	Red River Coop, Winnipeg (Can)	Std Rectangle	-	Picture of Coop
9.	1982	Piggly Wiggly Supermarket, Memphis, TN	Std Rectangle	-	Collage
10.	1983	100th Anniversary, Kroger Supermarket	Sm Oval	-	Picture, Wagon
11.	1984	50th Anniversary Big Bear Supermarkets (OH)	Lge Rectangle	-	Repro 1935 Santa Ad
12.	1986	NAC, Nat'l Assoc of Concessionaires	Deep Round	-	Graphics, ShoWest '86
13.	c.1988	7-11 & Coke, Can't Beat the Feeling	Flat Rectangle	-	Picture, Baseball
14.	1990	35th Anniversary, Bob's IGA	Lge Rectangle	-	Repro 1924 Ad, Touring Car
15.	1991	Kroger Opening, Savannah, GA	Sm Rectangle	-	Repro 1921 Summer Girl, Picture, Store
16.	1999	Steak n' Shake Comm and Promotion	Deep Round	est 10,000	Collage of Products*

COCA-COLA COLLECTOR EVENTS

#	Yr Issued	Subject	Shape	Volume	Type (Repro, Picture)
1.	1981	Springtime in Atlanta	Std Rectangle	2,000	Collage
2.	1981	7th National Convention Kansas City	Lge Deep Oval	1,500	Hot Air Balloons
3.	1982	8th National Convention Nashville	Std Rectangle	2,000	Repro Ad, 1951 Sprite Boy
4.	1983	9th National Convention Washington, D.C.	Flat Round	2,000	Antique Truck
5.	1984	10th National Convention Sacramento, CA	Sm Oval	1,600	Picture, Covered Wagon
6.	1985	Ohio Winterfest	Deep Round	-	Sm Graphics w/Balloons
7.	1986	Winter Festival, Zephyrhills, FL	Lge Rectangle	-	Collage Graphics
8.	1989	15th National Convention Anaheim, CA	Std Rectangle	-	Picture, Plant
9.	1992	18th National Convention Orlando, FL	Std Rectangle	-	Picture, Shuttle Lift-off
10.	1993	10th Anniv, Springtime in Atlanta	Std Rectangle	-	Repro Ad, 1945
11.	1997	10th Anniv, Badger Spring Pause	Flat Rectangle	-	Repro Ad, 1941 Work Refreshed
12.	1997	23rd National Convention Colorado Springs, CO	Std Rectangle	2,000	Smokey Bear
13.	1998	15th Anniv, Springtime in Atlanta	Std Rectangle	2,000	Repro 1958 Santa Ad
14.	1998	24th National Convention Minneapolis, MN	Std Rectangle	2,000	Repro Ad, 1936 Woman at Helm

EVENT COMMEMORATIVES

#	Yr Issued	Subject	Shape	Volume	Type (Repro, Picture)
1.	1967	100th Anniversary Canadian Federation	Std Rectangle	-	Symbols, Stainless Steel
2.	1972	Black History Month	TV Tray w/Legs	17,600	Collage of Leaders and Others
3.	1978	James Cook Landing, Nakoota Sound, BC (Can)	Flat Oval	-	Map & Picture
4.	1978	Employee, W.C.K. Ohio Art Tribute	Std Rectangle	-	Collage
5.	1982	Centennial, Branton, Manitoba (Can)	Std Rectangle	-	Picture, Collage
6.	1982	World's Fair, Knoxville, TN	Flat Round	-	Artist Rendition, Fairgrounds

7.	1984	Restoration, Special Train, Memphis, TN	Std Rectangle	-	Artist Rendition, Train
8.	1986	Expo '86, Vancouver, BC (Can)	Std Rectangle	-	Picture, Fireworks
9.	1986	Expo' 86, Vancouver, BC (Can)	Std Rectangle	-	Picture, Map
10.	1993	Strawberry Festival, Portage, LaPrairie (Can)	Std Rectangle	-	Picture, Location

SPORTS EVENT COMMEMORATIVES

#	Yr Issued	Subject	Shape	Volume	Type (Repro, Picture)
1.	1975	Coaches' Last Game, Alabama/Auburn (Football)	Std Rectangle	224,000	Collage
2.	1975	Fortitude Valley, Australia (Rugby)	Lge Rectangle	-	Team Picture*
3.	1976	Paterno, Nittany Lions, Penn State (Football)	Lge Rectangle	est 75,000	Collage
4.	1976	NCAA Champs, Indian Univ & Coach (Basketball)	Round	125,000	Collage
5.	1976	Cotton Bowl, Arkansas & Coach (Football)	Std Rectangle	53,600	Collage
6.	1977	"A" Grade, Australia, Past Brothers (Rugby)	Flt Rectangle	-	Collage
7.	1980	75th Anniv Normandeau Cup (Can) (Horses)	Std Rectangle	-	Collage*
8.	1981	Nat'l Champs, Georgia Bulldogs (Football)	Lge Rectangle	-	Collage
9.	1984	Memphis Chicks Baseball Team, Memphis, TN	Std Rectangle	-	Collage
10.	1986	World Cup Mexico (Soccer)	Round	-	Logo, issued in Germany

PLACE COMMEMORATIVES

#	Yr Issued	Subject	Shape	Volume	Type (Repro, Picture)
1.	1980	25th Anniversary Santa Village, Bracebridge (Can)	Std Rectangle	-	Repro Ad, 1963 Santa
2.	1981	Anniversary Shasta Dam (PA)	Lge Deep Oval	-	Repro Ad, 1922 Four Seasons*
3.	1981	Renovation, Peabody Hotel, Memphis, TN	Std Rectangle	-	Picture of Hotel
4.	1983	Renovation, Beale Street, Memphis, TN	Std Rectangle	-	Collage
5.	1984	City Attractions, Memphis, TN	Lge Rectangle	-	Collage
x.	1984	Y-Bridge, Zanesville, OH (also 75th Commem)	Std Rectangle	5,000	Picture, Leslie Cope
6.	1985	The Headly Inn, Zanesville, OH	Std Rectangle	-	Picture, Leslie Cope
7.	1985	50th Anniversary Hoover Dam	Std Rectangle	-	Picture
8.	1988	The B&O Railroad Station, Zanesville, OH	Std Rectangle	-	Picture, Leslie Cope
9.	1989	Market House, Zanesville, OH	Std Rectangle	-	Picture, Leslie Cope
10.	1992	Dresden Village, Zanesville, OH	Std Rectangle	-	Picture, Leslie Cope

OLYMPIC GAMES AND COMMONWEALTH GAMES COMMEMORATIVES

#	Yr Issued	Subject	Shape	Volume	Type (Repro, Picture)
1.	1976	XXI, Montreal, Can (Olympic)	Flat Rectangle	-	Icons of Sports
2.	1976	XXI, Montreal, Can (Olympic, VIP Edition)	Std Rectangle	1,976	Nine Pictures
3.	1978	Edmonton, Can (Commonwealth)	Std Rectangle	-	Collage (Pink)
4.	1978	Edmonton, Can (Commonwealth)	Std Rectangle	-	Collage (Tan)
5.	1984	XXIII, USA Records (Olympic)	Lge Deep Oval	-	Collage
6.	1987	XV Winter Games, Calgary (Can) (Olympic)	Std Rectangle	-	Posters
7.	1988	Calgary & Seoul, Winter & Summer (Olympic)	Lge Rectangle	-	Posters
8.	1991	XXV Barcelona Games (Olympic)	Std Rectangle	-	Posters
9.	2000	XXVII Sydney Games (Olympic)	Lge Rectangle	-	Characters*

COCA-COLA 100TH ANNIVERSARY COMMEMORATIVES

#	Yr Issued	Subject	Shape	Volume	Type (Repro, Picture)
x.	1986	Coca-Cola 100th Anniv, Italy, Bottler	Deep Round	-	Repro 1923 Flapper Girl
1.	1986	Coca-Cola 100th Anniv, Canada	Std Rectangle	-	Collage
2.	1986	Coca-Cola 100th Anniv, Statue of Liberty, Hotel	Std Rectangle	-	Picture of each
3.	1986	Coca-Cola 100th Anniv, Celebration of the Century	Lge Rectangle	-	Collage

"x" - this tray counted in Bottler Commemmorative trays
*Indicates a tray that is not pictured in the chronological Chapters

The short life of commemorative trays is documented in the numbers below. Bottler and sports commemoratives peaked in the 1970s while all other types peaked in the 1980s.

Category	1960s	1970s	1980s	1990s	Total
Bottler Anniversary	2	36	22	2	62
Other Bottler Events	1	3	9	0	13
Total	**3**	**39**	**31**	**2**	**75**
Customer	0	3	10	3	16
Coke Collector	0	0	8	6	14
Events	1	3	5	1	10
Sports Events	0	6	4	0	10
Places	0	0	9	1	10
Olympic Games	0	4	3	2	9
Coke 100th	0	0	3	0	3
Total	**1**	**16**	**42**	**13**	**72**
Total All	**4**	**55**	**73**	**15**	**147**

V. Tray Series

Many examples of groups or series of trays with similar themes can be found. The text and captions in the chronological Chapters provide information on them. A few such groups are listed below. The emphasis here is on later trays, as many groups have already been identified from the earlier trays. Earlier examples include the red-border group and women in bathing suits.

(1) In the 1970s and 1980s eight trays were issued in a series commemorating fifty years of Coca-Cola bottling in Italy.

(2) The *Refreshed* Series contains four long rectangle trays dated in the early 1990s with a similar advertising theme.

(3) Norman Rockwell calendars from the 1930s were reproduced on three trays in the early 1980s.

(4) In the early 1990s a series of small rectangle trays from Italy contained three unique calendars reproductions from 1891, 1901, and 1901.

(5) Another group of three Italian trays featured outdoor scenes where some part of the image was shaped like a Coke bottle.

(6) *Circus* and *Court Day* are two trays from 1990 and 1991 that reproduce ads from the 1920s and show detailed scenes of small town life.

(7) The Manitoba, Canada bottler issued at least three trays on various events and activities in the mid-1980s.

(8) The Vancouver, Canada bottler had a group of three trays from 1980 commemorating the 60th Anniversary of that operation. Two pictures are striking *then* and *now* pictures while the third is a reproduction of a 1920 tray. In 1986 two additional trays promoted Expo '86, also in Vancouver.

(9) The Memphis, Tennessee bottler was active in the early 1980s with trays promoting local attractions. A group of six is varied and attractive. *Peabody Hotel, Beale Street, Memphis Chicks,* and *Special Train* promote specific Memphis attractions; *Piggly Wiggly* commemorates a large customer's HQ move to Memphis; and *Memphis, A Good Place to Be* is an early example of a photo collage.

(10) In 1983 Leslie Cope was commissioned to produce a painting for use on a tray commemorating the 75th Anniversary, in 1984, of the Zanesville Bottling Company. That painting, *The Zanesville Y-Bridge,* was followed by additional works over the next eight years. Those five trays and a sixth collage tray form the *Zanesville Series.*

The Coca-Cola Company commissioned many recognized artists to create paintings or photographs to be used on advertising materials, including trays. That practice ceased, or at least became much less prominent, after the end of the classic collectible period in the late 1960s. Artists such as Pamela C. Renfroe, Jim Harrison, and others who have produced paintings used for advertising materials and trays in the 1990s are all certainly talented. But names such as Norman Rockwell, Gil Elvgren, N. C. Wyeth, and others from the past had instant name recognition. Perhaps somewhere between these two groups of artists is the best place to position the Ohio artist noted above, Leslie Cope.

To position the work he has done on Coca-Cola trays, the following background is provided. Mr. Cope has won honors and awards and has been recognized in both this country and Europe. His work can be found in locations such as the permanent collection of the Metropolitan Museum of Art in New York and the Carnegie Institute in Pittsburgh. Popular subjects in his paintings include work horses, Amish country, and village sketches, to name a few. Mr. Cope and his gallery are located in Roseville, Ohio a few miles from Zanesville. The Cope trays also have been featured in the *Americana* display at Epcot, Disney World, in Orlando. Note that each tray image contains *workhorses*, with at least one horse pulling a wagon of Coca-Cola. The paintings, filled with earth tones and gray skies, evoke a real feeling of the rigors of life early in the twentieth century. The back of each tray has extensive notations about the site.

The first four of the Zanesville trays picture sites found on the National Road (U.S. Route 40) around Zanesville. The first was issued in 1984, the year that the fourth Y-Bridge was dedicated. *Headly Inn* followed in 1985; *The B&O Railroad Station* was issued in 1988; and *Zanesville's Market House* is dated 1989. *Holiday,* a collage tray, was issued at the end of 1989. Cope's last tray is a brighter image with a sky blue border and no earth tones, titled *Dresden: All-American Hometown.* The subject deviates from the National Road and Zanesville theme. Other research material indicates that the last surviving business descendant of The American Artworks is located in Dresden. That company produced most of the beautiful classic trays issued from the 1920s, 1930s, and 1940s and was located in Coshocton, Ohio. Dresden is midway between Zanesville and Coshocton.

Chapter Eight

Tip or Change Trays,
A Small Review

Tip or change trays have generally not been included in this book's chronological review of serving trays. One exception is a group of Mexican trays, larger than most U.S. tip trays, and some with unique images. Although the number of Internet auctions for tip trays has been increasing, not enough were logged to include Internet dollar values in this review. Values from reference materials are included if available.

Fourteen tip trays have been identified from 1900-1920. This group becomes the *classics*. After that, the Mexican trays and one Canadian tray are about all that can be found until the reproductions of the 1970s, 1980s, and 1990s.

The Classics (1900-1920)

Beginning in 1900, at least one *tip tray* was issued for every image on a *serving tray* through 1920, *except* for the *Lillian Nordica Bottle and Glass Trays* in 1905. Nine of the fourteen trays are pictured here.

Name: Hilda with The Glass; **Issued:** 1903
Comments: No note on table, different coloring, different border; **Shape:** Round; **Size:** 4.125"; **Story:** —; **Country:** US; **Mfr/Dist:** —; **Border/Edge:** Gold, *Delicious* at top, *Refreshing* at Bottom; **Quantity:** —; *Courtesy of John E. Peterson.*
$ Value, References: $900-$2500 (1,2,4,5,6,8,x)

Name: Relieves Fatigue; **Issued:** c.1907-1908
Comments: First oval tip tray; **Shape:** Oval; **Size:** 4.375" x 6.0";
Story: —; **Country:** US; **Mfr/Dist:** Chas. W. Shonk Co.;
Border/Edge: Gold, black edge, cola bean trim; **Quantity:** —;
Courtesy of John E. Peterson.
$ Value, References: $650-$1300 (1,2,4,5,6,8,x)

Name: Juanita; **Issued:** 1906
Comments: One of two trays with border words; **Shape:** Round; **Size:** 4.25" **Story:** —; **Country:** US; **Mfr/Dist:** NY Metal Ceiling Co.; **Border/Edge:** Gold, *Delicious* at top, *Refreshing* at Bottom, cola bean trim; **Quantity:** —; *Courtesy of John E. Peterson.*
$ Value, References: $400-$1000 (1,2,4,5,6,x)

Name: Exhibition Girl; **Issued:** 1909
Comments: Slight change in image at bottom versus serving tray; **Shape:** Oval; **Size:** 4.5" x 6.25";
Story: —; **Country:** US; **Mfr/Dist:** H. D. Beech Co.;
Border/Edge: Blue, gold trim, cola beans; **Quantity:** —
; *Courtesy of John E. Peterson.*
$ Value, References: $275-$600 (1,2,4,5,6,8,x)

Name: The Coca-Cola Girl;
Issued: 1910
Comments: By Hamilton King, tray name and signature on tray face; **Shape:** Oval; **Size:** 4.375" x 6.125"; **Story:** —; **Country:** US; **Mfr/Dist:** The American Artworks; **Border/Edge:** Red, gold trim, cola beans; **Quantity:** —; *Courtesy of John E. Peterson.*
$ Value, References: $350-$850 (2,4,5,6,8,x)

Name: The Hamilton King Girl;
Issued: 1913
Comments: By Hamilton King, signature on tray; **Shape:** Oval; **Size:** 4.375" x 6.125"; **Story:** —; **Country:** US; **Mfr/Dist:** Passaic Metalware Company; **Border/Edge:** Black, gold edge; **Quantity:** —; *Courtesy of John E. Peterson.*
$ Value, References: $275-$675 (1,2,4,5,6,8,x)

Name: Elaine; **Issued:** 1916
Comments: Image cropped at bottom versus serving tray; **Shape:** Oval; **Size:** 4.375" x 6.125"; **Story:** —; **Country:** US; **Mfr/Dist:** Stelad Signs Passaic Metalware Company; **Border/Edge:** Gold, gold trim; **Quantity:** —; *Courtesy of John E. Peterson.*
$ Value, References: $175-$300 (1,2,4,5,6,8,x)

Name: Betty; **Issued:** 1914
Comments: Same image as serving tray; **Shape:** Oval; **Size:** 4.375"; x 6.5"; **Story:** —; **Country:** US; **Mfr/Dist:** Passaic Metalware Company; **Border/Edge:** Green, gold edge, gold trim; **Quantity:** —; *Courtesy of John E. Peterson.*
$ Value, References: $200-$575 (1,2,4,5,6,8,x)

Name: Golfer Girl; **Issued:** 1920
Comments: More of image shown than in oval serving tray, last of the classic tip trays to be issued; **Shape:** Oval; **Size:** 4.5" x 6.375"; **Story:** —; **Country:** US; **Mfr/Dist:** —; **Border/Edge:** Black, gold stripe; **Quantity:** —; *Courtesy of John E. Peterson.*
$ Value, References: $275-$500 (1,2,4,5,6,8,x)

1920-1970s, Mexico and Canada

No U.S. trays have been identified during the five decades after the 1920 *Golfer Girl* tip tray. Listed below are Mexican and Canadian tip trays found in this period. (Note that the Comments column includes Chapter number if the tray has been pictured or referenced in an earlier Chapter.)

Year	Title	Shape	Size (inches)	Color/Border	Country	Comments
1920	Golfer Girl*	Oval	4.5 x 6.375	Black, gold stripe	Canada (French)	—
1963	Woman with Bottle and Daisy	Sm Rectangle	6.625 x 7.875	Brown	Mexico	Chapter Three
1965	Woman in Red Sweater	Sm Rectangle	6.625 x 7.875	Brown	Mexico	Chapter Three
1968	Fruit Arrangement*	Sm Rectangle	6.625 x 7.875	Brown	Mexico	Matching TV tray, 1969
1969	Ornate Utensils*	Sm Rectangle	6.625 x 7.875	White	Mexico	Matching TV Tray, 1968
1969	Ornamin by Ornamold*	Sm Rectangle	6.25 x 7.75	Blue	Canada (French)	—
1970s	New Bottling Plant	Sm Rectangle	6.25 x 7.75	Brown	Mexico	Chapter Four
1970	Public Plaza with Buildings	Sm Rectangle	6.5 x 7.5	Brown	Mexico	Chapter Four, Matching TV tray, 1972
1974	Insigne Y. . . de Guadalupe	Sm Rectangle	6.5 x 7.5	Brown	Mexico	Chapter Four, Matching TV tray, 1975
1978	de mas Chispa	Sm Rectangle	6.5 x 7.5	Beige	Mexico	Chapter Four, Woman in Red T-shirt
1979	Woman in Red T-shirt, Straw Hat, and Coke*	Sm Rectangle	6.5 x 7.5	Beige	Mexico	Similar picture to 1960s round tray

*Indicates a tray that is not pictured in the chronological Chapters

1970s-1980s

Just as with U.S. serving trays, reproductions of earlier trays began to appear on tip trays in the 1970s. Some were authorized; others were obviously not authorized.

Six 1973 reproductions are of images on trays from 1906-1920. The group includes the only reproduction of the 1909 *Exhibition Girl*.

Name: Relieves Fatigue; **Issued:** 1973
Comments: Reproduction of 1907 tray; **Shape:** Oval; **Size:** 4.5" x 6.125"; **Story:** —; **Country:** US; **Mfr/Dist:** J. V. Reed Company; **Border/Edge:** Gold; **Quantity:** 200,000.

Name: Exhibition Girl; **Issued:** 1973
Comments: Reproduction of 1909 tray; **Shape:** Oval; **Size:** 4.5" x 6.125"; **Story:** —; **Country:** US; **Mfr/Dist:** J. V. Reed Company; **Border/Edge:** Blue; **Quantity:** 200,000.

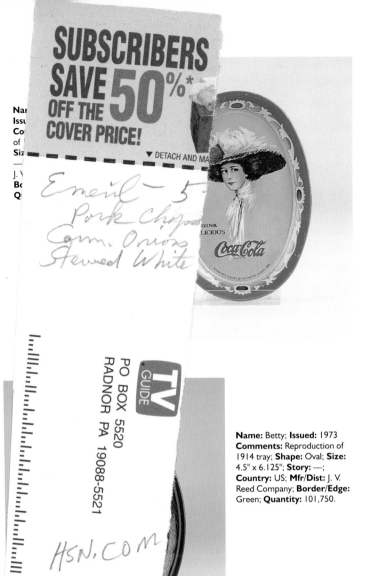

Emeril - 5
Pork Chop
Corn. Onions
Stewed White

HSN.COM

Name: Betty; **Issued:** 1973
Comments: Reproduction of 1914 tray; **Shape:** Oval; **Size:** 4.5" x 6.125"; **Story:** —; **Country:** US; **Mfr/Dist:** J. V. Reed Company; **Border/Edge:** Green; **Quantity:** 101,750.

Name: Golfer Girl; **Issued:** 1973
Comments: Reproduction of 1920 tray; **Shape:** Oval; **Size:** 4.5" x 6.125"; **Story:** —; **Country:** US; **Mfr/Dist:** J. V. Reed Company; **Border/Edge:** Green; **Quantity:** 101,750.

Several tip trays of dubious repute are listed here, c.1970s-1980s.

Name: Elaine; **Issued:** 1973
Comments: Reproduction of 1916 tray; **Shape:** Oval; **Size:** 4.5" x 6.125"; **Story:** —; **Country:** US; **Mfr/Dist:** J. V. Reed Company; **Border/Edge:** Green; **Quantity:** 200,000.

Name: Boxed set of four trays; **Issued:** 1982
Comments: Inferior reproductions but a set in the original box; *Courtesy of John E. Peterson.*

Name: Elaine; **Issued:** 1982
Comments: One of the trays in the 1982 boxed set, a poor reproduction.

Name: Duster Girl;
Issued: c.1980s
Comments: Reproduction of 1911 ad, irregular oval shape; *Courtesy of John E. Peterson.*

Name: The Coca-Cola Girl;
Issued: c.1980s
Comments: Reproduction of 1910 tray, irregular oval shape; *Courtesy of John E. Peterson.*

Name: Girl with Glass;
Issued: 1980s
Comments: Reproduction of Marion Davies, 1919 distributor calendar, a poor reproduction, irregular oval shape; *Courtesy of John E. Peterson.*

1980s-1990s

Following is a list of all other tip trays that were identified during the research for this book.

#	Year	Name	Shape	Size (inches)	Color	Country	Mfr/Dist	Comments
1.	c.1980s	Barefoot Boy	Round	4.5	Red	Mexico	—	Repro tray, 1931, by N. Rockwell
2.	c.1980s	Girl with Glass	Round	4.5	Red	US	—	Repro calendar, 1919, Marion Davies
3.	c.1980s	Betty	Oval	4.375 x 6.125	Green	Can (French)	—	Repro tray, 1914
4.	1989	Trolley Ad	Sm Rect	4.5 x 6.5	Red	US	Dist by Trademark	Repro 1907 ad, couple at soda fountain
5.	1989	Trolley Ad	Sm Rect	4.5 x 6.5	Red	US	Dist by Trademark	Repro 1907 ad, man drinking a Coke
6.	c.1990s	Coke and Ice	Sm Rect	4.5 x 6.5	White	Mexico	—	Logo tray
7.	c.1990s	Winter Coat	Round	4.5	Yellow	Italy	—	Repro ad, c.1920s
8.	c.1990s	—	Round	4.5	—	Italy	—	Repro ad, c.1920s
9.	c.1990s	Out Fishin'	Round	4.5	—	US	—	Repro calendar, 1932, by N. Rockwell
10.	1990s	Glass in Snow	Sm Rect	4.5 x 6.5	Red	US	Dist by Trademark	Repro ad, 1935
11.	1990s	Bottle in Snow	Sm Rect	4.5 x 6.5	Red	US	Dist by Trademark	Repro ad, 1937
12.	1990s	Calendar Girls	Sm Rect	4.5 x 6.5	Various	US	Dist by Trademark	Repro various calendar girls, set of six
13.	1990s	Decades	Sm Rect	4.5 x 6.5	Various	US	Dist by Trademark	3 Decades 40s, 3 Decades 50s, Trays dated 1998
14.	1995	Girl in Chair	Sm Rect	4.5 x 6.5	White	US	Dist by Trademark	Repro ad, 1919
15.	1995	Soda Jerk	Sm Rect	4.5 x 6.5	White	US	Dist by Trademark	Repro ad, c.1930s
16.	1995	Girl with Umbrella	Sm Rect	4.5 x 6.5	Red	US	Dist by Trademark	Repro ad, 1926
17.	1995	Sprite Boy w/Bottle	Sm Rect	4.5 x 6.5	White	US	Dist by Trademark	Repro ad, 1948
18.	1995	1900 Coupon	Sm Rect	4.5 x 6.5	Green	US	Dist by Trademark	Repro coupon, 1900, same image as 1992 tray
19.	1995	Couple Swimming	Sm Rect	4.5 x 6.5	Blue	US	Dist by Trademark	Repro ad, 1915
20.	c.1995	Button with Bottle	Square	5.0	White	Germany	—	Repro sign, c.1950s
21.	1996	Sprite Boy w/Carton	Sm Rect	4.5 x 6.5	Green	US	Dist by Trademark	Repro ad, 1946, also repro on 1960 & 1992 tray
22.	1997	Polar Bear & Cubs	Sm Rect	4.5 x 6.5	Red	US	Dist by Trademark	In snow, drinking Coke
23.	1998	Signature Series	Sm Rect	4.5 x 6.5	Various	US	Dist by Trademark	2 by P. Renfroe, 2 by J. Mack, 2 by J. Harrison
24.	1998	Toy Truck	Sm Rect	4.5 x 6.5	Green	US	Dist by Trademark	Repro w/picture, 1948 Buddy-L wooden truck
25.	1998	Vending Machine	Sm Rect	4.5 x 6.5	Green	US	Dist by Trademark	Repro w/picture, c.1940s Jacob's #26 vending machine
26.	1998	Toy Truck	Sm Rect	4.5 x 6.5	Red	US	Dist by Trademark	Repro w/picture, tin truck, Marx #1090, 1956-57
27.	1998	Waterfall	Sm Rect	4.5 x 6.5	Red	US	Dist by Trademark	Repro w/picture, Waterfall Light-up Sign, c.1950s

Appendix

The Appendix contains seven sections with additional information for review by readers. The first two sections contain tables that provide tray data. The first summarizes data on all trays and the second lists volumes and top sellers for recent trays.

Four sections provide details on the documented Internet auctions. One shows auctions and bids by decade; one lists the top selling trays from documented auctions; the third compares auctions prices to the "Dollar Values" of the expert references; and the fourth contains some suggestions for those participating in Internet auctions.

The last section contains captions for the sixty-five trays not pictured in Chapters One through Six, plus captions for five classic era tip trays not pictured in Chapter Eight. That section begins with a Decade/Chapter summary of the sixty-five serving trays.

I. Tray Data (#1): Details by Decade

This section summarizes the tray data by decades and groups them by Chapter. The information is totaled from the captions in Chapters One through Six and the Appendix, Section VII. The column names represent the following: **(Decade & Chap)** decade and Chapter number; **(# Trays)** number of trays; **(Country)** number of trays by country; **(# Shapes)** number of trays by shape; **(Mfr)** number of trays with manufacturer information; **(Vol)** number of trays with quantities; **(#Pic)** number of trays with photographs; and **(First Seen)** number of trays not found in other reference materials.

Decade & Chap	#Trays	Country	# Shapes	Mfr	Vol	#Pic	First Seen
1897-1909	16	US-16	Round-7 / Oval/Oblong-9	14	1	15	0
1910-1919	6	US-6	Round-0 / Oval/Oblong-2 / Std Rect-3 / Lng Rect/Sq-1	6	0	6	0
Chap One	**22**	US-22	Round-7 / Oval/Lg Oval-11 / Std Rect-3 / Lng Rect/Sq-1	20	1	21	0
1920-1929	15	US-14 / Canada-0 / Mexico-1	Round-0 / Oval/Oblong-1 / Std Rect-14	12	0	13	0
1930-1939	17	US-11 / Canada-5 / Mexico-1	Round-0 / Oval/Oblong-0 / Std Rect-17	17	1	13	0
1940-1949	11	US-6 / Canada-2 / Mexico-3	Round-1 / Oval/Oblong-0 / Std Rect-10	5	0	5	0
Chap Two	**43**	US-31 / Canada-7 / Mexico-5	Round-1 / Oval/Oblong-1 / Std Rect-41	34	1	31	0
1950-1959	32	US-9 / Canada-13 / Mexico-7 / Germany-2 / Oriental-1	Round-6 / Std Rect-21 / Lge Rect/TV-5 / Flat/Sm Rect-0	4	0	25	3
1960-1969	40	US-5 / Canada-8 / Mexico-26	Round-13 / Std Rect-7 / Lge Rect/TV-10	13	5	29	8
1960-1969(cont'd)		Germany-0 / Oriental-0 / Arabic-1	Flt/Sm Rect-10				
Chap Three	**72**	US-14 / Canada-21 / Mexico-33 / Germany-2 / Oriental-1 / Arabic-1	Round-19 / Std Rect-28 / Lge Rect/TV-15 / Flt/Sm Rect-10	17	5	54	11
1970-1979	115	US-64 / Canada-23 / Mexico-19 / Italian-2 / Germany-2 / UK-3 / Australia-2	Round-41 / Oval/Oblong-16 / Std Rect-25 / Lge Rect/TV-8 / Lng Rect/Sq-4 / Flt/Sm Rect-21	49	55	101	25
Chap Four	**115**	115	115	49	55	101	25
1980-1989	155	US-104 / Canada-30 / Mexican-4 / Italian-11 / German-3 / Chile-1 / Belgium-1 / Scandinavia-1	Round-28 / Oval/Oblong-20 / Std Rect-70 / Lge Rect/TV-23 / Lng Rect/Sq-5 / Flat/Sm Rect-9	24	31	143	45
Chap Five	**155**	155	155	24	31	143	45
1990-1999 (incl. 2000)	175	US-138 / Canada -1 / Mexico-1 / Italy-28 / Germany-1 / Argentina-3 / Thailand-1 / France-1 / Belgium-1	Round-31 / Oval/Oblong-8 / Std Rect-39 / Lge Rect/TV-37 / Lng Rect/Sq-10 / Flt/Sm Rect-50	144	98	167	81
Chap Six	**175**	175	175	144	98	167	81
TOTAL ALL	**582**	US-373 / Canada-82 / Mexico-62 / Italian-41 / German-8 / UK-3 / Argentina-3 / Australia-2 / Belgium-2 / Chile, Scandinavia, 1 each / Orient, Arabic, 1 each / France, Thailand, 1 each	Round-127 / Oval/Oblong-56 / Std Rect-206 / Lge Rect/TV-83 / Lng Rect/Sq-20 / Flt/Sm Rect-90	288	191	517	162
TOTAL ALL	**582**	582	582	288	191	517	162
				50%	33%	89%	28%

US: 373 (64%)   Canada: 82 (14%)   Mexico: 62 (11%)
Italy: 41(7%)   Germany: 8 (1%)   All Other: 16 (3%)

II. Tray Data (#2): Quantities of Licensed Trays Distributed by Trademark Marketing, International

Over one hundred trays issued in the late 1980s and 1990s were licensed by The Coca-Cola Company and distributed by Trademark Marketing, International. Quantities, when available, are listed on *all* trays in the captions under pictures in Chapters One through Six and Section VII of this Appendix. Note that these volumes are those sold from the Distributor. In this chart, volumes are listed from high to low and are not rounded off as some of the quantities in the captions. Note also that marketing promotions and other special situations may have influenced the quantities distributed.

Sixteen trays or sixty-four percent of the following *Top Twenty-Five* list are trays from reproductions of earlier ads, including one from an earlier tray. Six trays, or twenty-four percent, are *The Signature Series* trays, two are collages, and one is a logo tray. While Haddon Sundblom created the images on four of these best sellers, Pamela C. Renfroe has five.

Tray volumes in this section provided courtesy of Trademark Marketing, International.

Year	Tray Name	Tray Description	Shape	Volume
1. 1985, '90	Through All the Yrs	Collage Coke Items	Std Rect	200,394
2. 1995	Sign Art	Collage Coke Items	Lng Rect	89,282
3. 1993	Always Cool	Repro 1992 ad, Bears	Std Rect	73,675
4. 1991	Have a Coke	Repro 1948 ad, Couple	Lge Rect	65,704
5. 1987	Touring Car	Repro 1924 ad, Red Car	Lge Rect	64,484
6. 1990	Four Seasons	Repro 1922 Festoon	Sm Rect	62,625
7. 1993	The Pause that...	P. Renfroe #1	Lge Rect	59,394
8. 1989	Dear Santa	Repro 1963 ad, at Chimney	Std Rect	57,701
9. 1994	Coca-Cola w/Bottle	Repro 1951 Button Sign	Round	54,832
10. 1991	He's Coming Home	Repro 1944 ad, w/Wagon	Flt Rect	54,147
11. 1990	Drive Refreshed	Repro 1950 ad, Car	Lng Rect	52,614
12. 1989	Soda Fountain	Repro 1908 ad, Fountain	Lge Rect	50,478
13. 1995	1905 Summer Bridge	Jim Harrison #1	Lge Rect	47,632
14. 1988	Sea Captain	Repro 1936 Calendar	Flt Rect	46,074
15. 1988	When Friends Drop In	Repro 1961 ad, Santa/Dog	Round	46,008
16. 1988	Lady in Red	Repro 1908 Calendar	Lge Oval	45,239
17. 1996	The Gathering Place	P. Renfroe #3	Lge Rect	44,800
18. 1994	Sign of Good Taste	P. Renfroe #2	Std Rect	43,551
19. 1996	Polar Bear Push	Repro 1990s ad, Cubs	Small Oval	40,673
20. 1991	Barefoot Boy	Repro 1931 Tray	Flt Rect	38,347
21. 1991	Welcome	Repro 1943 ad, Uniform	Lng Rect	37,117
22. 1992	Be Really Refreshed	Repro 1958 ad, Umpire	Flt Rect	36,965
23. 1989	Baseball (Massengale)	Repro 1907 ad, in Stands	Std Rect	35,031
24. 1996	(DQ#1) Winning	P. Renfroe #5	Std Rect	34,654
25. 1996	Fillin' Up	P. Renfroe #6	Std Rect	28,499

The next twenty-five trays (#26-50) have average volumes of *20,700* each. Trays #51-75 average *12,750* each and #76-100 average *7,200* each.

III. Internet Data (#1): Number of Auctions and Number of Bids, by Decade.

The following information lists details of Internet auction data, by decade. The chart contains the number of auctions, sales, and bids in each decade. The column headings list **(Decade)**, **(# Trays)** the total trays identified in those years, **(# w/Auc)** # of different trays seen in at least one auction, with the **(%)** of total trays, **(# Auc)** auctions for the trays of that decade, and **(# Bids)** bids in the auctions.

After the totals for each decade additional data is provided detailing four types of auctions. These types are: **(# Sales, VG+)** trays *sold* in Very Good or better condition, **(# Sales, G-)** trays *sold* in Good or worse condition, **(# Auc, res not met)** *reserve* auctions in which the tray was *not sold* because no bids reached the seller's desired price, and **(# Auc, no bid)** no bid auctions, which means unsold trays because no bids were recorded. The **(%)** numbers after types of auctions indicate what percent of the total (#w/Auc), (#Auc), and (#Bids) each type of auction represents.

An interesting comparison is found in the *average bids per auction*. The review shows clearly that *recent* trays, while sold in volume, receive *fewer* bids per tray (*no bid* auctions are not included in this calculation). Auctions that resulted in sales for trays from 1897-1919 received an average of *9.5* bids per auction. Trays of the 1920s, 1930s, and 1940s attracted the *most* bids with sale auctions that averaged *11.5* bids each. The 1930s, at *14.1* bids per auction, is the top decade. The decades of the 1950s and 1960s average *4.8* bids per sale while the 1970s have an average of *2.6* and 1980s average *3.2*. Auctions with sales in the 1990s average *1.98* bids each, the lowest number of any decade.

Decade	#Trays	#w/Auc	%	#Auc	%	#Bids	%
1897-1909	16	7	44%	12	—	115	—
# Sales VG+		0	0%	0	0%	0	0%
# Sales G-		5	71%	8	67%	88	77%
# Auc, res not met				4	33%	27	23%
# Auc, no bid				0	0%	0	0%
1910-1919	6	4	66%	22	—	169	—
# Sales VG+		0	0%	0	0%	0	0%
# Sales G-		3	75%	7	32%	49	29%
# Auc, res not met				11	50%	120	71%
# Auc, no bid				4	18%	0	0%
1920-1929	15	12	80%	96	—	687	—
# Sales, VG+		10	83%	27	28%	361	53%
# Sales, G-				19	20%	150	22%
# Auc, res not met				41	43%	176	25%
# Auc, no bid				9	9%	0	0%
1930-1939	17	12	65%	188	—	2376	—
# Sales, VG+		11	92%	77	41%	820	35%
# Sales, G-				52	28%	595	25%
# Auc, res not met				40	21%	961	40%
# Auc, no bid				19	10%	0	0%
1940-1949	11	5	45%	162	—	1494	—
# Sales, VG+		4	80%	54	34%	731	49%
# Sales, G-				41	25%	292	20%
# Auc, res not met				44	27%	471	31%
# Auc, no bid				23	14%	0	0%
1950-1959	32	22	69%	545	—	1958	—
# Sales, VG+		18	82%	299	55%	1555	79%
# Sales G-				31	69%	85	4%
# Auc, res not met				62	11%	318	16%
# Auc, no bid				153	28%	0	0%
1960-1969	40	25	63%	199	—	620	—
# Sales, VG+		20	80%	130	65%	562	91%
# Sales, G-				12	6%	37	6%
# Auc, res not met				6	3%	21	3%
# Auc, no bid				51	26%	0	0%
1970-1979	115	77	67%	941	—	1459	—
# Sales, VG+		69	90%	473	50%	1236	85%
# Sales, G-				73	8%	190	13%
# Auc, res not met				12	1%	33	2%
# Auc, no bid				383	41%	0	0%
1980-1989	155	108	70%	539	—	1107	—
# Sales, VG+		81	75%	297	55%	951	86%
# Sales, G-				43	8%	131	12%
# Auc, res not met				8	1%	25	2%
# Auc, no bid				191	35%	0	0%

Decade	#Trays	#w/Auc	%	#Auc	%	#Bids	%
1990-1999	**175**	**137**	**78%**	**1855**	—	**920**	—
# Sales, VG+		112	82%	444	24%	873	95%
# Sales, G-				13	1%	25	3%
# Auc, res not met				7	0%	22	2%
# Auc, no bid				1391	75%	0	0%
Auctions Dropped*	—	—		469	—	469	—
# Sales, VG+		—		20	4%	224	48%
# Sales, G-				19	4%	168	36%
# Auc, res not met				4	1%	77	16%
# Auc, no bid				426	91%	0	0%
TOTAL	**582**	**409**	**70%**	**5028**	—	**11374**	—
# Sales, VG+		325	79%	1821	36%	7313	64%
# Sales, G-		8	2%	318	6%	1810	16%
# Auc, res not met				239	5%	2251	20%
# Auc, no bid				2650	53%	0	0%

*Reasons for dropping an auction include no available picture, questions on the data, and other miscellaneous reasons.

Trays seen in at least one auction total 409, or *70%* of the total trays identified. And, 333 different trays, or *81%* of the trays auctioned, were sold at least once in an auction recorded for this material.

It can be seen that the numbers and relative percents vary widely by decade. But, in total, about forty percent of the recorded auctions ended in a successful sale.

IV. Internet Data (#2): Top Selling Trays in Auctions

Following is an overall top ten list and top sellers by decade, up to a maximum of ten trays. *This information is from the seventy days of auctions reviewed over the first ten months of the year 2000.* Listed are trays that sold the most number of times (ranked by sales, in acceptable quality). For comparison, also included are the number of auctions for that tray that ended in a sale in *good* or worse condition, a *reserve* (Res) auction, or a *no bid* (NB) auction. A tray is *not* listed unless it was recorded in more than three sales.

First listed are the *ten* trays that sold the highest number of times, regardless of decade. It is interesting to note that all ten trays are dated in the 1950s or 1970s.

In reviewing the listing by decade, note that the 1910s and 1920s have the highest rate of reserve auctions versus other decades. The 1920s and 1930s record the highest rate of sales in less than Good condition although over forty percent of the 1930s trays are listed as best sellers.

In the 1950s top seller list, the *no bid* auctions outnumber *reserve* auctions for the first time, and continue to do so in the following decades. Top seller auctions in the 1960s and 1980s have the highest rate of sales versus total auctions. Sixty-seven percent of these auctions result in sales.

Reproduction trays of 1973 and 1974 contribute to the 1970s record as top decade for actual number of trays sold. Finally, *no bid* auctions account for seventy percent of the 1990s top seller auctions, the highest of any decade.

#	Year	Name	VG+	G-	Res	NB	Total
Top Ten							
1.	1953	Menu Girl	134	15	34	64	247
2.	1973	Betty (Repro 1914)	55	1	0	33	89
3.	1973	Elaine (Repro 1916)	48	1	1	19	69
4.	1950	Girl with Wind in Hair	41	8	4	19	72
5.	1974	Party Girl (Repro 1925)	36	0	1	56	93
6.	1974	Autumn Girl (Repro 1922)	33	3	2	14	52
7.	1973	The Hamilton King Girl (Repro 1913)	32	2	1	35	70
8.	1956	Snacks	31	3	1	45	80
9.	1972	The Coca-Cola Girl (Repro 1910)	29	5	1	46	81
10.	(tie)1958	Picnic Cart (Std Rect shape)	26	1	5	5	37
	(tie)1974	Flapper Girl (Repro 1923)	26	0	1	52	79

#	Year	Name	VG+	G-	Res	NB	Total
By Decade							
1.	1916	Elaine	4	1	5	1	11
2.	1914	Betty	3	0	1	3	7
Tot 1910s			7	1	6	4	18
1.	1923	Flapper Girl	5	4	3	2	14
2.	1926	Golfers	3	2	2	1	8
3.	1929	Girl in Swimsuit, with Bottle	3	2	1	1	7
Tot 1920s			11	8	6	4	29
1.	1938	Girl at Shade	24	14	5	7	50
2.	1939	Springboard Girl	14	10	6	2	32
3.	1937	Running Girl	9	8	12	3	32
4.	1936	Hostess Girl	5	6	7	4	22
5.	1934	Tarzan	5	2	2	2	11
6.	1931	Barefoot Boy	4	1	4	1	10
7.	1930	Bather Girl	4	2	0	0	6
Tot 1930s			65	43	36	19	163
1.	1940	Sailor Girl	23	15	13	5	56
2.	1941	Two Girls at Car	18	16	18	9	61
3.	1942	Skater Girl	12	8	12	9	41
Tot 1940s			53	39	43	23	158
1.	1953	Menu Girl	134	15	34	64	247
2.	1950	Girl with Wind in Hair	41	8	4	19	72
3.	1956	Snacks	31	3	1	45	80
4.	1958	Picnic Cart (Std Rect shape)	26	1	5	5	37
5.	1957	Rooster Tray (Fr Can)	11	1	2	0	14
6.	1958	Picnic Cart (TV)	10	1	4	5	20
7.	1957	Birdhouse Tray (Eng Can)	9	0	1	1	11
8.	1957	Rooster Tray (Eng Can)	8	0	2	4	14
9.	1958	Picnic Cart (Fishtail logo, Fr Can)	8	0	2	4	14
10.	1957	Girl with the Umbrella (Fr Can)	5	3	0	0	8
Tot 1950s			283	32	55	147	517
1.	1961	Harvest (TV)	25	0	1	12	38
2.	1961	Pansy Garden (Coke Ref)	25	1	1	5	32
3.	1961	Pansy Garden (Be Really, Rect logo)	21	4	2	15	42
4.	1961	Pansy Garden (Be Really, Fishtail logo)	15	4	0	0	19
5.	1962	Candlelight (TV)	14	0	0	5	19
6.	1961	Pansy Garden (Fishtail logo, Fr Can)	12	0	0	4	16
Tot 1960s			112	9	4	41	166
1.	1973	Betty (Repro 1914)	55	1	0	33	89
2.	1973	Elaine (Repro 1916)	48	1	1	19	69
3.	1974	Party Girl (Repro 1925)	36	0	1	56	93
4.	1974	Autumn Girl (Repro 1922)	33	3	2	14	52
5.	1973	The Hamilton King Girl (Repro 1913)	32	2	1	35	70
6.	1972	The Coca-Cola Girl (Repro 1910)	29	5	1	46	81
7.	1974	Flapper Girl (Repro 1923)	26	0	1	52	79
8.	1970s	Tarzan (Repro 1934)	24	0	0	10	34
9.	1976	Indiana University	13	0	0	5	18
10.	1975	L. Nordica (Repro 1905, Atlanta)	12	0	0	5	17
Tot 1970s			308	12	7	275	602
1.	1983	Kroger 100th Anniv	11	0	0	3	14
2.	1986	Expo '86, Fireworks	11	0	0	2	13
3.	1987	Hospitality (Repro 1948 ad)	11	0	0	1	12
4.	1987	Girls at the Seashore (Repro 1917 ad)	10	0	0	3	13
5.	1981	Boy Fishing (Repro 1935 ad)	9	0	0	3	12
6.	1982	The 1982 World's Fair	9	0	0	17	26
7.	1983	Good Boys and Girls (Repro 1951 ad)	9	1	0	2	12
8.	1982	Hawaii, 75th Anniv	9	0	0	0	9
9.	1985	Through All the Years	8	0	0	8	16
10.	1986	Things go better (Repro 1964 ad)	8	0	0	4	12
Tot 1980s			95	1	0	43	139

#	Year	Name	VG+	G-	Res	NB	Total
1.	1998	Coke By the Sea (Mack #9)	24	0	0	38	62
2.	1998	Coca-Cola Goes Along (Renfroe #10)	15	0	0	79	94
3.	1999	Boston Lighthouse (Mack #11)	14	0	0	2	16
4.	1998	Always (Baby Bears)	13	0	0	19	32
5.	1999	Summer Smiles (Sandridge #5)	12	0	0	52	64
6.	1999	Varsity (with Menu)	11	0	0	25	36
7.	1996	Last Drip (Sandridge #3)	9	0	0	5	14
8.	1997	Smokey Bear	9	0	5	0	14
9.	1998	REA (Renfroe #11)	9	0	0	50	59
10.	1998	Refreshing Times (Renfroe #8)	9	0	0	17	26
Tot 1990s			125	0	5	287	417

Decade	#Trays	#w/Auc	#Not Sold	#Sold	+	=	-
Chap Three	72	47	9	38	3	16	19
1970-1979	115	77	8	69	0	38	31
Chap Four	115	77	8	69	0	38	31
1980-1989	155	108	27	81	7	53	21
Chap Five	155	108	27	81	7	53	21
1990-1999	175	137	25	112	2	75	35
Chap Six	175	137	25	112	2	75	35
Total All	582	409	76	333	12	205	116
Total Trays in Auction	70%						
Trays in Auctions, not sold		19%					
Trays in Auctions, sold			81%				
Trays sold, av above Ref range				4%			
Trays sold, av within Ref range					62%		
Trays sold, av below Ref range							35%

V. Internet Data (#3): Internet Dollar Values versus Reference Material Dollar Values

To review information previously noted, Dollar Values are listed two ways in the caption detail for Chapters One through Six: *Reference Guide* prices are compiled from eight price guides plus dealer/collector transactions. *Internet* prices are logged from actual tray auctions.

Reference Guide prices are sometimes criticized for pricing *too low*. And, they are also sometimes criticized for pricing *too high*. Comparisons to the *actual* prices paid in Internet auctions might prove a useful comparison, and is the purpose of this chart.

The dollar values used in this book from References are expressed in a range, allowing for differences in tray conditions. The Internet price is a specific price that is an average of prices from each recorded sale. The condition of the trays that sold obviously varied, but except for early trays most were in Very Good or better condition. Trays from the late 1990s were assumed to be in Near Mint condition.

Columns below indicate **(Decade)**, **(# Trays)** the total number of trays in that decade, **(# w/Auc)** the number of trays seen in at least one auction, **(# Not Sold)** the number of trays seen in at least one auction that did not sell, and **(# Sold)** the number of different trays from that decade that were seen in at least one auction and that sold successfully at least once. The trays are then categorized by whether the average final price is **(+)** above the dollar range of the reference price, **(=)** within the dollar range, or **(-)** below the dollar range. Note that the final price for a tray can be the result of one auction or the average price from one hundred auctions, as seen in the individual caption details.

Internet average sale prices underscore the importance of a tray's condition, especially in older trays. Trays sold dating from 1897 through the 1970s averaged a price (+) *above* or (=) *equal to* the Reference dollar value in 57% of the trays. Auctions of trays dating from the 1980s and 1990s averaged a sale price (+) *above* or (=) *equal to* the Reference dollar value in 71% of the trays. Overall, the chart demonstrates that dealer prices are generally consistent with actual market conditions and that Internet shoppers, while getting good values and some great values, are not generally paying unreasonable prices, high or low.

Decade	#Trays	#w/Auc	#Not Sold	#Sold	+	=	-
1897-1909	16	7	2	5	0	1	4
1910-1919	6	4	1	3	0	1	2
Chap One	22	11	3	8	0	2	6
1920-1929	15	12	2	10	0	9	1
1930-1939	17	12	1	11	0	8	3
1940-1949	11	5	1	4	0	4	0
Chap Two	43	29	4	25	0	21	4
1950-1959	32	22	4	18	0	13	5
1960-1969	40	25	5	20	3	3	14

Note that over sixty percent of the sales were within the Reference Material price range; about one-third were below the range, and a small percent were above the range. Sellers and buyers could benefit from checking captions for price information on a specific tray before selling or bidding to buy.

VI. Internet Data (# 4): Suggestions (a short list)

Over 97,000 auctions were checked on seventy specific days to identify the 5,028 auctions reviewed in detail for the Internet Dollar Values. Looking at that many auctions created a short list of suggestions, mostly for sellers.

Sellers: Listing multiple trays in one auction can be a problem since a collector may already have one or more of the trays and would not want to bid on the entire group.

Sellers: If a tray is a commemorative describe the nature of the commemorative. Sounds obvious but that detail is omitted in many of the reviewed auctions.

Sellers: All trays come from somewhere and many are acquired from flea markets, estate sales, and dusty attics. Unless it is a special situation, that information is usually not helpful. An example of acquisition information that *is* useful would be if the owner was a previous collector or bottler or trays were acquired in volume.

Sellers: Over-used words and phrases that aren't usually helpful include *Vintage* (whatever that means), *Mint except for that big chip, Looks better than the photograph, Could be a reproduction but I don't see any indication* (hint, look on the rim).

Buyers: Ask questions.

VII. Caption Details, Trays Not Pictured

Pictures of all identified trays were not available. However, in this section a caption has been provided for each tray not pictured that contains all the details available for that tray. Below is a chart summarizing the data, by Chapter, for these captions. The chart is similar to the summary chart of all trays by decade, in Section One of this Appendix. One difference in this chart is to indicate the number of unique *images* not pictured. The columns are as follows: **(Decade)** decade and chapter of the book; **(# Trays)** number of trays in the decade without a picture; **(Country)** country of the trays; **(# Shapes)** number of shapes of these trays; **(Mfr)** number of these trays with manufacturer information; **(Vol)** number of these trays with volume information; and **(# Images)** number of unique images on these trays—that is, an image not seen on any of the trays with pictures.

Decade	# Trays	Country	# Shapes	Mfr	Vol	# Images
1897-1909	1	US-1	Oblong/Oval-1	1	0	0
1910-1919	0	0	0	0	0	0
Chap One	1	US-1	Oblong/Oval-1	1	0	0
1920-1929	2	US-1	Round-0	2	0	0
		Canada-0	Std Rectangle-2			
		Mexico-1				
1930-1939	4	US-0	Round-0	4	0	0
		Canada-4	Std Rectangle-4			
		Mexico-0				
1940-1949	6	US-3	Round-1	1	0	4
		Canada-1	Std Rectangle-5			
		Mexico-2				
Chap Two	12	US-4	Round-1	7	0	4
		Canada-5	Std Rectangle-11			
		Mexico-3				
1950-1959	7	US-3	Round-1	1	0	2
		Canada-1	Std Rectangle-5			
		Mexico-2	Lge Rectangle/TV-1			
		German-1	Flat/Sm Rectangle-0			
1960-1969	11	US-0	Round-3	2	1	7
		Canada-2	Std Rectangle-0			
		Mexico-9	Lge Rectangle/TV-4			
		German-0	Flat/Sm Rectangle-4			
Chap Three	18	US-3	Round-4	3	1	9
		Canada-3	Std Rectangle-5			
		Mexico-11	Lge Rectangle/TV-5			
		German-1	Flat/Sm Rectangle-4			
1970-1979	14	US-6	Round-7	5	3	8
		Canada-1	Lge Rectangle/TV-2			
		Mexico-4	Lng Rectangle/Sq-1			
		Italy-1	Flat/Sm Rectangle-4			
		Germany-1				
		Australia-1				
Chap Four	14	14	14	5	3	8
1980-1989	12	US-6	Round-2	0	0	7
		Canada-3	Oblong/Oval-3			
		Italy-2	Std Rectangle-4			
		Belgium-1	Lge Rectangle/TV-2			
			Lng Rectangle/Sq-1			
Chap Five	12	12	12	0	0	7
1990-1999	8	US-4	Round-2	3	2	6
		Mexico-1	Std Rectangle-1			
		Italy-3	Lge Rectangle/TV-1			
			Flat/Sm Rectangle-4			
Chap Six	8	8	8	3	2	6
TOTALS	65	US-24	Round-16	19	6	34
		Canada-12	Oblong/Oval-4			
		Mexico-19	Std Rectangle-21			
		Italy-6	Lge Rectangle/TV-10			
		German-2	Flat/Sm Rectangle-12			
		Australia-1	Lng Rectangle/Sq-2			
		Belgium-1				
TOTALS	65	65	65	19	6	34

Trays not pictured: 65 (11%)
Images not pictured: 34 (7%)

Trays Not Pictured, *Chapter One*

Name: Hilda with The Glass (Pewter Holder), *or* Big Hilda; **Issued:** 1903, also on calendar
Comments: Differs in color and sharpness from other version. Also, note does not list the Boston Branch; **Shape:** Large Oval; **Size:** 15.125" x 18.625"; **Story:** —; **Country:** US; **Mfr/Dist:** Chas. W. Shonk Company **Border/Edge:** Red, flower trim; **Quantity:** —.
$ Value, References: est $3,500-$8,300 (3,5)
$ Value, Internet Auctions: —; **# Sales:** —

Trays Not Pictured, *Chapter Two*

Name: Smiling Girl; **Issued:** 1924, also on calendar
Comments: Issued in two versions, differing only in border colors, calendar picture has glass *and* bottle, maroon version is more scarce; **Shape:** Std Rectangle; **Size:** 10.5" x 13.25"; **Story:** —; **Country:** US; **Mfr/Dist:** The American Artworks; **Border/Edge:** Maroon, gold stripe; **Quantity:** —.
$ Value, References: $325-$1100 (5,7,8)
$ Value, Internet Auctions: —; **# Sales:** —

Name: Girl With The Bobbed Hair *or* Bobbed Hair Girl; **Issued:** 1928, ©1927
Comments: First known tray also issued in a Mexican edition, *Tome*, or *Drink*, first person on tray sipping Coke (from a bottle) through a straw; **Shape:** Std Rectangle; **Size:** 10.5" x 13.25"; **Story:** —; **Country:** US for Mexican market; **Mfr/Dist:** The American Artworks; **Border/Edge:** Red, gold edge band; **Quantity:** —.
$ Value, References: est $275-$975 (4,5)
$ Value, Internet Auctions: —; **# Sales:** —

Name: Hostess Girl *or* Hostess Tray; **Issued:** c.1936-1937, ©1936
Comments: By Hayden Hayden, tray reverses the colors in red border trays; **Shape:** Std Rectangle; **Size:** 10.5" x 13.25"; **Story:** —; **Country:** US for Canadian (English) market; **Mfr/Dist:** The American Artworks; **Border/Edge:** Gold, w/red edge; **Quantity:** —.
$ Value, References: est $175-$650 (4,5)
$ Value, Internet Auctions: —; **# Sales:** —.

Name: Hostess Girl *or* Hostess Tray; **Issued:** c.1936-1937, ©1936
Comments: By Hayden Hayden, tray reverses the colors in red border trays; **Shape:** Std Rectangle; **Size:** 10.5" x 13.25"; **Story:** —; **Country:** US for Canadian (French) market; **Mfr/Dist:** The American Artworks; **Border/Edge:** Gold, with red edge; **Quantity:** —.
$ Value, References: est $175-$650 (4,5)
$ Value, Internet Auctions: $72 (for info only); **# Sales:** 1

Name: Girl at Shade *or* Girl in the Afternoon *or* Girl in Yellow Hat; **Issued:** 1938, ©1938, similar calendar image
Comments: By Bradshaw Crandell; **Shape:** Std Rectangle; **Size:** 10.5" x 13.25"; **Story:** —; **Country:** US for Canadian (English) market; **Mfr/Dist:** The American Artworks; **Border/Edge:** Gold, with red edge; **Quantity:** —.
$ Value, References: $125-$325 (4,5,x)
$ Value, Internet Auctions: —; **# Sales:** —

Name: Springboard Girl; **Issued:** 1939, ©1939
Comments: By Haddon Sundblom, with signature on tray, ninth and last of red border swimsuit trays, expanded top logo drops below border; **Shape:** Std Rectangle; **Size:** 10.5" x 13.25"; **Story:** —; **Country:** US for Canadian (English) market; **Mfr/Dist:** The American Artworks; **Border/Edge:** Red, thin silver lines, w/ silver edge; **Quantity:** —.
$ Value, References: $175-$325 (1,2,3,4,5,7,8,x)
$ Value, Internet Auctions: —; **# Sales:** —

Name: Sailor Girl; **Issued:** 1940, ©1940
Comments: Third horizontal image; **Shape:** Std Rectangle; **Size:** 10.5" x 13.25"; **Story:** —; **Country:** US for Canadian (English) market; **Mfr/Dist:** The American Artworks; **Border/Edge:** Red, thin silver lines, with silver edge; **Quantity:** —.
$ Value, References: est $100-$350 (4,5)
$ Value, Internet Auctions: —; **# Sales:** —

Name: Coca-Cola, Logo Tray; **Issued:** c.1941
Comments: Found in one reference book, no price data, words on tray read: *Trademark Reg. U.S. Pat.*; **Shape:** Std Rectangle; **Size:** 10.5" x 13.25"; **Story:** —; **Country:** US; **Mfr/Dist:** —; **Border/Edge:** Black; **Quantity:** —.
$ Value, References: est $100-$250 (x)
$ Value, Internet Auctions: —; **# Sales:** —

Name: Coca-Cola, Logo Tray; **Issued:** c.1941
Comments: Found in one reference book, no price data, words on tray read: *Reg. U.S. Pat. Off.*; **Shape:** Std Rectangle; **Size:** 10.5" x 13.75"; **Story:** —; **Country:** US; **Mfr/Dist:** —; **Border/Edge:** White; **Quantity:** —.
$ Value, References: est $100-$250 (x)
$ Value, Internet Auctions: —; **# Sales:** —

Name: Drink Coca-Cola, Delicious and Refreshing; **Issued:** c.1940s
Comments: Logo tray, rim with curved lip; **Shape:** Round; **Size:** 12.75"; **Story:** —; **Country:** US; **Mfr/Dist:** —; **Border/Edge:** —; **Quantity:** —.
$ Value, References: est $275-$375; (2,7)
$ Value, Internet Auctions: —; **# Sales:** —

Name: Woman in Evening Gown, with Bottle; **Issued:** c.1940s
Comments: Early Mexican tray, dark red strapless gown; **Size:** 10.5" x 13.25"; **Story:** —; **Country:** Mexico; **Mfr/Dist:** —; **Border/Edge:** Ivory; **Quantity:** —.
$ Value, References: est $750-$900; (4)
$ Value, Internet Auctions: —; **# Sales:** —

Name: Woman in Cowboy Dress, with Bottle; **Issued:** c.1940s
Comments: Early Mexican tray; **Shape:** Std Rectangle; **Size:** 10.5" x 13.25"; **Story:** —; **Country:** Mexico; **Mfr/Dist:** —; **Border/Edge:** Ivory; **Quantity:** —.
$ Value, References: est $900-$1050; (2,4)
$ Value, Internet Auctions: —; **# Sales:** —

Trays Not Pictured, *Chapter Three*

Name: Trink Coca Cola; **Issued:** c.1950s
Comments: Logo tray, words: *Eiskalt* (Ice Cold). One of two that are the first known *logo* trays from outside North America and the first identified trays from Germany; **Shape:** Deep Round; **Size:** 13.5" dia. x 1.75" depth; **Story:** —; **Country:** Germany; **Mfr/Dist:** —; **Border/Edge:** White with red back; **Quantity:** —.
$ Value, References: est $20-$50 (x)
$ Value, Internet Auctions: $20 (for info only); **# Sales:** 1

Name: World with Bottle; **Issued:** c.1950
Comments: Coca-Cola in eight languages, plastic; **Shape:** Large Rectangle; **Size:** 12.0" x 16.5"; **Story:** —; **Country:** US; **Mfr/Dist:** —; **Border/Edge:** —; **Quantity:** —.
$ Value, References: est $200-$300 (x)
$ Value, Internet Auctions: —; **# Sales:** —

Name: Girl with Wind in Hair *or* Girl with Red Hair; **Issued:** 1950-1952, on 1948 calendars for the U.S. (Mar/Apr page) and Canada (Jan/Feb page)
Comments: By Haddon Sundblom, some disagreement on issue date vs. 1948, first tray with ad words on all four sides, this version has a darker screen in bottom half of tray face vs. the other US version; **Shape:** Std Rectangle; **Size:** 10.5" x 13.25"; **Story:** —; **Country:** US; **Mfr/Dist:** —; **Border/Edge:** Red, with silver edge; **Quantity:** —.
$ Value, References: $75-$400 (4,5,8)
$ Value, Internet Auctions: $170 (for info only); **# Sales:** 2

Name: Menu Girl *or* Girl with Menu; **Issued:** 1953-c.1960, on 1951 calendar, U.S. (Mar/Apr page)
Comments: End of red border trays, slight change in rectangle size, banners in border have different wording: *Thirst Quencher* replaces *Have a Coke*. This version is rare; **Shape:** Std Rectangle; **Size:** 10.625" x 13.25"; **Story:** —; **Country:** US; **Mfr/Dist:** —; **Border/Edge:** Fourteen small pictures of year around activities; **Quantity:** —.
$ Value, References: est $100-$275 (x)
$ Value, Internet Auctions: —; **# Sales:** —

Name: Menu Girl *or* Girl with Menu; **Issued:** 1953-c.1960, on 1951 calendar, U.S. (Mar/Apr page)
Comments: Red border tray still exists on this version, slight change in rectangle size, Tray words: *Deliciosa* and *Refraichissant*; **Shape:** Std Rectangle; **Size:** 10.625" x 13.25"; **Story:** —; **Country:** US for Mexican Market; **Mfr/Dist:** —; **Border/Edge:** Red; **Quantity:** —.
$ Value, References: $90-$200 (2,4,5,8)
$ Value, Internet Auctions: —; **# Sales:** —

Name: Picnic Cart *or* Picnic Basket; **Issued:** c.1958
Comments: Fishtail or Arciform Logo, *Drink Coca-Cola*, some references list different size dimensions but this data has not been verified; **Shape:** Std Rectangle; **Size:** 10.75" x 13.25"; **Story:** —; **Country:** US for Canadian (English) market; **Mfr/Dist:** Donaldson Art Company; **Border/Edge:** Brown lines with a wicker look; **Quantity:** —.
$ Value, References: est $40-$75 (4,8)
$ Value, Internet Auctions: $17 (for info only); **# Sales:** 2

Name: Woman with Braids; **Issued:** c.1951, also on 1951 Mexican calendar
Comments: Reproduction of 1950 US ad; **Shape:** Std Rectangle; **Size:** 10.75" x 13.25"; **Story:** —; **Country:** Mexico; **Mfr/Dist:** —; **Border/Edge:** Yellow, red stripe; **Quantity:** —.
$ Value, References: est $450-$600 (8,x)
$ Value, Internet Auctions: —; **# Sales:** —

Name: Woman with Bottle, Large Straw Hat; **Issued:** 1960s
Comments: Same image as a tip tray of the 1970s; **Shape:** Deep Round; **Size:** 13.25" dia. x 1.5" depth; **Story:** —; **Country:** Mexico; **Mfr/Dist:** —; **Border/Edge:** Red; **Quantity:** —.**$ Value, References:** est $70-$100 (x)
$ Value, Internet Auctions: $20 (for info only); **# Sales:** 1

Name: Plate of Snacks; **Issued:** 1960s
Comments: Food, with Coke, tray listed in one reference; **Shape:** TV; **Size:** 13.5" x 18.25"; **Story:** —; **Country:** Mexico; **Mfr/Dist:** —; **Border/Edge:** —; **Quantity:** —.
$ Value, References: est $30-$50 (8)
$ Value, Internet Auctions: —; **# Sales:** —

Name: Bottles in an Ice Bucket; **Issued:** 1963
Comments: Coke, roast chicken, flowers; **Shape:** TV; **Size:** 13.5" x 18.75"; **Story:** —; **Country:** Mexico; **Mfr/Dist:** —; **Border/Edge:** Brown, lattice trim; **Quantity:** —.
$ Value, References: est $70-90 (4)
$ Value, Internet Auctions: —; **# Sales:** —

Name: Spooning out Beans; **Issued:** 1963
Comments: Beans and Rice; **Shape:** TV; **Size:** 13.5" x 18.25"; **Story:** —; **Country:** Mexico; **Mfr/Dist:** —; **Border/Edge:** —; **Quantity:** —.
$ Value, References: est $40-$65 (4)
$ Value, Internet Auctions: —; **# Sales:** —

Name: Woman in Red Sweater; **Issued:** 1965
Comments: Same image as a tip tray of the same year; **Shape:** Deep Round; **Size:** 13.25" dia. x 1.5" depth; **Story:** —; **Country:** Mexico; **Mfr/Dist:** —; **Border/Edge:** Red; **Quantity:** —.
$ Value, References: $85-$125 (4,7,8)
$ Value, Internet Auctions: —; **# Sales:** —

Name: Fruit Arrangement; **Issued:** 1968
Comments: Food, with Coke, same image as 1969 TV Tray; **Shape:** Small Rectangle; **Size:** 6.625" x 7.875"; **Story:** —; **Country:** Mexico; **Mfr/Dist:** —; **Border/Edge:** Brown; **Quantity:** —.
$ Value, References: est $30-$45 (4)
$ Value, Internet Auctions: —; **# Sales:** —

Name: Embotelladora Pacifico, S.A.; **Issued:** 1968
Comments: Artist rendition of new Bottling Plant, *first* such commemorative tray; **Shape:** TV; **Size:** 13.5" x 18.75"; **Story:** Yes; **Country:** Mexico; **Mfr/Dist:** —; **Border/Edge:** —; **Quantity:** —.
$ Value, References: est $90-$120 (6)
$ Value, Internet Auctions: —; **# Sales:** —

Name: Ornate Utensils; **Issued:** 1969
Comments: Coffee service and other utensils, same image as 1968 TV tray; **Shape:** Small Rectangle; **Size:** 6.625" x 7.875"; **Story:** —; **Country:** Mexico; **Mfr/Dist:** —; **Border/Edge:** White; **Quantity:** —.
$ Value, References: est $30-$45 (4)
$ Value, Internet Auctions: $29 (for info only); **# Sales:** 1

Name: Woman Lounging on Beach Mat; **Issued:** 1969
Comments: Close-up of face; **Shape:** Deep Round; **Size:** 13.25" dia. x 1.5" depth; **Story:** —; **Country:** Mexico; **Mfr/Dist:** —; **Border/Edge:** White, red edge; **Quantity:** —.
$ Value, References: est $40-$65 (4)
$ Value, Internet Auctions: $83 (for info only); **# Sales:** 2

Name: Lillian Nordica with Bottle; **Issued:** 1968
Comments: Reproduction of 1905 tray, same image as 1968 French Canadian version; **Shape:** Flat Rectangle; **Size:** 10.75" x 14.75"; **Story:** —; **Country:** Canada (English); **Mfr/Dist:** Ballanoff; **Border/Edge:** Green; **Quantity:** 50,000.
$ Value, References: $40-$85 (1,3,4,7,8)
$ Value, Internet Auctions: $30 (for info only); **# Sales:** 2

Name: Ornamin by Ornamold; **Issued:** c.1969
Comments: Cartoon with cup of frozen Coke, plastic; **Shape:** Small Rectangle; **Size:** 6.25" x 7.75"; **Story:** —; **Country:** Canada; **Mfr/Dist:** Ornamold; **Border/Edge:** —; **Quantity:** —.
$ Value, References: est $65-$90 (4)
$ Value, Internet Auctions: —; **# Sales:** —

Trays Not Pictured, *Chapter Four*

Note that three 1970s trays not pictured have captions included in groupings of commemorative trays listed in Chapter Four. One is in the *Hilda with Glass and Note* commemoratives for 1977 and two are in the 1978 *Bottle 5¢* commemoratives.

Name: Enjoy Coke; **Issued:** 1970
Comments: Logo tray, plastic; **Shape:** Deep Square; **Size:** 14.0" x 14.0"; **Story:** —; **Country:** US; **Mfr/Dist:** —; **Border/Edge:** Red; **Quantity:** —.
$ Value, References: est $10-$18 (x)
$ Value, Internet Auctions: —; **# Sales:** —

Name: Candlelight; **Issued:** 1972
Comments: Reproduction of 1962 TV tray, Ham and Coke, by candlelight, noted in reference material as produced for Coke's Sales Development; **Shape:** TV; **Size:** 13.5" x 18.5"; **Story:** —; **Country:** US; **Mfr/Dist:** Donaldson Art Company; **Border/Edge:** Brown; **Quantity:** 25,000.
$ Value, References: est $15-$30 (4)
$ Value, Internet Auctions: —; **# Sales:** —

Name: Bottle and Bowl of Beans; **Issued:** 1970
Comments: Beans and Rice; **Shape:** Deep Round; **Size:** 13.25" dia. x 1.5" depth; **Story:** —; **Country:** Mexico; **Mfr/Dist:** —; **Border/Edge:** —; **Quantity:** —.
$ Value, References: est $15-$30 (4,7,8)
$ Value, Internet Auctions: —; **# Sales:** —

Name: disfrute la Chispa dela vita; **Issued:** 1970
Comments: Bottle with colorful waves; **Shape:** Deep Round; **Size:** 13.25" dia. x 1.5" depth; **Story:** —; **Country:** Mexico; **Mfr/Dist:** —; **Border/Edge:** White; **Quantity:** —.
$ Value, References: est $15-$30 (4)
$ Value, Internet Auctions: $28 (for info only) **# Sales:** 2

Name: The Coca-Cola Girl; **Issued:** 1971
Comments: Reproduction of 1910 tray, by Hamilton King, repro has signature;
Shape: Flat Rectangle; **Size:** 10.5" x 14.5"; **Story:** Rim; **Country:** Canada (English);
Mfr/Dist: Ballonoff; **Border/Edge:** Red; **Quantity:** 50,000
$ Value, References: $15-$25 (1,3,4,6)
$ Value, Internet Auctions: —; **# Sales:** —

Name: Flapper Girl; **Issued:** 1974
Comments: Reproduction of 1925 tray; **Shape:** Round; **Size:** 12.0" dia.; **Story:** —;
Country: Germany; **Mfr/Dist:** Harlekin Geschenke Mfg.; **Border/Edge:** Green, gold
edge; **Quantity:** —.
$ Value, References: est $15-$30 (x)
$ Value, Internet Auctions: $25 (for info only); **# Sales:** 1

Name: Dear Santa or Santa at Chimney; **Issued:** 1975
Comments: Reproduction of 1963 ad, by Haddon Sundblom; **Shape:** Flat Rectangle;
Size: 10.5" x 14.5"; **Story:** —; **Country:** US; **Mfr/Dist:** Ohio Art Company; **Border/
Edge:** Green, no trim, no logo; **Quantity:** 7,500.
$ Value, References: est $15-$25 (3,x)
$ Value, Internet Auctions: $10; **# Sales:** 3

Name: The Fortitide Valley Rugby League Football Club, 1st Grade Team; **Issued:** 1975
Comments: Photo of players and coaches, Coke logos; **Shape:** Large Rectangle; **Size:**
13.5" x 19"; **Story:** Yes; **Country:** Australia; **Mfr/Dist:** —; **Border/Edge:** White;
Quantity: —. **$ Value, References:** est $12-$25 (x)
$ Value, Internet Auctions: $13 (for info only); **# Sales:** 1

Name: Lillian Nordica with Bottle; **Issued:** 1977
Comments: Reproduction of 1905 tray, first in a series of eight trays issued from 1977 to
1988 commemorating fifty years of Coke bottling in Italy; **Shape:** Flat Standard; **Size:**
10.5" x 14.5"; **Story:** Yes; **Country:** Italy; **Mfr/Dist:** —; **Border/Edge:** Verde Scuro (Dark
Green); **Quantity:** —.
$ Value, References: est $30-$50 (x)
$ Value, Internet Auctions: —; **# Sales:** —

Name: Women with bottles of Coke; **Issued:** 1976
Comments: Reproduction of 1929 calendar and a current model, Hay que compartir –
Coca-Cola y ya; **Shape:** Deep Round; **Size:** 13.25"; **Story:** —; **Country:** Mexico; **Mfr/
Dist:** —; **Border/Edge:** —; **Quantity:** —. **$ Value, References:** est $15-$30 (4,x)
$ Value, Internet Auctions: $26 (for info only); **# Sales:** 1

Name: Woman with red T-shirt, straw hat and Coke; **Issued:** 1979
Comments: Same image as 1960s round tray and 1979 round tray and 1978 tip tray;
words similar to 1979 round tray: Tome Coca-Cola Bien Fria; **Shape:** Small Rectangle; **Size:**
6.5" x 7.5"; **Story:** —; **Country:** Mexico; **Mfr/Dist:** —; **Border/Edge:** —; **Quantity:** —.
$ Value, References: est $45-$85 (x)
$ Value, Internet Auctions: —; **# Sales:** —

Trays Not Pictured, Chapter Five

Name: Candy Girl; **Issued:** c.1980s
Comments: Woman in white shorts riding a stick with a red candy heart at one end;
Shape: Round; **Size:** 11.75"; **Story:** —; **Country:** ?Belgium; **Mfr/Dist:** —; **Border/Edge:**
Silver; **Quantity:** —.
$ Value, References: est $10-$18 (x)
$ Value, Internet Auctions: —, **# Sales:** —

Name: St. Johns Grand Opening; **Issued:** c.1980s
Comments: Commemorative of bottler plant opening, Geo W Bennett Bryson & Co.,
Ltd, Newfoundland; **Shape:** Long Rectangle; **Size:** —; **Story:** —; **Country:** Canada; **Mfr/
Dist:** —; **Border/Edge:** —; **Quantity:** —.
$ Value, References: est $12-$20 (x)
$ Value, Internet Auctions: —; **# Sales:** —

Name: Coca-Cola Relieves Fatigue; **Issued:** c.1980s
Comments: Logo tray, glass tray face in wooden base, slotted handles; **Shape:** Large
Rectangle; **Size:** 12.0" x 15.5"; **Story:** —; **Country:** US; **Mfr/Dist:** —; **Border/Edge:**
Wood; **Quantity:** —.
$ Value, References: est $15-$20 (x)
$ Value, Internet Auctions: —; **# Sales:** —

Name: The Coca-Cola Girl; **Issued:** c.1980s
Comments: Reproduction of 1910 tray, by Hamilton King, glass face. Tray words: Delicious and
Refreshing, bamboo sides and handles; **Shape:** Large Rectangle; **Size:** 12.5" x 15.5"; **Story:** —;
Country: US; **Mfr/Dist:** —; **Border/Edge:** Bamboo; **Quantity:** —.
$ Value, References: est $15-$20 (x)
$ Value, Internet Auctions: —; **# Sales:** —

Name: Girl with Glass; **Issued:** 1980s
Comments: A poor quality image made of thin metal. However, it appears to be a
reproduction of a 1919 distributor calendar featuring the movie star Marion Davies. The
hair and extended fingers are the same as the calendar, the image is also on a large
rectangle tray and tip tray; **Shape:** Round; **Size:** 12.0"; **Story:** —; **Country:** US; **Mfr/
Dist:** —; **Border/Edge:** Red; **Quantity:** —.
$ Value, References: est $5-$8 (4)
$ Value, Internet Auctions: $6 (for info only); **# Sales:** 1

Name: Antique Car, Imperial Oil; **Issued:** 1980
Comments: Commemorates customer, 100th Anniversary of Imperial Oil Company,
largest oil company in Canada, picture of antique car at gas pump; **Shape:** Std Rectangle;
Size: 10.5" x 13.25"; **Story:** Yes; **Country:** Canada; **Mfr/Dist:** —; **Border/Edge:** —;
Quantity: —.
$ Value, References: est $15-$20 (x)
$ Value, Internet Auctions: $18 (for info only); **# Sales:** 2

Name: Normandeau Cup; **Issued:** 1980
Comments: Commemorates sports event, 75th Anniversary, Alberta, Canada. Pictures
horses jumping in competition; **Shape:** Std Rectangle; **Size:** 10.5" x 13.25"; **Story:** Yes;
Country: Canada (French); **Mfr/Dist:** —; **Border/Edge:** —;
Quantity: —.
$ Value, References: est $20-$30 (3,x)
$ Value, Internet Auctions: —; **# Sales:** —

Name: Four Seasons; **Issued:** 1981
Comments: Reproduction of 1922 Festoon, commemorates the Shasta Dam; **Shape:**
Large Deep Oval; **Size:** 12.5" x 15.5"; **Story:** Yes; **Country:** US; **Mfr/Dist:** —;
Border/Edge: Black, yellow edge; **Quantity:** —.
$ Value, References: est $5-$15 (x)
$ Value, Internet Auctions: —; **# Sales:** —

Name: 1927 Calendar Girl; **Issued:** 1981
Comments: Reproduction of 1927 calendar, third in the series of eight trays to
commemorate fifty years of Coca-Cola bottling in Italy; **Shape:** Std Rectangle; **Size:** 10.5"
x 13.25"; **Story:** Yes; **Country:** Italy; **Mfr/Dist:** —; **Border/Edge:** Blu scuro (Dark Blue);
Quantity: —.
$ Value, References: est $15-$30 (x)
$ Value, Internet Auctions: —; **# Sales:** —

Name: Summer Girl or Baseball Girl; **Issued:** 1984
Comments: Reproduction of 1921 tray, fifth in the series of eight trays to commemorate
fifty years of Coca-Cola bottling in Italy; **Shape:** Std Rectangle; **Size:** 10.5" x 13.25";
Story: Yes; **Country:** Italy; **Mfr/Dist:** —; **Border/Edge:** Crema, (Beige); **Quantity:** —.
$ Value, References: est $15-$30 (x)
$ Value, Internet Auctions: —; **# Sales:** —

Name: Four Seasons; **Issued:** 1984
Comments: Reproduction of 1922 Festoon, commemorates 45th Anniversary and new
plant opening, The Bottling Company of Cape Cod; **Shape:** Large Deep Oval; **Size:** 12.5" x
15.5"; **Story:** Yes; **Country:** US; **Mfr/Dist:** —; **Border/Edge:** Black, yellow edge;
Quantity: —.
$ Value, References: est $15-$25 (x)
$ Value, Internet Auctions: —; **# Sales:** —

Name: Duster Girls; **Issued:** 1988
Comments: Reproduction of 1912 ad, commemorates the anniversary of a bottler in
Arkansas; **Shape:** Large Deep Oval; **Size:** 12.5" x 15.5"; **Story:** Yes; **Country:** US;
Dist: —; **Border/Edge:** —; **Quantity:** —.
$ Value, References: est $5-$10 (3,x)
$ Value, Internet Auctions: —; **# Sales:** —
Trays Not Pictured, Chapter Six

Name: Out Fishin'; **Issued:** c.1992-1995
Comments: Commemorates customer, by Norman Rockwell; **Shape:** Small
Rectangle; **Size:** 8.0" x 11.0" x 1.0"; **Story:** —; **Country:** Italy; **Mfr/Dist:** Scatolificio
Lecchese; **Border/Edge:** —; **Quantity:** —.
$ Value, References: est $15-$30 (6)
$ Value, Internet Auctions: —; **# Sales:** —

Name: Drink Coca-Cola, 5¢ at Fountains; **Issued:** c.1992-1995
Comments: Reproduction of 1901 ad; **Shape:** Small Rectangle; **Size:** 8.0" x 11.0" x 1.0"; **Story:**
—; **Country:** Italy; **Mfr/Dist:** Scatolificio Lecchese; **Border/Edge:** —; **Quantity:** —.
$ Value, References: est $15-$30 (6)
$ Value, Internet Auctions: —; **# Sales:** —

Name: Barefoot Boy, Boy with Dog, or The Rockwell Tray; **Issued:** c.1992-1995
Comments: Reproduction of 1931 tray and calendar, by Norman Rockwell; **Shape:** Std
Rectangle; **Size:** 10.5" x 13.25"; **Story:** —; **Country:** Italy; **Mfr/Dist:** —; **Border/Edge:**
Yellow, with trim; **Quantity:** —.
$ Value, References: est $100-$150 (x)
$ Value, Internet Auctions: —; **# Sales:** —

Name: Thirst Asks Nothing More; **Issued:** 1992-1995
Comments: Reproduction of c.1930s ad, large glass with people seated at a table; **Shape:**
Small Flat Rectangle; **Size:** 10.5" x 14.0"; **Story:** —; **Country:** US; **Mfr/Dist:** Ohio Art
Company, Distributed by Trademark Marketing; **Border/Edge:** Orange; **Quantity:**
12,000.
$ Value, References: est $12-$22 (3)
$ Value, Internet Auctions: —; **# Sales:** —

Name: Group of Eleven Polar Bears; **Issued:** 1994
Comments: Reproduction of 1990s TV ad, eleven bears with scarves and Coke watching the aurora borealis. Same image as 1993 metal tray. Plastic w/molded handles in the shape of bows; **Shape:** Deep Round; **Size:** 12.0"; **Story:** —; **Country:** US; **Mfr/Dist:** —; **Border/Edge:** Blue; **Quantity:** —.
$ Value, References: est $5-$10 (x)
$ Value, Internet Auctions: —; **# Sales:** —

Name: You Can't Beat the Feeling; **Issued:** c.1995
Comments: Bottle, stars, words: *You Can't Beat the Feeling, Atlanta, Georgia*, possibly a 1996 Olympic Games promotion; **Shape:** Small Rectangle; **Size:** 7.0" x 9.5"; **Story:** —; **Country:** US; **Mfr/Dist:** —; **Border/Edge:** Blue; **Quantity:** —.
$ Value, References: est $5-$10 (x)
$ Value, Internet Auctions: $5 (for info only); **# Sales:** 1

Name: Steak & Shake; **Issued:** c.1999
Comments: Commemorative for customer, *Steak & Shake*. Customer logo and eight Coke product logos surround a bottle. Reference material indicates that twenty-four trays were provided to each Steak & Shake location. **Shape:** Deep Round; **Size:** est 13.5"; **Story:** —; **Country:** US; **Mfr/Dist:** —; **Border/Edge:** White; **Quantity:** est 24,000.
$ Value, References: est $10-$20 (x)
$ Value, Internet Auctions: $15 (for info only); **# Sales:** 2

Name: Sydney 2000 Olympic Games; **Issued:** c.2000
Comments: Commemorative featuring Olympic logo and three cartoon-like characters from the Games' promotion, all drinking Coke; **Shape:** Large Rectangle; **Size:** 15.25" x 18.5"; **Story:** —; **Country:** Mexico; **Mfr/Dist:** —; **Border/Edge:** Red; **Quantity:** —.
$ Value, References: est $15-$20 (x)
$ Value, Internet Auctions: $20 (for info only); **# Sales:** 1

Trays Not Pictured, *Chapter Eight*

Name: Hilda with Glass and Note; **Issued:** 1900, ©1899, also on calendar
Comments: Note reads *Coca-Cola makes flow of thought more easy and reasoning power more vigorous.* Book on table indicates branches in Philadelphia, Chicago, Los Angeles, and Dallas; **Shape:** Round; **Size:** 5.5"; **Story:** —; **Country:** US; **Mfr/Dist:** Standard Advertising Company; **Border/Edge:** Yellow with cola beans, blue/red edge; **Quantity:** —.
$ Value, References: $500-$2,500 (4,5,6,8)

Name: Hilda with The Roses; **Issued:** 1901, ©1900, also on calendar
Comments: First tray to show a price for Coca-Cola, branches are listed in Philadelphia, Chicago, Los Angeles, and Dallas; **Shape:** Round; **Size:** 5.625"; **Story:** —; **Country:** US; **Mfr/Dist:** Meek & Beech Company; **Border/Edge:** Yellow with cola beans, blue/red edge, higher edge rim; **Quantity:** —.
$ Value, References: $1,500-$4,000 (4,5,6)

Name: Hilda with The Roses; **Issued:** 1901, ©1900, also on calendar
Comments: First tray to show a price for Coca-Cola, branches are listed in Philadelphia, Chicago, Los Angeles, and Dallas; **Shape:** Round; **Size:** 5.625"; **Story:** —; **Country:** US; **Mfr/Dist:** Meek & Beech Company; **Border/Edge:** Yellow with cola beans, blue/red edge; **Quantity:** —.
$ Value, References: $500-$2,800 (4,5,6,8)

Name: Hilda with The Glass (Pewter Holder); **Issued:** 1903, also on calendar
Comments: Fourth year of Hilda trays, branch list adds New York and Boston; **Shape:** Round; **Size:** 6.0"; **Story:** —; **Country:** US; **Mfr/Dist:** Chas. W. Shonk Company; **Border/Edge:** Gold, flower trim; **Quantity:** —.
$ Value, References: $900-$2,500 (4,5,6,8)

Name: Bottle 5¢; **Issued:** c.1903-1912
Comments: Tray words: *The Most Refreshing Drink in the World.* Last classic round shape; **Shape:** Round; **Size:** 6.0"; **Story:** —; **Country:** US; **Mfr/Dist:** Chas. W. Shonk Co.; **Border/Edge:** Gold; **Quantity:** —.
$ Value, References: est $3,500-$8,500 (5,6)

Bibliography

This Bibliography lists books, catalogues, pamphlets and magazine articles researched in the preparation of this book. The reference material is divided into three sections.

Section I lists those reference books with specific Coca-Cola trays mentioned and/or pictured that *also* contain dollar values of trays used to compile the information shown in the captions after the heading *$ Value, References*. These items are numbered, and the numbers are also used in parenthesis after the actual values in the *$ Value, References* line. This numbering allows readers to further pursue specific tray values.

Section II lists other reference materials with specific tray information. These items may contain prices, but they were not used in creating the dollar value ranges because the data was published more that four years ago.

Section III lists all other reference materials.

Readers wanting to further explore the history of The Coca-Cola Company and other aspects of collecting Coca-Cola memorabilia will find a wealth of information in these books, most of which are still in print.

Section I.

References with pictures and/or words on specific trays AND that were used in compiling the *$ Values* listed in the captions.

(1) Hill, Deborah Goldstein. *Price Guide to Vintage Coca-Cola Collectibles: 1896-1965*. Iola, Wisconsin: Krause Publications, 1999.

(2) Huxford, Sharon, and Bob Huxford. *Huxford's Collectible Advertising Third Edition*. Paducah, Kentucky: Collector Books, 1997.

(3) McClintock, William. *Coca-Cola Trays, Revised and Expanded 2nd Edition With Price Guide*. Atglen, Pennsylvania: Schiffer Publishing Ltd., 2000.

(4) Petretti, Allan. *Petretti's Coca-Cola Collectibles Price Guide 10th Edition*. Dubuque, Iowa: Antique Trader Books, 1997.

(5) Petretti, Allan, and Chris Beyer. *Classic Coca-Cola Serving Trays*. Dubuque, Iowa: Antique Trader Books, 1998.

(6) Sherrod, Ann Poppenheimer. *Pop's Mail Order Collectibles*. Bells, Tennessee: (Catalogue), 2000.

(7) Summers, B.J. *B.J. Summers Guide to Coca-Cola, Identifications, Current Values, Circa Dates. Second Edition*. Paducah, Kentucky: Collector Books, A Division of Schroeder Publishing Co., Inc., 1999.

(8) Wilson, Al, and Helen Wilson. *Wilson's Coca-Cola Price Guide 3rd Edition, Updated Values*. Atglen, Pennsylvania: Schiffer Publishing Ltd., 2000.

Section II

All other references with pictures and/or comments on specific trays.

Coca-Cola Company, The, An Illustrated Profile. Compiled by The Coca-Cola Company. Atlanta, Georgia: The Coca-Cola Company, 1974.

"For Your Information." *The Cola Call* Vol. 2 No. 6 (Nov/Dec 1978): 8-9. A letter from Coca-Cola lists some 1970s trays and production volumes.

Goldstein, Shelly, and Helen Goldstein. *Coca-Cola Collectibles (Volume 1)*. Woodland Hills, California, 1971.

Goldstein, Shelley, and Helen Goldstein. *Goldstein's Coca-Cola Collectibles, An Illustrated Value Guide*. Compiled by the Publisher from Volumes 1 through 4 of Coca-Cola Collectibles by Shelley and Helen Goldstein. Paducah, Kentucky: Collector Books, 1993.

Hoy, Anne (text). *Coca-Cola: The First Hundred Years Revised Edition*. Atlanta, Georgia: The Coca-Cola Company, 1990.

Munsey, Cecil. *The Illustrated Guide To The Collectibles of Coca-Cola*. New York: Hawthorn Books, Inc., 1972.

Schaeffer, Randy, and Bill Bateman. *Coca-Cola, A Collector's Guide to New and Vintage Coca-Cola Memorabilia*. Philadelphia: Courage Books, 1995.

Schmidt, Bill, and Jan Schmidt. *The Schmidt Museum Collection of Coca-Cola Memorabilia Volume One*. Elizabethtown, Kentucky: Schmidt Books, 1981.

Shartar, Martin, and Norma Shavin. *The Wonderful World of Coca-Cola*. Atlanta, Georgia: Perry Communications, 1978.

Weinberger, Marty, and Don Weinberger. *Coca-Cola Trays from Mexico and Canada*. Willow, Grove, Pennsylvania: Marty and Don Weinberger, 1979.

Wilson, Al. *Collectors Guide To Coca-Cola Items Volumes 1 & 2 7th Printing*. Gas City, Indiana: L-W Book Sales, 1993.

Section III

All other references.

Beverage World's Coke's First 100 Years . . . and a look into the future. Compiled by *Beverage World Magazine*. Shepherdsville, Kentucky: Keller Publishing Corp., 1986.

Charles, Barbara Fahs, and J. R. Taylor. *Dream of Santa, Haddon Sundblom's Advertising Paintings for Christmas, 1931-1964*. New York: Gramercy Books, 1992.

Garrett, Franklin. *Coca-Cola A Chronological History * 1886 – 1964*. Atlanta, Georgia: Public Relations Dept., The Coca-Cola Company, 1965.

Kahn, E. J. Jr. *The Big Drink The Story of Coca-Cola*. New York: Random House, 1960.

Kaiser, Laura Fisher, and Michael Kaiser. *The Official ebay Guide to Buying, Selling, and Collecting Just About Anything*. New York: Fireside, 1999

Oliver, Thomas. *The Real Coke, The Real Story*. New York: Random House, Inc., 1986.

Spontak, Joyce. *Commemorative Coca-Cola Bottles An Unauthorized Guide*. Atglen, Pennsylvania: Schiffer Publishing Ltd., 1998.

Pendergrast, Mark. *For God, Country and Coca-Cola, The Unauthorized History of the Great American Soft Drink and the Company that makes it*. New York: Charles Scribner's Sons Macmillan Publishing Company, 1993.

Petretti, Allan, and Chris Beyer. *Classic Coca-Cola Calendars*. Iola, Wisconsin: Krause Publications, Antique Trader Books, 1999.

Watters, Pat. *Coca-Cola An Illustrated History*. Garden City, New York: Doubleday and Company, Inc., 1978.

Wrynn, V. Dennis. *Coke Goes to War*. Missoula, Montana: Pictorial Histories Publishing Co., 1996.

Index

This index is divided into three sections: trays, ads, and tip trays. Tray entries are listed in alphabetical order by the primary name appearing in the captions, followed by the year issued and, on some entries, other identifying information. A page number containing a picture of the tray is indicated in *italics*. Some tray entries will be followed by a "*See also*" notation to direct readers to a related tray or trays. Also, several alternate tray names and name variations are listed with a "*See*" notation to direct readers to the primary tray name entry. An asterisk (*) indicates a tray entry without a picture. Trays that are reproductions of earlier trays and ads each have an Index entry. Each entry also contains page number references to the lists of reproductions in Chapter Seven. Therefore, any "Reproduction of…" information in the "Comments" of captions is not indexed.